IMPERIUM 1

THE ADEPTUS ASTARTES

CONTENTS

PRODUCED BY GAMES WORKSHOP IN NOTTINGHAM

With thanks to the Mournival for their additional playtesting services

Index: Imperium 1 © Copyright Games Workshop Limited 2017. Index: Imperium 1, GW, Games Workshop, Space Marine, 40K, Warhammer, Warhammer 40,000, the 'Aquila' Double-headed Eagle logo, and all associated logos, illustrations, images, names, creatures, races, vehicles, locations, weapons, characters, and the distinctive likenesses thereof, are either ® or TM, and/or © Games Workshop Limited, variably registered around the world. All Rights Reserved.

Games Workshop Ltd, Willow Rd, Lenton, Nottingham, NG7 2WS

games-workshop.com

INTRODUCTION

Welcome to *Index: Imperium 1*, one of five tomes which together contain updated rules for every unit of miniatures in Warhammer 40,000. If you have an army of Space Marines, Blood Angels, Dark Angels, Space Wolves, Deathwatch, Grey Knights or Legion of the Damned, this volume allows you to field your models in the new edition of Warhammer 40,000.

Within these pages are detailed rules entries, known as datasheets, for every Citadel Miniature within the Space Marines, Blood Angels, Dark Angels, Space Wolves, Deathwatch, Grey Knights and Legion of the Damned Factions. When taken together with the *Warhammer 40,000* rulebook, you will have everything you need to field the Adeptus Astartes on the battlefield. The wisdom contained within allows you to lead the Emperor's finest warriors into battle, the better to defend the Imperium of Man from the horrors of a hostile galaxy.

The Space Marines are the Emperor's finest warriors, each worth at least ten lesser men. Possessing specialist warriors and war machines tailored to every aspect of warfare, it is the resilience, the courage and the martial might of these superhuman warriors that allows the Imperium to

endure. Now, with the addition of the Primaris Space Marines to their ranks, the Adeptus Astartes are mightier than ever before. While many Space Marine Chapters follow the tenets of the sacred Codex Astartes, there are those who practise their own, more specialised ways of war. From the tragically noble Blood Angels and the secretive, deadly Dark Angels, to the feral warriors of the Space Wolves, each such Chapter has its own unique strengths. The Grey Knights, meanwhile, are the Imperium's finest Daemon hunters, masters of counter-malefic warfare, while the Deathwatch are the vigilant blade that strikes down the xenos threat. Strangest of all are the Legion of the Damned, mysterious and ghostly Space Marines wreathed in spectral fire, who strike from nowhere when the hour seems darkest for the Adeptus Astartes and vanish without a trace of their passing.

INSIDE YOU WILL FIND:

- **Army Lists:** The first fifteen sections of this book present all of the datasheets that you will need in order to use your Space Marines miniatures in games of Warhammer 40,000, along with the additional rules and psychic disciplines that make each of these Factions unique.

- **Battle-forged Armies:** This presents a guide on how to organise your miniatures into an army for matched play games, including photocopiable Army Roster sheets.

- **Appendix:** This section contains all of the profiles and rules for the weapons and wargear carried by the units covered in this book, as well as all of the points values you will need to use your army in matched play games.

DATASHEETS

1. Battlefield Role

This is typically used when making a Battle-forged army.

2. Power Rating

The higher this is, the more powerful the unit! You can determine the Power Level of your entire army by adding up the Power Ratings of all the units in your army.

3. Unit Name

Models move and fight in units, which can have one or more models. Here you'll find the name of the unit.

4. Profiles

These contain the following characteristics that tell you how mighty the models in the unit are:

Move (M): This is the speed at which a model moves across the battlefield.

Weapon Skill (WS): This tells you a model's skill at hand-to-hand fighting. If a model has a Weapon Skill of '-' it is unable to fight in melee and cannot make close combat attacks at all.

Ballistic Skill (BS): This shows how accurate a model is when shooting with ranged weapons. If a model has a Ballistic Skill of '-' it has no proficiency with ranged weapons and cannot make shooting attacks at all.

Strength (S): This indicates how strong a model is and how likely it is to inflict damage in hand-to-hand combat.

Toughness (T): This reflects the model's resilience against physical harm.

Wounds (W): Wounds show how much damage a model can sustain before it succumbs to its injuries.

Attacks (A): This tells you how many times a model can strike blows in hand-to-hand combat.

Leadership (Ld): This reveals how courageous, determined or self-controlled a model is.

Save (Sv): This indicates the protection a model's armour gives.

TERMINATOR ANCIENT

NAME	M	WS	BS	S	T	W	A	Ld	Sv
Terminator Ancient	5"	3+	3+	4	4	5	3	8	2+

A Terminator Ancient is a single model armed with a lightning claw.

WEAPON	RANGE	TYPE	S	AP	D	ABILITIES
Lightning claw	Melee	Melee	User	-2	1	You can re-roll failed wound rolls for this weapon. If a model is armed with two lightning claws, each time it fights it can make 1 additional attack with them.
Thunder hammer	Melee	Melee	x2	-3	3	When attacking with this weapon, you must subtract 1 from the hit roll.

WARGEAR OPTIONS	• This model may replace his lightning claw with a thunder hammer.

ABILITIES

And They Shall Know No Fear (pg 88)

Teleport Strike: During deployment, you can set up this unit in a teleportarium chamber instead of placing it on the battlefield. At the end of any of your Movement phases this unit can teleport into battle – set it up anywhere on the battlefield that is more than 9" away from any enemy models.

Terminator Armour: This model has a 5+ invulnerable save.

Archangel Standard: Friendly **Blood Angels** units within 6" of an Archangel standard add 1 to their Leadership characteristic, and you can re-roll failed hit rolls for them in the Fight phase.

FACTION KEYWORDS	**Imperium, Adeptus Astartes, Blood Angels**
KEYWORDS	**Character, Infantry, Ancient, Terminator, Terminator Ancient**

5. Unit Composition & Wargear

This tells you what models are in the unit and covers the basic weapons and equipment the models are armed with.

6. Weapons

The weapons that a unit comes equipped with are described using a set of characteristics as follows:

Range: How far the weapon can shoot. Weapons with a range of 'Melee' can only be used in hand-to-hand combat. All other weapons are referred to as ranged weapons.

Type: These are all explained under the Shooting and Fight phases of the core rules.

Strength (S): How likely the weapon is to inflict damage. If a weapon's Strength lists 'User', it is equal to the wielder's current Strength. If a weapon lists a modifier such as '+1' or 'x2', you should modify the user's current Strength characteristic as shown to determine the weapon's Strength. For example, if a weapon's Strength was 'x2', and the user had a Strength characteristic of 6, that weapon has Strength 12.

Armour Penetration (AP): How good it is at getting through armour.

Damage (D): The amount of damage inflicted by a successful hit.

7. Wargear Options

Some units have a number of choices as to which gear they take into battle – this section describes these options. Weapons which a unit may take as an optional choice are typically described in the appendix.

8. Abilities

Many units have exciting special abilities that are not covered by the core rules; these will be described here.

9. Keywords

All datasheets have a list of keywords, sometimes separated into Faction keywords and other keywords. The former can be used as a guide to help decide which models to include in your army, but otherwise both sets of keywords are functionally the same. Sometimes a rule will say that it applies to models that have a specific keyword. For example, a rule might say that it applies to 'all **Blood Angels** models'. This means it would only apply to models that have the Blood Angels keyword on their datasheet.

'They shall be my finest warriors, these men who give themselves to me.

Like clay I shall mould them and in the furnace of war I shall forge them.

They will be of iron will and steely muscle.

In great armour shall I clad them and with the mightiest guns shall they be armed.

They will be untouched by plague or disease, no sickness will blight them.

They will have tactics, strategies and machines such that no foe will best them in battle.

They are my bulwark against the Terror.

They are the Defenders of Humanity.

They are my Space Marines

...and they shall know no fear.'

- *The Emperor of Mankind*

ADEPTUS ASTARTES

The Adeptus Astartes are the Imperium's Angels of Death. They descend from the skies upon trails of fire to bring swift and bloody destruction to the enemies of Mankind, sweeping the corruption of Chaos and the spoor of the xenos foe from the galaxy with bolter and chainsword. No conquest is beyond them, for they are the Space Marines, and they know no fear.

The Space Marines are superhuman warriors who can trace their lineage to the golden era of Mankind's ascension. Each is an echo of the strength of the Primarchs, the demi-gods that served as the Emperor's generals during the expansion of the Imperium. Ten thousand years ago the Space Marines were organised into Legions, each containing many thousands of warriors. At the height of their power, the Legiones Astartes was a force whose might was unmatched in all the galaxy. Then the unthinkable happened. Horus, Primarch of the Luna Wolves, raised his banner in rebellion, and fully half of the Primarchs and their Legions followed him into damnation. The glorious future of Mankind was lost to betrayal and heresy, and the Emperor was brought low by the hand of Horus, his favoured son.

Yet those loyal Primarchs who survived the Horus Heresy refused to abandon the work of their gene-father. Roboute Guilliman, Primarch of the Ultramarines, created the Codex Astartes, a document of strategy and organisational doctrine that would define the future of the Space Marines. In what has become known as the Second Founding, the Legions of old were disassembled, and in their place rose the Adeptus Astartes, a new fighting force consisting of smaller Space Marine Chapters each comprising no more than a thousand souls. Never again would a single commander wield the awesome destructive power of an entire Legion. In the millennia since this momentous event, the warriors of the Adeptus Astartes have embraced their destiny, fighting against impossible odds to save the Imperium of Man from anarchy and chaos.

The gene-seed that transforms an Adeptus Astartes initiate from mortal warrior to legendary champion is part of the Emperor's own arcane science, and it bestows a suite of superhuman abilities upon those who survive the implantation process. Each battle-brother harbours within him not only this inheritance from the Primarchs, but a score of strange biological organs that lend him the strength to tear a man limb from limb, and the resilience to survive serious injury. A Space Marine can breathe underwater, enter a hibernation state, learn of the foe by consuming his flesh, survive in the cold vacuum of space and even spit acid should the need arise.

Recruited in the prime of his youth, the Space Marine is not only transformed physically by his Chapter's induction process, but mentally and even spiritually. Under extensive autohypnotic suggestion, prolonged meditation and extensive psychological training, his mind is transformed into a fortress of surety, enabling him to wage endless war in a hostile universe and still retain his sanity. A Space Marine can operate at the height of his mental faculties even in the direst circumstances. His soul too is strengthened by this process; under the guidance of his designated company's Chaplain, a Space Marine is kept sharp and true no matter the horrors that he is called upon to face – or to commit.

Already transformed into a living weapon, the Space Marine is made deadlier still by heirloom wargear bestowed upon him in great ceremony. After the implantation of the interface known as the black carapace, he bonds with a suit of advanced power armour that further increases his strength and makes him all but invulnerable to small arms fire. There are even records of Space Marines shrugging off direct hits from anti-tank weaponry and fighting on to cut down the impertinent foe.

Foremost amongst the weapons of the Adeptus Astartes is the bolter, a form of which is bequeathed to all Space Marines at one time or another as they advance through the Chapter. This is a sacred weapon with a fierce and often ancient machine spirit. The self-propelled shells it fires detonate after penetrating the target, causing horrendous damage from within. And this is but the most basic of tools available to the Chapters; at their disposal is an arsenal of devastating weaponry, as well as a massive armoury of battle tanks, gunships, bikes and skimmers to bear them to battle.

A NEW GENERATION

In an event that sent shock waves across the galaxy, the Primarch Roboute Guilliman – who for many centuries had lain in temporal stasis on the Ultramarines' home planet of Macragge – was awoken from his slumber to bestride the Imperium once more. With his miraculous resurrection came another momentous event. Ten thousand years ago, the Archmagos Belisarius Cawl was tasked by Guilliman with the creation of a new army, a force of genetically enhanced warriors mightier even than the noble Space Marines. Hidden away in his sprawling forge-complexes deep beneath the surface of Mars, Cawl lost himself in experimentation, creating countless technological wonders and refining the gene-seed. Now, after playing a crucial role in the Primarch's return, he has unleashed his most miraculous creation: the Primaris Space Marines. Taller and stronger than the last generation of Adeptus Astartes, the warriors of this new breed are clad in advanced Mark X power armour and wield devastating new weaponry.

Recognising the dire threats facing the Imperium, Roboute Guilliman swiftly deployed the new-found Primaris Space Marines in an event known as the Ultima Founding. Alongside several new Chapters comprised entirely of these peerless warriors, many existing Chapters found their ranks bolstered by Primaris reinforcements. Currently, the Codex-compliant Chapters of the Adeptus Astartes adhere to the time-honoured directives of that hallowed tome, deploying the Primaris Space Marines as battleline troops. There are whispers, though, that Guilliman, the reinstated Lord Commander of the Imperium, is already turning his ingenious mind towards codifying a new tactical doctrine – one that will ensure that the enhanced combat prowess and advanced weaponry of the Primaris Space Marines are utilised to the most devastating effect.

CHAPTER ORGANISATION

Guilliman's Codex Astartes was designed to prevent a disaster like the Horus Heresy ever taking place again. By providing a strict organisational doctrine for the new Space Marine Chapters to follow, it would limit the possibility for corruption and rebellion, whilst still maintaining the strength and martial adaptability the Legions had known. This hallowed document dictates the core tenets around which the majority of Space Marine Chapters are organised.

At the head of each Chapter stands the Chapter Master, a warrior of consummate skill, possessed of a keen strategic mind honed by centuries of warfare. His is the final word in all matters, though he is advised by both his company Captains and the four pillars of his command structure. The Reclusiam, represented by the Master of Sanctity, is the spiritual core of the Chapter, and home to its Chaplains. The Apothecarion is responsible for the training and deployment of Apothecaries, and the retrieval of gene-seed from fallen warriors. The Master of the Forge commands the Armoury, and provides the Chapter with arms, armour and equipment, and performs the re-sanctification of the same. Finally, the Librarius is home to the Chapter's Librarian psykers, warrior-scholars whose expertise regarding the endless vagaries of the warp is of the utmost value.

Each Codex-compliant Chapter numbers ten companies. These organised fighting forces of Space Marine battle-brothers are each led by a Captain – a champion and officer of particular distinction who is assigned his orders by the Chapter Master and granted the autonomy to command in whatever manner he deems most effective. The 1st Company is comprised of one hundred veteran warriors, the elite of their Chapter. Detachments from the 1st are deployed upon the most fiercely contested battlefields, for these warriors are capable of extraordinary feats of martial skill. The majority of these battle-brothers go to war clad in hulking suits of Terminator plate – each a relic of priceless antiquity – and all wield the finest weapons and artefacts that the Chapter possesses. It is common for veteran squads of the 1st Company to periodically join the ranks of the Battle Companies, where the

surety and skill with which they slaughter the foe provides glorious inspiration to their battle-brothers.

The 2nd through 5th Companies are the Battle Companies, the main fighting force of the Chapter. The typical Battle Company is a mixed arms force. Led by a Captain and built around a core of infantry, it has fast-striking elements that operate as a vanguard, heavy firepower in the form of cannon-toting marksmen and nigh-indestructible tanks, and psychic and spiritual support from the Librarians and Chaplains that are often assigned to it. If the tactical situation calls for it, each Battle Company can also make use of various support and operational vehicles; Rhino and Razorback transports, as well as Drop Pods, all of which are maintained in sufficient numbers to facilitate a swift armoured deployment.

The endless wars fought by the Chapters of the Adeptus Astartes mean that casualties among the Battle Companies are inevitable, and thus it is important that they can swiftly replenish their ranks. The 6th through 9th Companies are designated the Reserve Companies, and formerly were only deployed against the enemy in the gravest of situations, such as if the Chapter's home world was under attack. Of late, however, the rising tide of Chaos has necessitated their full committal to front-line combat – the forces of the Imperium simply cannot afford to hold such valuable reinforcements in reserve. Instead, squads of Space Marines from these companies take the place of brothers from the Battle Companies who have fallen in combat, or have been sequestered or deployed elsewhere. It is a mark of how rigorous and exacting the training regimes of the Reserve Companies are that these newcomers are warmly welcomed when they arrive to take the places of the slain. The 6th and 7th Companies typically comprise versatile battleline squads, and the Codex Astartes dictates that such warriors are trained in bike-mounted warfare and piloting respectively – this ensures that the Battle Companies are never short of the specialist skills of combat and transport pilots. The 8th Company consists entirely of close support squads, masters of brutal close-quarters combat, while the ranks of the 9th are comprised of heavy support squads whose high-calibre, long-ranged weapons are capable of dealing extreme damage.

To ensure that it can continue to prosecute its endless war against the Emperor's enemies, each Space Marine Chapter must ensure that it maintains a steady flow of new recruits. These neophyte warriors are inducted into the 10th Company, where they begin their lifelong study of the art of war. Designated as Space Marine Scouts, these novitiates are trained by veteran officers in the arts of guerrilla warfare and covert operations. Wearing light, manoeuvrable battle-plate and wielding specialist weapons such as sniper rifles and heavy bolters, the Scouts learn their trade in the white-hot furnace of a war zone. They are seconded to the Battle Companies to range ahead of the larger strike force, performing reconnaissance and harrying the enemy whenever possible. Scouts must prove themselves upon many battlefields before their assigned officer will consider promoting them to become fully fledged battle-brothers.

Though the Codex Astartes has achieved almost religious significance to many Space Marine Chapters, the governing rulers of the Imperium have never decreed that it must be adhered to by law. Such a decree would be almost impossible to enact in any case, for the Chapters of the Adeptus Astartes are proudly autonomous, and have little time for the interference of human bureaucrats. The idiosyncrasies of gene-seed and the thousands of cultural deviations that have taken place in the years since the Second Founding mean that many warrior brotherhoods organise themselves in a different manner to the dictates of Guilliman. So long as such Chapters continue to slaughter the enemies of Mankind and submit to the ultimate will of Terra, such individualism is tolerated – subject to the approval of the ever-vigilant Inquisition.

SPACE MARINES ARMY LIST

This section contains all of the datasheets that you will need in order to fight battles with your Space Marines miniatures. Each datasheet includes the characteristics profiles of the unit it describes, as well as any wargear and abilities it may have. Some rules are common to several Space Marines units – these are described below and referenced on the datasheets.

KEYWORDS

Throughout this book you will come across a keyword that is within angular brackets, specifically <Chapter>. This is shorthand for a keyword of your own choosing, as described below.

<Chapter>

All Space Marine units are drawn from a Chapter. Some datasheets specify what Chapter the unit is drawn from (e.g. Marneus Calgar has the Ultramarines keyword, so is drawn from the Ultramarines Chapter). If an Adeptus Astartes datasheet does not specify which Chapter it is drawn from, it will have the <Chapter> keyword. When you include such a unit in your army, you must nominate which Chapter that unit is from. You then simply replace the <Chapter> keyword in every instance on that unit's datasheet with the name of your chosen Chapter.

For example, if you were to include a Captain in your army, and you decided he was from the Blood Ravens Chapter, his <Chapter> Faction keyword is changed to Blood Ravens and his Rites of Battle ability would then say 'You can re-roll hit rolls of 1 made for friendly Blood Ravens units within 6" of this model.'

Note that Adeptus Astartes Psykers cannot be from the Black Templars Chapter.

While this section of the book provides rules for all Space Marine Chapters, those that are more unique – such as the Blood Angels (pg 88) or Space Wolves (pg 128) – have certain restrictions, datasheets and army special rules that can be found in their own sections later in the book. The Legion of the Damned keyword can only be taken by Damned Legionnaires, while the other Chapters are described later in this book, with each description covering which units can be part of each Chapter. If you wish to see which units each Chapter can include, we recommend reading the relevant section first.

ABILITIES

The following ability is common to several Adeptus Astartes units:

And They Shall Know No Fear

You can re-roll failed Morale tests for this unit.

LIBRARIUS DISCIPLINE

Before the battle, generate the psychic powers for Psykers that can use powers from the Librarius discipline using the table below. You can either roll a D3 to generate their powers randomly (re-roll any duplicate results), or you can select the psychic powers you wish the psyker to have.

LIBRARIUS DISCIPLINE

D3	PSYCHIC POWER
1	**Veil of Time** *Veil of Time* has a warp charge value of 6. If manifested, pick an Adeptus Astartes unit within 18" of the psyker. Until the start of your next Psychic phase, you can re-roll charge rolls and Advance rolls for that unit and they always fight first in the Fight phase, even if they didn't charge. If the enemy also has units that have charged, or that have a similar ability, then alternate choosing units to fight with, starting with the player whose turn is taking place.
2	**Might of Heroes** *Might of Heroes* has a warp charge value of 6. If manifested, select an Adeptus Astartes model within 12" of the psyker. Until the start of your next Psychic phase, add 1 to that model's Strength, Toughness and Attacks characteristics.
3	**Null Zone** *Null Zone* has a warp charge value of 8. If manifested, then until the start of your next Psychic phase, while they are within 6" of the psyker, enemy models cannot take invulnerable saves and must halve the result of any Psychic tests (rounding up) that they take.

'Of the Tactical Space Marine, bedrock of his Chapter and paragon to his brothers, I shall tell thee.

He shall be steeped in the lore of battle and schooled in all manner of weapon and strategy. With combat blade, boltgun and grenade he shall assail the foe.

But these are mere tools; a Tactical Space Marine's true weapons are his courage, his wits and his dedication to his brothers.

He will bring his foe to battle in a manner and time of his choosing, never himself caught unready or ill-prepared for the task at hand. In defence he shall be stalwart as the mountain, a bulwark stood firm against the enemies of Man. In attack he shall strike with the wrath of the Immortal Emperor, felling the foe without mercy, remorse or fear.'

- *From the teachings of Roboute Guilliman as laid down in the Apocrypha of Skaros*

WARGEAR

Many of the units you will find on the following pages reference one or more of the wargear lists below. When this is the case, the unit may take any item from the appropriate list below. The profiles for the items in these lists can be found in the appendix (pg 206-209).

SERGEANT EQUIPMENT

Up to two weapons can be chosen from the following list:
- Bolt pistol
- Grav-pistol
- Plasma pistol
- Chainsword
- Power sword
- Power axe
- Power maul
- Lightning claw
- Power fist
- Thunder hammer [1]

One weapon can be chosen from the following list:
- Boltgun
- Combi-flamer
- Combi-grav
- Combi-melta
- Combi-plasma
- Storm bolter

[1] Cannot be taken by a Sternguard Veteran Sergeant

PISTOLS
- Bolt pistol
- Plasma pistol
- Grav-pistol

COMBI-WEAPONS
- Storm bolter
- Combi-plasma
- Combi-flamer
- Combi-melta
- Combi-grav

MELEE WEAPONS
- Chainsword
- Power sword
- Power axe
- Power maul
- Power lance
- Power fist
- Lightning claw
- Thunder hammer

SPECIAL WEAPONS
- Flamer
- Plasma gun
- Meltagun
- Grav-gun

HEAVY WEAPONS
- Missile launcher
- Heavy bolter
- Multi-melta
- Lascannon
- Grav-cannon and grav-amp
- Plasma cannon

TERMINATOR MELEE WEAPONS
- Lightning claw
- Power fist
- Thunder hammer
- Storm shield

TERMINATOR COMBI-WEAPONS
- Storm bolter
- Combi-plasma
- Combi-flamer
- Combi-melta

TERMINATOR HEAVY WEAPONS
- Heavy flamer
- Assault cannon
- Cyclone missile launcher and storm bolter

DREADNOUGHT HEAVY WEAPONS
- Twin heavy flamer
- Twin autocannon
- Twin heavy bolter
- Twin lascannon
- Assault cannon
- Heavy plasma cannon
- Multi-melta

CAPTAIN

5 POWER

NAME	M	WS	BS	S	T	W	A	Ld	Sv
Captain	6"	2+	2+	4	4	5	4	9	3+

A Captain is a single model armed with a chainsword, a master-crafted boltgun, frag grenades and krak grenades.

WEAPON	RANGE	TYPE	S	AP	D	ABILITIES
Master-crafted boltgun	24"	Rapid Fire 1	4	-1	2	-
Chainsword	Melee	Melee	User	0	1	Each time the bearer fights, it can make 1 additional attack with this weapon.
Frag grenade	6"	Grenade D6	3	0	1	-
Krak grenade	6"	Grenade 1	6	-1	D3	-

WARGEAR OPTIONS
- This model may replace its master-crafted boltgun with an item from the *Pistols, Combi-weapons* or *Melee Weapons* lists.
- This model may replace its chainsword with a storm shield, relic blade or an item from the *Melee Weapons* list.
- This model may take a jump pack (**Power Rating +1**). If it does, its Move characteristic is increased to 12" and it gains the **JUMP PACK** and **FLY** keywords.

ABILITIES

And They Shall Know No Fear (pg 10)

Rites of Battle: You can re-roll hit rolls of 1 made for friendly <CHAPTER> units within 6" of this model.

Iron Halo: This model has a 4+ invulnerable save.

Storm Shield: A model equipped with a storm shield has a 3+ invulnerable save.

Jump Pack Assault: During deployment, if this model has a jump pack, you can set it up high in the skies instead of placing it on the battlefield. At the end of any of your Movement phases this model can assault from above – set it up anywhere on the battlefield that is more than 9" away from any enemy models.

FACTION KEYWORDS IMPERIUM, ADEPTUS ASTARTES, <CHAPTER>

KEYWORDS CHARACTER, INFANTRY, CAPTAIN

CAPTAIN
IN TERMINATOR ARMOUR

8 POWER

NAME	M	WS	BS	S	T	W	A	Ld	Sv
Captain in Terminator Armour	5"	2+	2+	4	4	6	4	9	2+

A Captain in Terminator Armour is a single model armed with a power sword and storm bolter.

WEAPON	RANGE	TYPE	S	AP	D	ABILITIES
Storm bolter	24"	Rapid Fire 2	4	0	1	-
Wrist-mounted grenade launcher	12"	Assault D3	4	1	1	-
Chainfist	Melee	Melee	x2	-4	2	When attacking with this weapon, you must subtract 1 from the hit roll.
Power sword	Melee	Melee	User	-3	1	-
Relic blade	Melee	Melee	+2	-3	D3	-

WARGEAR OPTIONS
- This model may replace its storm bolter with an item from the *Terminator Combi-weapons* or *Terminator Melee Weapons* lists.
- This model may replace its power sword with a relic blade, chainfist, storm shield or an item from the *Terminator Melee Weapons* list.
- A Captain in Terminator Armour with a power fist can also be equipped with a wrist-mounted grenade launcher.

ABILITIES

And They Shall Know No Fear (pg 10)

Iron Halo: This model has a 4+ invulnerable save.

Storm Shield: A model equipped with a storm shield has a 3+ invulnerable save.

Rites of Battle: You can re-roll hit rolls of 1 made for friendly <CHAPTER> units within 6" of this model.

Teleport Strike: During deployment, you can set up this model in a teleportarium chamber instead of placing it on the battlefield. At the end of any of your Movement phases this model can teleport into battle – set it up anywhere on the battlefield that is more than 9" away from any enemy models.

FACTION KEYWORDS IMPERIUM, ADEPTUS ASTARTES, <CHAPTER>

KEYWORDS CHARACTER, INFANTRY, TERMINATOR, CAPTAIN

CAPTAIN
IN CATAPHRACTII ARMOUR

8 POWER

NAME	M	WS	BS	S	T	W	A	Ld	Sv
Captain in Cataphractii Armour	4"	2+	2+	4	4	6	4	9	2+

A Captain in Cataphractii Armour is a single model armed with a power sword and combi-bolter.

WEAPON	RANGE	TYPE	S	AP	D	ABILITIES
Combi-bolter	24"	Rapid Fire 2	4	0	1	-
Chainfist	Melee	Melee	x2	-4	2	When attacking with this weapon, you must subtract 1 from the hit roll.
Power sword	Melee	Melee	User	-3	1	-
Relic blade	Melee	Melee	+2	-3	D3	-

WARGEAR OPTIONS
- This model may replace its combi-bolter with an item from the *Combi-weapons* or *Terminator Melee Weapons* lists.
- This model may replace its power sword with a relic blade, a chainfist or an item from the *Terminator Melee Weapons* list.

ABILITIES

And They Shall Know No Fear (pg 10)

Cataphractii Armour and Iron Halo: This model has a 3+ invulnerable save, but you must halve the result of the dice rolled when determining how far this model Advances.

Rites of Battle: You can re-roll hit rolls of 1 made for friendly <Chapter> units within 6" of this model.

Teleport Strike: During deployment, you can set up this model in a teleportarium chamber instead of placing it on the battlefield. At the end of any of your Movement phases this model can teleport into battle – set it up anywhere on the battlefield that is more than 9" away from any enemy models.

FACTION KEYWORDS | IMPERIUM, ADEPTUS ASTARTES, <CHAPTER>

KEYWORDS | CHARACTER, INFANTRY, TERMINATOR, CAPTAIN

CAPTAIN
IN GRAVIS ARMOUR

7 POWER

NAME	M	WS	BS	S	T	W	A	Ld	Sv
Captain in Gravis Armour	5"	2+	2+	4	5	6	5	9	3+

A Captain in Gravis Armour is a single model armed with a master-crafted power sword and a boltstorm gauntlet.

WEAPON	RANGE	TYPE	S	AP	D	ABILITIES
Boltstorm gauntlet (shooting)	12"	Pistol 3	4	0	1	-
Boltstorm gauntlet (melee)	Melee	Melee	x2	-3	D3	When attacking with this weapon, you must subtract 1 from the hit roll.
Master-crafted power sword	Melee	Melee	User	-3	2	-

ABILITIES

And They Shall Know No Fear (pg 10)

Iron Halo: This model has a 4+ invulnerable save.

Rites of Battle: You can re-roll hit rolls of 1 made for friendly <Chapter> units within 6" of this model.

FACTION KEYWORDS | IMPERIUM, ADEPTUS ASTARTES, <CHAPTER>

KEYWORDS | CHARACTER, INFANTRY, Mk X GRAVIS, PRIMARIS, CAPTAIN

CAPTAIN
ON BIKE

7 POWER

NAME	M	WS	BS	S	T	W	A	Ld	Sv
Captain on Bike	14"	2+	2+	4	5	6	4	9	3+

A Captain on Bike is a single model armed with a chainsword, a master-crafted boltgun, frag grenades and krak grenades. His Space Marine bike is equipped with a twin boltgun.

WEAPON	RANGE	TYPE	S	AP	D	ABILITIES
Master-crafted boltgun	24"	Rapid Fire 1	4	-1	2	-
Twin boltgun	24"	Rapid Fire 2	4	0	1	-
Chainsword	Melee	Melee	User	0	1	Each time the bearer fights, it can make 1 additional attack with this weapon.
Frag grenade	6"	Grenade D6	3	0	1	-
Krak grenade	6"	Grenade 1	6	-1	D3	-

WARGEAR OPTIONS	• This model may replace its master-crafted boltgun with an item from the *Pistols*, *Combi-weapons* or *Melee Weapons* lists. • This model may replace its chainsword with a storm shield or an item from the *Melee Weapons* list.	
ABILITIES	**And They Shall Know No Fear** (pg 10) **Iron Halo:** This model has a 4+ invulnerable save. **Storm Shield:** A model equipped with a storm shield has a 3+ invulnerable save.	**Rites of Battle:** You can re-roll hit rolls of 1 made for friendly <**Chapter**> units within 6" of this model. **Turbo-boost:** When this model Advances, add 6" to its Move characteristic for that Movement phase instead of rolling a dice.
FACTION KEYWORDS	**Imperium, Adeptus Astartes, <Chapter>**	
KEYWORDS	**Biker, Character, Captain**	

LIBRARIAN

6 POWER

NAME	M	WS	BS	S	T	W	A	Ld	Sv
Librarian	6"	3+	3+	4	4	4	3	9	3+

A Librarian is a single model armed with a force stave, a bolt pistol, frag grenades and krak grenades.

WEAPON	RANGE	TYPE	S	AP	D	ABILITIES
Bolt pistol	12"	Pistol 1	4	0	1	-
Boltgun	24"	Rapid Fire 1	4	0	1	-
Force axe	Melee	Melee	+1	-2	D3	-
Force stave	Melee	Melee	+2	-1	D3	-
Force sword	Melee	Melee	User	-3	D3	-
Frag grenade	6"	Grenade D6	3	0	1	-
Krak grenade	6"	Grenade 1	6	-1	D3	-

WARGEAR OPTIONS	• This model may replace its bolt pistol with a boltgun or an item from the *Pistols* or *Combi-weapons* lists. • This model may replace its force stave with a force sword or a force axe. • This model may take a jump pack (**Power Rating +1**). If it does, its Move characteristic is increased to 12" and it gains the **Jump Pack** and **Fly** keywords.
ABILITIES	**And They Shall Know No Fear** (pg 10) **Psychic Hood:** You can add 1 to Deny the Witch tests you take for this model against enemy **Psykers** within 12". **Jump Pack Assault:** During deployment, if this model has a jump pack, you can set it up high in the skies instead of placing it on the battlefield. At the end of any of your Movement phases this model can assault from above – set it up anywhere on the battlefield that is more than 9" away from any enemy models.
PSYKER	This model can attempt to manifest two psychic powers in each friendly Psychic phase, and attempt to deny one psychic power in each enemy Psychic phase. It knows the *Smite* power and two psychic powers from the Librarius discipline (pg 10).
FACTION KEYWORDS	**Imperium, Adeptus Astartes, <Chapter>**
KEYWORDS	**Character, Infantry, Psyker, Librarian**

LIBRARIAN
IN TERMINATOR ARMOUR

NAME	M	WS	BS	S	T	W	A	Ld	Sv
Librarian in Terminator Armour	5"	3+	3+	4	4	5	3	9	2+

A Librarian in Terminator Armour is a single model armed with a force stave and storm bolter.

WEAPON	RANGE	TYPE	S	AP	D	ABILITIES
Storm bolter	24"	Rapid Fire 2	4	0	1	-
Force axe	Melee	Melee	+1	-2	D3	-
Force stave	Melee	Melee	+2	-1	D3	-
Force sword	Melee	Melee	User	-3	D3	-

WARGEAR OPTIONS	• This model may replace its storm bolter with a storm shield or an item from the *Terminator Combi-weapons* list. • This model may replace its force stave with a force sword or a force axe.

ABILITIES	**And They Shall Know No Fear** (pg 10) **Crux Terminatus:** This model has a 5+ invulnerable save. **Storm Shield:** A model with a storm shield has a 3+ invulnerable save.	**Psychic Hood:** You can add 1 to Deny the Witch tests you take for this model against enemy **PSYKERS** within 12". **Teleport Strike:** During deployment, you can set up this model in a teleportarium chamber instead of placing it on the battlefield. At the end of any of your Movement phases this model can teleport into battle – set it up anywhere on the battlefield that is more than 9" away from any enemy models.

PSYKER	This model can attempt to manifest two psychic powers in each friendly Psychic phase, and attempt to deny one psychic power in each enemy Psychic phase. It knows the *Smite* power and two psychic powers from the Librarius discipline (pg 10).

FACTION KEYWORDS	IMPERIUM, ADEPTUS ASTARTES, <CHAPTER>
KEYWORDS	CHARACTER, INFANTRY, TERMINATOR, PSYKER, LIBRARIAN

LIBRARIAN
ON BIKE

NAME	M	WS	BS	S	T	W	A	Ld	Sv
Librarian on Bike	14"	3+	3+	4	5	5	3	9	3+

A Librarian on Bike is a single model armed with a force stave, a bolt pistol, frag grenades and krak grenades. His Space Marine bike is equipped with a twin boltgun.

WEAPON	RANGE	TYPE	S	AP	D	ABILITIES
Bolt pistol	12"	Pistol 1	4	0	1	-
Boltgun	24"	Rapid Fire 1	4	0	1	-
Twin boltgun	24"	Rapid Fire 2	4	0	1	-
Force axe	Melee	Melee	+1	-2	D3	-
Force stave	Melee	Melee	+2	-1	D3	-
Force sword	Melee	Melee	User	-3	D3	-
Frag grenade	6"	Grenade D6	3	0	1	-
Krak grenade	6"	Grenade 1	6	-1	D3	-

WARGEAR OPTIONS	• This model may replace its bolt pistol with a boltgun or an item from the *Pistols* or *Combi-weapons* lists. • This model may replace its force stave with a force sword or a force axe.

ABILITIES	**And They Shall Know No Fear** (pg 10) **Psychic Hood:** You can add 1 to Deny the Witch tests you take for this model against enemy **PSYKERS** within 12".	**Turbo-boost:** When this model Advances, add 6" to its Move characteristic for that Movement phase instead of rolling a dice.

PSYKER	This model can attempt to manifest two psychic powers in each friendly Psychic phase, and attempt to deny one psychic power in each enemy Psychic phase. It knows the *Smite* power and two psychic powers from the Librarius discipline (pg 10).

FACTION KEYWORDS	IMPERIUM, ADEPTUS ASTARTES, <CHAPTER>
KEYWORDS	BIKER, CHARACTER, PSYKER, LIBRARIAN

TECHMARINE

NAME	M	WS	BS	S	T	W	A	Ld	Sv
Techmarine	6"	3+	2+	4	4	4	3	8	2+

A Techmarine is a single model armed with a power axe, a servo-arm, a bolt pistol, frag grenades and krak grenades.

WEAPON	RANGE	TYPE	S	AP	D	ABILITIES
Bolt pistol	12"	Pistol 1	4	0	1	-
Boltgun	24"	Rapid Fire 1	4	0	1	-
Conversion beamer	42"	Heavy D3	6	0	1	Attacks from a conversion beamer that target enemies at over half its range are resolved at Strength 8, AP -1 and Damage 2.
Flamer	8"	Assault D6	4	0	1	This weapon automatically hits its target.
Plasma cutter	When attacking with this weapon, choose one of the profiles below.					
- Standard	12"	Assault 1	7	-3	1	-
- Supercharge	12"	Assault 1	8	-3	2	On a hit roll of 1, the bearer is slain.
Power axe	Melee	Melee	+1	-2	1	-
Servo-arm	Melee	Melee	x2	-2	3	Each servo-arm can only be used to make one attack each time this model fights. When a model attacks with this weapon, you must subtract 1 from the hit roll.
Frag grenade	6"	Grenade D6	3	0	1	-
Krak grenade	6"	Grenade 1	6	-1	D3	-

WARGEAR OPTIONS	• This model may replace its bolt pistol with a boltgun or an item from the *Pistols* or *Combi-weapons* lists. • This model may replace its power axe with an item from the *Melee Weapons* list. • This model may replace its servo-arm with a conversion beamer. • This model may take a servo-harness (**Power Rating +1**), which comprises an additional servo-arm, a plasma cutter and a flamer. If it does this, neither servo-arm may be replaced with a conversion beamer.
ABILITIES	And They Shall Know No Fear (pg 10) **Blessing of the Omnissiah:** At the end of your Movement phase this model can repair a single <CHAPTER> VEHICLE within 1". That model regains D3 lost wounds. A model can only be repaired once per turn.
FACTION KEYWORDS	IMPERIUM, ADEPTUS ASTARTES, <CHAPTER>
KEYWORDS	CHARACTER, INFANTRY, TECHMARINE

SERVITORS

NAME	M	WS	BS	S	T	W	A	Ld	Sv
Servitor	5"	5+	5+	3	3	1	1	6	4+

This unit contains 4 Servitors. Each model is armed with a servo-arm.

WEAPON	RANGE	TYPE	S	AP	D	ABILITIES
Heavy bolter	36"	Heavy 3	5	-1	1	-
Multi-melta	24"	Heavy 1	8	-4	D6	If the target is within half range of this weapon, roll two dice when inflicting damage with it and discard the lowest result.
Plasma cannon	When attacking with this weapon, choose one of the profiles below.					
- Standard	36"	Heavy D3	7	-3	1	-
- Supercharge	36"	Heavy D3	8	-3	2	On a hit roll of 1, the bearer is slain after all of this weapon's shots have been resolved.
Servo-arm	Melee	Melee	x2	-2	3	Each servo-arm can only be used to make one attack each time this model fights. When a model attacks with this weapon, you must subtract 1 from the hit roll.

WARGEAR OPTIONS	• Up to two Servitors may replace their servo-arm with a heavy bolter, plasma cannon or multi-melta.
ABILITIES	**Mindlock:** Servitors improve both their Weapon Skill and Ballistic Skill to 4+, and their Leadership to 9, whilst they are within 6" of any friendly TECHMARINES.
FACTION KEYWORDS	IMPERIUM, ADEPTUS ASTARTES, <CHAPTER>
KEYWORDS	INFANTRY, SERVITORS

TECHMARINE
ON BIKE

NAME	M	WS	BS	S	T	W	A	Ld	Sv
Techmarine on Bike	14"	3+	2+	4	5	5	3	8	2+

A Techmarine on Bike is a single model armed with a power axe, a servo-arm, a bolt pistol, frag grenades and krak grenades. His Space Marine bike is equipped with a twin boltgun.

WEAPON	RANGE	TYPE	S	AP	D	ABILITIES
Bolt pistol	12"	Pistol 1	4	0	1	-
Boltgun	24"	Rapid Fire 1	4	0	1	-
Conversion beamer	42"	Heavy D3	6	0	1	Attacks from a conversion beamer that target enemies at over half its range are resolved at Strength 8, AP -1 and Damage 2.
Flamer	8"	Assault D6	4	0	1	This weapon automatically hits its target.
Plasma cutter	When attacking with this weapon, choose one of the profiles below.					
- Standard	12"	Assault 1	7	-3	1	-
- Supercharge	12"	Assault 1	8	-3	2	On a hit roll of 1, the bearer is slain.
Twin boltgun	24"	Rapid Fire 2	4	0	1	-
Power axe	Melee	Melee	+1	-2	1	-
Servo-arm	Melee	Melee	x2	-2	3	Each servo-arm can only be used to make one attack each time this model fights. When a model attacks with this weapon, you must subtract 1 from the hit roll.
Frag grenade	6"	Grenade D6	3	0	1	-
Krak grenade	6"	Grenade 1	6	-1	D3	-

WARGEAR OPTIONS	
	• This model may replace its bolt pistol with a boltgun or an item from the *Pistols* or *Combi-weapons* lists.
	• This model may replace its power axe with an item from the *Melee Weapons* list.
	• This model may replace its servo-arm with a conversion beamer.
	• This model may take a servo-harness (**Power Rating +1**), which comprises an additional servo-arm, a plasma cutter and a flamer. If it does this, neither servo-arm may be replaced with a conversion beamer.

ABILITIES	
And They Shall Know No Fear (pg 10) **Turbo-boost:** When this model Advances, add 6" to its Move characteristic for that Movement phase instead of rolling a dice.	**Blessing of the Omnissiah:** At the end of your Movement phase this model can repair a single **<CHAPTER> VEHICLE** within 1". That model regains D3 lost wounds. A model can only be repaired once per turn.

FACTION KEYWORDS	IMPERIUM, ADEPTUS ASTARTES, <CHAPTER>
KEYWORDS	BIKER, CHARACTER, TECHMARINE

CHAPLAIN

NAME	M	WS	BS	S	T	W	A	Ld	Sv
Chaplain	6"	2+	3+	4	4	4	3	9	3+

A Chaplain is a single model armed with a crozius arcanum, a bolt pistol, frag grenades and krak grenades.

WEAPON	RANGE	TYPE	S	AP	D	ABILITIES
Bolt pistol	12"	Pistol 1	4	0	1	-
Boltgun	24"	Rapid Fire 1	4	0	1	-
Crozius arcanum	Melee	Melee	+1	-1	2	-
Power fist	Melee	Melee	x2	-3	D3	When attacking with this weapon, you must subtract 1 from the hit roll.
Frag grenade	6"	Grenade D6	3	0	1	-
Krak grenade	6"	Grenade 1	6	-1	D3	-

WARGEAR OPTIONS	• This model may replace its bolt pistol with a boltgun, power fist or an item from the *Pistols* or *Combi-weapons* lists. • This model may take a jump pack (**Power Rating +1**). If it does, its Move characteristic is increased to 12" and it gains the **JUMP PACK** and **FLY** keywords.

ABILITIES	**And They Shall Know No Fear** (pg 10)	**Rosarius:** This model has a 4+ invulnerable save.
	Litanies of Hate: You can re-roll failed hit rolls in the Fight phase for friendly **<CHAPTER>** units within 6" of this model.	**Jump Pack Assault:** During deployment, if this model has a jump pack, you can set it up high in the skies instead of placing it on the battlefield. At the end of any of your Movement phases this model can assault from above – set it up anywhere on the battlefield that is more than 9" away from any enemy models.
	Spiritual Leaders: All friendly **<CHAPTER>** units within 6" of this model can use the Chaplain's Leadership instead of their own.	

FACTION KEYWORDS	**IMPERIUM, ADEPTUS ASTARTES, <CHAPTER>**
KEYWORDS	**CHARACTER, INFANTRY, CHAPLAIN**

Chaplains stir the spirits of their fellow battle-brothers with rousing litanies of righteous hatred.

CHAPLAIN
IN TERMINATOR ARMOUR

7 POWER

NAME	M	WS	BS	S	T	W	A	Ld	Sv
Chaplain in Terminator Armour	5"	2+	3+	4	4	5	3	9	2+

A Chaplain in Terminator Armour is a single model armed with a crozius arcanum and a storm bolter.

WEAPON	RANGE	TYPE	S	AP	D	ABILITIES
Storm bolter	24"	Rapid Fire 2	4	0	1	-
Crozius arcanum	Melee	Melee	+1	-1	2	-

WARGEAR OPTIONS
- This model may replace its storm bolter with an item from the *Terminator Combi-weapons* list.

ABILITIES

And They Shall Know No Fear (pg 10)

Litanies of Hate: You can re-roll failed hit rolls in the Fight phase for friendly <CHAPTER> units within 6" of this model.

Spiritual Leaders: All friendly <CHAPTER> units within 6" of this model can use the Chaplain's Leadership instead of their own.

Rosarius: This model has a 4+ invulnerable save.

Teleport Strike: During deployment, you can set up this model in a teleportarium chamber instead of placing it on the battlefield. At the end of any of your Movement phases this model can teleport into battle – set it up anywhere on the battlefield that is more than 9" away from any enemy models.

FACTION KEYWORDS IMPERIUM, ADEPTUS ASTARTES, <CHAPTER>

KEYWORDS CHARACTER, INFANTRY, TERMINATOR, CHAPLAIN

CHAPLAIN
ON BIKE

6 POWER

NAME	M	WS	BS	S	T	W	A	Ld	Sv
Chaplain on Bike	14"	2+	3+	4	5	5	3	9	3+

A Chaplain on Bike is a single model armed with a crozius arcanum, a bolt pistol, frag grenades and krak grenades. His Space Marine bike is equipped with a twin boltgun.

WEAPON	RANGE	TYPE	S	AP	D	ABILITIES
Bolt pistol	12"	Pistol 1	4	0	1	-
Boltgun	24"	Rapid Fire 1	4	0	1	-
Twin boltgun	24"	Rapid Fire 2	4	0	1	-
Crozius arcanum	Melee	Melee	+1	-1	2	-
Power fist	Melee	Melee	x2	-3	D3	When attacking with this weapon, you must subtract 1 from the hit roll.
Frag grenade	6"	Grenade D6	3	0	1	-
Krak grenade	6"	Grenade 1	6	-1	D3	-

WARGEAR OPTIONS
- This model may replace its bolt pistol with a boltgun, power fist or an item from the *Pistols* or *Combi-weapons* lists.

ABILITIES

And They Shall Know No Fear (pg 10)

Litanies of Hate: You can re-roll failed hit rolls in the Fight phase for friendly <CHAPTER> units within 6" of this model.

Rosarius: This model has a 4+ invulnerable save.

Turbo-boost: When this model Advances, add 6" to its Move characteristic for that Movement phase instead of rolling a dice.

Spiritual Leaders: All friendly <CHAPTER> units within 6" of this model can use the Chaplain's Leadership instead of their own.

FACTION KEYWORDS IMPERIUM, ADEPTUS ASTARTES, <CHAPTER>

KEYWORDS BIKER, CHARACTER, CHAPLAIN

APOTHECARY

NAME	M	WS	BS	S	T	W	A	Ld	Sv
Apothecary	6"	3+	3+	4	4	4	3	8	3+

An Apothecary is a single model armed with a bolt pistol, chainsword, frag grenades and krak grenades.

WEAPON	RANGE	TYPE	S	AP	D	ABILITIES
Bolt pistol	12"	Pistol 1	4	0	1	-
Chainsword	Melee	Melee	User	0	1	Each time the bearer fights, it can make 1 additional attack with this weapon.
Frag grenade	6"	Grenade D6	3	0	1	-
Krak grenade	6"	Grenade 1	6	-1	D3	-

| ABILITIES | And They Shall Know No Fear (pg 10)

Narthecium: At the end of any of your Movement phases, the Apothecary can attempt to heal or revive a single model. Select a friendly <CHAPTER> INFANTRY or BIKER unit within 3" of the Apothecary. If that unit contains a wounded model, it immediately regains D3 lost wounds. If the chosen unit contains no wounded models but one or more of its models have been slain during the battle, roll a D6. On a 4+ a single slain model is returned to the unit with 1 wound remaining. If the Apothecary fails to revive a model he can do nothing else for the remainder of the turn (shoot, charge, fight, etc.) as he recovers the gene-seed of the fallen warrior. A unit can only be the target of the Narthecium ability once in each turn. |
|---|---|
| **FACTION KEYWORDS** | IMPERIUM, ADEPTUS ASTARTES, <CHAPTER> |
| **KEYWORDS** | CHARACTER, INFANTRY, APOTHECARY |

APOTHECARY
ON BIKE

NAME	M	WS	BS	S	T	W	A	Ld	Sv
Apothecary on Bike	14"	3+	3+	4	5	5	3	8	3+

An Apothecary on Bike is a single model armed with a bolt pistol, chainsword, frag grenades and krak grenades. His Space Marine bike is equipped with a twin boltgun.

WEAPON	RANGE	TYPE	S	AP	D	ABILITIES
Bolt pistol	12"	Pistol 1	4	0	1	-
Twin boltgun	24"	Rapid Fire 2	4	0	1	-
Chainsword	Melee	Melee	User	0	1	Each time the bearer fights, it can make 1 additional attack with this weapon.
Frag grenade	6"	Grenade D6	3	0	1	-
Krak grenade	6"	Grenade 1	6	-1	D3	-

| ABILITIES | And They Shall Know No Fear (pg 10)

Narthecium: At the end of any of your Movement phases, the Apothecary can attempt to heal or revive a single model. Select a friendly <CHAPTER> INFANTRY or BIKER unit within 3" of the Apothecary. If that unit contains a wounded model, it immediately regains D3 lost wounds. If the chosen unit contains no wounded models but one or more of its models have been slain during the battle, roll a D6. On a 4+ a single slain model is returned to the unit with 1 wound remaining. If the Apothecary fails to revive a model he can do nothing else for the remainder of the turn (shoot, charge, fight, etc.) as he recovers the gene-seed of the fallen warrior. A unit can only be the target of the Narthecium ability once in each turn.

Turbo-boost: When this model Advances, add 6" to its Move characteristic for that Movement phase instead of rolling a dice. |
|---|---|
| **FACTION KEYWORDS** | IMPERIUM, ADEPTUS ASTARTES, <CHAPTER> |
| **KEYWORDS** | BIKER, CHARACTER, APOTHECARY |

PRIMARIS LIEUTENANTS

NAME	M	WS	BS	S	T	W	A	Ld	Sv
Primaris Lieutenant	6"	2+	3+	4	4	5	4	8	3+

This unit contains a single Primaris Lieutenant. It can include 1 additional Primaris Lieutenant (**Power Rating +4**). Each model is armed with a master-crafted auto bolt rifle, a bolt pistol, frag grenades and krak grenades.

WEAPON	RANGE	TYPE	S	AP	D	ABILITIES
Bolt pistol	12"	Pistol 1	4	0	1	-
Master-crafted auto bolt rifle	24"	Assault 2	4	0	2	-
Power sword	Melee	Melee	User	-3	1	-
Frag grenade	6"	Grenade D6	3	0	1	-
Krak grenade	6"	Grenade 1	6	-1	D3	-

WARGEAR OPTIONS	• Any model may replace his master-crafted auto bolt rifle with a power sword.

ABILITIES	**And They Shall Know No Fear** (pg 10) **Tactical Precision:** You can re-roll wound rolls of 1 for friendly <CHAPTER> units that are within 6" of this model.	**Company Heroes:** During deployment, all models in this unit must be set up at the same time, though they do not need to be set up in unit coherency. From that point onwards, each Primaris Lieutenant is treated as a separate unit.

FACTION KEYWORDS	IMPERIUM, ADEPTUS ASTARTES, <CHAPTER>

KEYWORDS	CHARACTER, INFANTRY, PRIMARIS, LIEUTENANTS

COMPANY ANCIENT

4 POWER

NAME	M	WS	BS	S	T	W	A	Ld	Sv
Company Ancient	6"	3+	3+	4	4	4	3	8	3+

A Company Ancient is a single model armed with a bolt pistol, frag grenades and krak grenades.

WEAPON	RANGE	TYPE	S	AP	D	ABILITIES
Bolt pistol	12"	Pistol 1	4	0	1	-
Boltgun	24"	Rapid Fire 1	4	0	1	-
Frag grenade	6"	Grenade D6	3	0	1	-
Krak grenade	6"	Grenade 1	6	-1	D3	-

WARGEAR OPTIONS	• This model may replace its bolt pistol with a boltgun, or an item from the *Pistols*, *Combi-weapons* or *Melee Weapons* lists.

ABILITIES	**And They Shall Know No Fear** (pg 10) **Astartes Banner:** <CHAPTER> units within 6" of any friendly <CHAPTER> ANCIENTS add 1 to their Leadership. In addition, roll a D6 each time a <CHAPTER> INFANTRY model is destroyed within 6" of any friendly <CHAPTER> ANCIENTS, before removing the model as a casualty. On a 4+ that model musters one last surge of strength before succumbing to its wounds; it can either shoot with one of its weapons as if it were the Shooting phase, or make a single attack as if it were the Fight phase.

FACTION KEYWORDS	IMPERIUM, ADEPTUS ASTARTES, <CHAPTER>
KEYWORDS	CHARACTER, INFANTRY, ANCIENT, COMPANY ANCIENT

COMPANY ANCIENT
ON BIKE

5 POWER

NAME	M	WS	BS	S	T	W	A	Ld	Sv
Company Ancient on Bike	14"	3+	3+	4	5	5	3	8	3+

A Company Ancient on Bike is a single model armed with a bolt pistol, frag grenades and krak grenades. His Space Marine bike is equipped with a twin boltgun.

WEAPON	RANGE	TYPE	S	AP	D	ABILITIES
Bolt pistol	12"	Pistol 1	4	0	1	-
Boltgun	24"	Rapid Fire 1	4	0	1	-
Twin boltgun	24"	Rapid Fire 2	4	0	1	-
Frag grenade	6"	Grenade D6	3	0	1	-
Krak grenade	6"	Grenade 1	6	-1	D3	-

WARGEAR OPTIONS	• This model may replace its bolt pistol with a boltgun, or an item from the *Pistols*, *Combi-weapons* or *Melee Weapons* lists.

ABILITIES	**And They Shall Know No Fear** (pg 10) **Astartes Banner:** <CHAPTER> units within 6" of any friendly <CHAPTER> ANCIENTS add 1 to their Leadership. In addition, roll a D6 each time a <CHAPTER> INFANTRY model is destroyed within 6" of any friendly <CHAPTER> ANCIENTS, before removing the model as a casualty. On a 4+ that model musters one last surge of strength before succumbing to its wounds; it can either shoot with one of its weapons as if it were the Shooting phase, or make a single attack as if it were the Fight phase. **Turbo-boost:** When this model Advances, add 6" to its Move characteristic for that Movement phase instead of rolling a dice.

FACTION KEYWORDS	IMPERIUM, ADEPTUS ASTARTES, <CHAPTER>
KEYWORDS	BIKER, CHARACTER, ANCIENT, COMPANY ANCIENT

PRIMARIS ANCIENT

4 POWER

NAME	M	WS	BS	S	T	W	A	Ld	Sv
Primaris Ancient	6"	3+	3+	4	4	5	4	8	3+

A Primaris Ancient is a single model armed with a bolt rifle, bolt pistol, frag grenades and krak grenades.

WEAPON	RANGE	TYPE	S	AP	D	ABILITIES
Bolt pistol	12"	Pistol 1	4	0	1	-
Bolt rifle	30"	Rapid Fire 1	4	-1	1	-
Frag grenade	6"	Grenade D6	3	0	1	-
Krak grenade	6"	Grenade 1	6	-1	D3	-

ABILITIES	And They Shall Know No Fear (pg 10)
	Astartes Banner: <CHAPTER> units within 6" of any friendly <CHAPTER> ANCIENTS add 1 to their Leadership. In addition, roll a D6 each time a <CHAPTER> INFANTRY model is destroyed within 6" of any friendly <CHAPTER> ANCIENTS, before removing the model as a casualty. On a 4+ that model musters one last surge of strength before succumbing to its wounds; it can either shoot with one of its weapons as if it were the Shooting phase, or make a single attack as if it were the Fight phase.
FACTION KEYWORDS	IMPERIUM, ADEPTUS ASTARTES, <CHAPTER>
KEYWORDS	CHARACTER, INFANTRY, PRIMARIS, ANCIENT

COMPANY CHAMPION

4 POWER

NAME	M	WS	BS	S	T	W	A	Ld	Sv
Company Champion	6"	2+	3+	4	4	4	3	8	3+

A Company Champion is a single model armed with a bolt pistol, master-crafted power sword, frag grenades and krak grenades.

WEAPON	RANGE	TYPE	S	AP	D	ABILITIES
Bolt pistol	12"	Pistol 1	4	0	1	-
Master-crafted power sword	Melee	Melee	User	-3	2	-
Frag grenade	6"	Grenade D6	3	0	1	-
Krak grenade	6"	Grenade 1	6	-1	D3	-

ABILITIES	And They Shall Know No Fear (pg 10)
	Honour or Death: This model must make a Heroic Intervention if it is able to do so. In addition, you can re-roll any failed hit rolls for this model in the Fight phase when targeting a CHARACTER.
	Combat Shield: This model has a 5+ invulnerable save.
FACTION KEYWORDS	IMPERIUM, ADEPTUS ASTARTES, <CHAPTER>
KEYWORDS	CHARACTER, INFANTRY, COMPANY CHAMPION

COMPANY CHAMPION
on Bike

NAME	M	WS	BS	S	T	W	A	Ld	Sv
Company Champion on Bike	14"	2+	3+	4	5	5	3	8	3+

A Company Champion on Bike is a single model armed with a bolt pistol, master-crafted power sword, frag grenades and krak grenades. His Space Marine bike is equipped with a twin boltgun.

WEAPON	RANGE	TYPE	S	AP	D	ABILITIES
Bolt pistol	12"	Pistol 1	4	0	1	-
Twin boltgun	24"	Rapid Fire 2	4	0	1	-
Master-crafted power sword	Melee	Melee	User	-3	2	-
Frag grenade	6"	Grenade D6	3	0	1	-
Krak grenade	6"	Grenade 1	6	-1	D3	-

ABILITIES	
	And They Shall Know No Fear (pg 10)
	Honour or Death: This model must make a Heroic Intervention if it is able to do so. In addition, you can re-roll any failed hit rolls for this model in the Fight phase when targeting a **Character**.
	Combat Shield: This model has a 5+ invulnerable save.
	Turbo-boost: When this model Advances, add 6" to its Move characteristic for that Movement phase instead of rolling a dice.
FACTION KEYWORDS	**Imperium, Adeptus Astartes, <Chapter>**
KEYWORDS	**Biker, Character, Company Champion**

COMPANY VETERANS

NAME	M	WS	BS	S	T	W	A	Ld	Sv
Space Marine Veteran	6"	3+	3+	4	4	1	2	8	3+
Veteran Sergeant	6"	3+	3+	4	4	1	3	9	3+

This unit contains 1 Veteran Sergeant and 1 Space Marine Veteran. It can include up to 3 additional Space Marine Veterans (**Power Rating +5**). Each model is armed with a bolt pistol, chainsword, frag grenades and krak grenades.

WEAPON	RANGE	TYPE	S	AP	D	ABILITIES
Bolt pistol	12"	Pistol 1	4	0	1	-
Boltgun	24"	Rapid Fire 1	4	0	1	-
Chainsword	Melee	Melee	User	0	1	Each time the bearer fights, it can make 1 additional attack with this weapon.
Frag grenade	6"	Grenade D6	3	0	1	-
Krak grenade	6"	Grenade 1	6	-1	D3	-

WARGEAR OPTIONS	• The Veteran Sergeant may replace his bolt pistol and chainsword with items from the *Sergeant Equipment* list. • Any Space Marine Veteran may replace their bolt pistol with a storm shield or an item from the *Melee Weapons* or *Pistols* lists. • Any Space Marine Veteran may replace their chainsword with a storm shield, a boltgun, or an item from the *Melee Weapons*, *Pistols*, *Combi-weapons* or *Special Weapons* list.
ABILITIES	**And They Shall Know No Fear** (pg 10) **Command Squad Bodyguard:** Roll a dice each time a friendly <CHAPTER> CHARACTER loses a wound whilst they are within 3" of this unit; on a 2+ a model from this squad can intercept that hit – the character does not lose a wound but this unit suffers a mortal wound. **Storm Shield:** A model equipped with a storm shield has a 3+ invulnerable save.
FACTION KEYWORDS	**IMPERIUM, ADEPTUS ASTARTES, <CHAPTER>**
KEYWORDS	**INFANTRY, COMPANY VETERANS**

The Command Squad, comprised of Company Veterans and specialists such as the Apothecary, bring swift death to their foes.

COMPANY VETERANS
on Bikes

NAME	M	WS	BS	S	T	W	A	Ld	Sv
Space Marine Veteran Biker	14"	3+	3+	4	5	2	2	8	3+
Veteran Biker Sergeant	14"	3+	3+	4	5	2	3	9	3+

This unit contains 1 Veteran Biker Sergeant and 1 Space Marine Veteran Biker. It can include up to 3 additional Space Marine Veteran Bikers (**Power Rating +8**). Each model is equipped with a bolt pistol, a chainsword, frag grenades and krak grenades. Each of their Space Marine bikes is equipped with a twin boltgun.

WEAPON	RANGE	TYPE	S	AP	D	ABILITIES
Bolt pistol	12"	Pistol 1	4	0	1	-
Boltgun	24"	Rapid Fire 1	4	0	1	-
Twin boltgun	24"	Rapid Fire 2	4	0	1	-
Chainsword	Melee	Melee	User	0	1	Each time the bearer fights, it can make 1 additional attack with this weapon.
Frag grenade	6"	Grenade D6	3	0	1	-
Krak grenade	6"	Grenade 1	6	-1	D3	-

WARGEAR OPTIONS	
	• The Veteran Biker Sergeant may replace his bolt pistol and chainsword with items from the *Sergeant Equipment* list.
	• Any Space Marine Veteran Biker may replace their bolt pistol with a storm shield or an item from the *Melee Weapons* or *Pistols* lists.
	• Any Space Marine Veteran Biker may replace their chainsword with a storm shield, a boltgun, or an item from the *Melee Weapons*, *Pistols*, *Combi-weapons* or *Special Weapons* list.

ABILITIES		
	And They Shall Know No Fear (pg 10)	**Turbo-boost:** When this model Advances, add 6" to its Move characteristic for that Movement phase instead of rolling a dice.
	Biker Bodyguard: Roll a dice each time a friendly <Chapter> Biker Character loses a wound whilst they are within 3" of this unit; on a 2+ a model from this squad can intercept that hit – the character does not lose a wound but this unit suffers a mortal wound.	**Storm Shield:** A model equipped with a storm shield has a 3+ invulnerable save.

FACTION KEYWORDS	IMPERIUM, ADEPTUS ASTARTES, <CHAPTER>
KEYWORDS	BIKER, COMPANY VETERANS

TACTICAL SQUAD

NAME	M	WS	BS	S	T	W	A	Ld	Sv
Space Marine	6"	3+	3+	4	4	1	1	7	3+
Space Marine Sergeant	6"	3+	3+	4	4	1	2	8	3+

This unit contains 1 Space Marine Sergeant and 4 Space Marines. It can include up to 5 additional Space Marines (**Power Rating +4**). Each model is armed with a boltgun, bolt pistol, frag grenades and krak grenades.

WEAPON	RANGE	TYPE	S	AP	D	ABILITIES
Bolt pistol	12"	Pistol 1	4	0	1	-
Boltgun	24"	Rapid Fire 1	4	0	1	-
Frag grenade	6"	Grenade D6	3	0	1	-
Krak grenade	6"	Grenade 1	6	-1	D3	-

WARGEAR OPTIONS	• The Space Marine Sergeant may replace his bolt pistol and boltgun with items from the *Sergeant Equipment* list. • If the unit contains fewer than ten models, one Space Marine may replace his boltgun with an item from the *Special Weapons* or *Heavy Weapons* list. • If the unit contains ten models, one Space Marine may replace his boltgun with an item from the *Special Weapons* list and one other Space Marine may replace his boltgun with an item from the *Heavy Weapons* list.
ABILITIES	**And They Shall Know No Fear** (pg 10) **Combat Squads:** Before any models are deployed at the start of the game, a Tactical Squad containing 10 models may be split into two units, each containing 5 models.
FACTION KEYWORDS	IMPERIUM, ADEPTUS ASTARTES, <CHAPTER>
KEYWORDS	INFANTRY, TACTICAL SQUAD

Tactical Squads are filled with versatile and deadly warriors armed with an arsenal of weaponry to counter any foe.

SCOUT SQUAD

NAME	M	WS	BS	S	T	W	A	Ld	Sv
Scout	6"	3+	3+	4	4	1	1	7	4+
Scout Sergeant	6"	3+	3+	4	4	1	2	8	4+

This unit contains 1 Scout Sergeant and 4 Scouts. It can include up to 5 additional Scouts (**Power Rating +4**). Each model is armed with a boltgun, bolt pistol, frag grenades and krak grenades.

WEAPON	RANGE	TYPE	S	AP	D	ABILITIES
Astartes shotgun	12"	Assault 2	4	0	1	If the target is within half range, add 1 to this weapon's Strength.
Bolt pistol	12"	Pistol 1	4	0	1	-
Boltgun	24"	Rapid Fire 1	4	0	1	-
Heavy bolter	36"	Heavy 3	5	-1	1	-
Missile launcher	When attacking with this weapon, choose one of the profiles below.					
- Frag missile	48"	Heavy D6	4	0	1	-
- Krak missile	48"	Heavy 1	8	-2	D6	-
Sniper rifle	36"	Heavy 1	4	0	1	This weapon may target a **CHARACTER** even if it is not the closest enemy unit. If you roll a wound roll of 6+ for this weapon, it inflicts a mortal wound in addition to its normal damage.
Combat knife	Melee	Melee	User	0	1	Each time the bearer fights, it can make 1 additional attack with this weapon.
Frag grenade	6"	Grenade D6	3	0	1	-
Krak grenade	6"	Grenade 1	6	-1	D3	-

WARGEAR OPTIONS	
	• The Scout Sergeant may replace his bolt pistol and boltgun with items from the *Sergeant Equipment* list. • Any model may replace his boltgun with a sniper rifle, an Astartes shotgun or a combat knife. • One Scout may replace his boltgun with a heavy bolter or a missile launcher. • Any model may take a camo cloak.

ABILITIES	
	And They Shall Know No Fear (pg 10) **Combat Squads:** Before any models are deployed at the start of the game, a Scout Squad containing 10 models may be split into two units, each containing 5 models.	**Concealed Positions:** When you set up this unit during deployment, it can be set up anywhere on the battlefield that is more than 9" from the enemy deployment zone. **Camo Cloaks:** If every model in a unit has a camo cloak you can add 2 to saving throws made for models in the unit when they receive the benefits of cover, instead of 1.

FACTION KEYWORDS	IMPERIUM, ADEPTUS ASTARTES, \<CHAPTER\>
KEYWORDS	INFANTRY, SCOUT, SCOUT SQUAD

Space Marine Scouts are trained in guerilla warfare and sabotage, and sow fear and confusion ahead of the main advance.

INTERCESSOR SQUAD

6 POWER

NAME	M	WS	BS	S	T	W	A	Ld	Sv
Intercessor	6"	3+	3+	4	4	2	2	7	3+
Intercessor Sergeant	6"	3+	3+	4	4	2	3	8	3+

This unit contains 1 Intercessor Sergeant and 4 Intercessors. Each model is armed with a bolt rifle, a bolt pistol, frag grenades and krak grenades.

WEAPON	RANGE	TYPE	S	AP	D	ABILITIES
Bolt pistol	12"	Pistol 1	4	0	1	-
Bolt rifle	30"	Rapid Fire 1	4	-1	1	-
Frag grenade	6"	Grenade D6	3	0	1	-
Krak grenade	6"	Grenade 1	6	-1	D3	-
ABILITIES	And They Shall Know No Fear (pg 10)					
FACTION KEYWORDS	IMPERIUM, ADEPTUS ASTARTES, <CHAPTER>					
KEYWORDS	INFANTRY, PRIMARIS, INTERCESSOR SQUAD					

IMPERIAL SPACE MARINE

3 POWER

NAME	M	WS	BS	S	T	W	A	Ld	Sv
Imperial Space Marine	6"	3+	3+	4	4	4	3	8	3+

The Imperial Space Marine is a single model. He is armed with a disintegration combi-gun, a disintegration pistol, frag grenades and krak grenades. Only one of this model may be included in your army.

WEAPON	RANGE	TYPE	S	AP	D	ABILITIES
Disintegration combi-gun	When attacking with this weapon, choose one or both of the profiles below. If you choose both, subtract 1 from all hit rolls for this weapon.					
- Boltgun	24"	Rapid Fire 1	4	0	1	-
- Disintegration gun	18"	Rapid Fire 1	5	-3	D6	-
Disintegration pistol	9"	Pistol 1	5	-3	D6	-
Frag grenade	6"	Grenade D6	3	0	1	-
Krak grenade	6"	Grenade 1	6	-1	D3	-
ABILITIES	And They Shall Know No Fear (pg 10)					
FACTION KEYWORDS	IMPERIUM, ADEPTUS ASTARTES, <CHAPTER>					
KEYWORDS	INFANTRY, CHARACTER, IMPERIAL SPACE MARINE					

HONOUR GUARD

POWER 2

NAME	M	WS	BS	S	T	W	A	Ld	Sv
Honour Guard	6"	3+	3+	4	4	2	2	9	2+

This unit contains 2 Honour Guard. Each model is armed with a boltgun, bolt pistol, power axe, frag grenades and krak grenades.

WEAPON	RANGE	TYPE	S	AP	D	ABILITIES
Boltgun	24"	Rapid Fire 1	4	0	1	-
Bolt pistol	12"	Pistol 1	4	0	1	-
Power axe	Melee	Melee	+1	-2	1	-
Power lance	Melee	Melee	+2	-1	1	-
Power maul	Melee	Melee	+2	-1	1	-
Power sword	Melee	Melee	User	-3	1	-
Relic blade	Melee	Melee	+2	-3	D3	-
Frag grenade	6"	Grenade D6	3	0	1	-
Krak grenade	6"	Grenade 1	6	-1	D3	-

WARGEAR OPTIONS	• Any model may replace his power axe with a power sword, power lance, power maul or relic blade.
ABILITIES	**And They Shall Know No Fear** (pg 10) **Honour Guard:** Roll a D6 each time a friendly \<CHAPTER> CHARACTER loses a wound whilst they are within 3" of this unit; on a 2+ a model from this unit can intercept that hit – the CHARACTER does not lose a wound but this unit suffers a mortal wound.
FACTION KEYWORDS	IMPERIUM, ADEPTUS ASTARTES, \<CHAPTER>
KEYWORDS	INFANTRY, HONOUR GUARD

The Honour Guard take to the field, the Chapter Champion and Chapter Ancient at the forefront of their advance.

CHAPTER ANCIENT

4 POWER

NAME	M	WS	BS	S	T	W	A	Ld	Sv
Chapter Ancient	6"	3+	3+	4	4	4	3	9	2+

The Chapter Ancient is a single model armed with a power sword, frag grenades and krak grenades. Only one of this model may be included in your army.

WEAPON	RANGE	TYPE	S	AP	D	ABILITIES
Power sword	Melee	Melee	User	-3	1	-
Frag grenade	6"	Grenade D6	3	0	1	-
Krak grenade	6"	Grenade 1	6	-1	D3	-

ABILITIES	**And They Shall Know No Fear** (pg 10)
	Astartes Banner: <CHAPTER> units within 6" of any friendly <CHAPTER> ANCIENTS add 1 to their Leadership. In addition, roll a D6 each time a <CHAPTER> INFANTRY model is destroyed within 6" of any friendly <CHAPTER> ANCIENTS, before removing the model as a casualty. On a 4+ that model musters one last surge of strength before succumbing to its wounds; it can either shoot with one of its weapons as if it were the Shooting phase, or make a single attack as if it were the Fight phase.

FACTION KEYWORDS	IMPERIUM, ADEPTUS ASTARTES, <CHAPTER>
KEYWORDS	CHARACTER, INFANTRY, ANCIENT, CHAPTER ANCIENT

CHAPTER CHAMPION

4 POWER

NAME	M	WS	BS	S	T	W	A	Ld	Sv
Chapter Champion	6"	2+	3+	4	4	4	4	9	2+

The Chapter Champion is a single model armed with a boltgun, a bolt pistol, a power sword, frag grenades and krak grenades. Only one of this model may be included in your army.

WEAPON	RANGE	TYPE	S	AP	D	ABILITIES
Bolt pistol	12"	Pistol 1	4	0	1	-
Boltgun	24"	Rapid Fire 1	4	0	1	-
Champion's blade	Melee	Melee	User	-2	1	Each time the bearer fights, it can make 1 additional attack with this weapon.
Power axe	Melee	Melee	+1	-2	1	-
Power lance	Melee	Melee	+2	-1	1	-
Power maul	Melee	Melee	+2	-1	1	-
Power sword	Melee	Melee	User	-3	1	-
Relic blade	Melee	Melee	+2	-3	D3	-
Thunder hammer	Melee	Melee	x2	-3	3	When attacking with this weapon, you must subtract 1 from the hit roll.
Frag grenade	6"	Grenade D6	3	0	1	-
Krak grenade	6"	Grenade 1	6	-1	D3	-

WARGEAR OPTIONS	• This model may replace his boltgun with a Champion's blade. • This model may replace his power sword with a power axe, power lance, power maul, thunder hammer or relic blade.
ABILITIES	**And They Shall Know No Fear** (pg 10) **Honour or Death:** This model must make a Heroic Intervention if it is able to do so. In addition, you can re-roll any failed hit rolls for this model in the Fight phase when targeting a CHARACTER.
FACTION KEYWORDS	IMPERIUM, ADEPTUS ASTARTES, <CHAPTER>
KEYWORDS	CHARACTER, INFANTRY, CHAPTER CHAMPION

CENTURION ASSAULT SQUAD

15 POWER

NAME	M	WS	BS	S	T	W	A	Ld	Sv
Centurion	4"	3+	3+	5	5	3	2	7	2+
Centurion Sergeant	4"	3+	3+	5	5	3	3	8	2+

This unit contains 1 Centurion Sergeant and 2 Centurions. It can include up to 3 additional Centurions (**Power Rating +15**). Each model is armed with siege drills, two flamers and Centurion assault launchers.

WEAPON	RANGE	TYPE	S	AP	D	ABILITIES
Flamer	8"	Assault D6	4	0	1	This weapon automatically hits its target.
Hurricane bolter	24"	Rapid Fire 6	4	0	1	-
Meltagun	12"	Assault 1	8	-4	D6	If the target is within half range of this weapon, roll two dice when inflicting damage with it and discard the lowest result.
Siege drills	Melee	Melee	x2	-4	3	-

WARGEAR OPTIONS	• Any model may replace its two flamers with two meltaguns. • Any model may replace its Centurion assault launchers with a hurricane bolter.

ABILITIES	**And They Shall Know No Fear** (pg 10) **Combat Squads:** Before any models are deployed at the start of the game, a Centurion Assault Squad containing 6 models may be split into two units, each containing 3 models.	**Centurion Assault Launchers:** If a model with Centurion assault launchers finishes a charge move within 1" of an enemy unit, roll a D6 – on a 4+ that unit suffers a mortal wound. **Omniscope:** Enemy units do not receive the benefit to their saving throws for being in cover against attacks made by a unit that includes a Centurion Sergeant.

FACTION KEYWORDS	IMPERIUM, ADEPTUS ASTARTES, <CHAPTER>
KEYWORDS	INFANTRY, CENTURION, CENTURION ASSAULT SQUAD

STERNGUARD VETERAN SQUAD

7 POWER

NAME	M	WS	BS	S	T	W	A	Ld	Sv
Space Marine Veteran	6"	3+	3+	4	4	1	2	8	3+
Veteran Sergeant	6"	3+	3+	4	4	1	3	9	3+

This unit contains 1 Veteran Sergeant and 4 Space Marine Veterans. It can include up to 5 additional Space Marine Veterans (**Power Rating +7**). Each model is equipped with a special issue boltgun, a bolt pistol, frag grenades and krak grenades.

WEAPON	RANGE	TYPE	S	AP	D	ABILITIES
Bolt pistol	12"	Pistol 1	4	0	1	-
Heavy flamer	8"	Heavy D6	5	-1	1	This weapon automatically hits its target.
Special issue boltgun	30"	Rapid Fire 1	4	-2	1	-
Frag grenade	6"	Grenade D6	3	0	1	-
Krak grenade	6"	Grenade 1	6	-1	D3	-

WARGEAR OPTIONS	• The Veteran Sergeant may replace his bolt pistol and special issue boltgun with items from the *Sergeant Equipment* list. • The Veteran Sergeant may replace his bolt pistol with an item from the *Sergeant Equipment* list. • Up to two Space Marine Veterans may replace their special issue boltgun with a heavy flamer or an item from the *Special Weapons, Heavy Weapons* or *Combi-weapons* list. • Any Space Marine Veteran may replace his special issue boltgun with a weapon from the *Combi-weapons* list.

ABILITIES	**And They Shall Know No Fear** (pg 10) **Combat Squads:** Before any models are deployed at the start of the game, a Sternguard Veteran Squad containing 10 models may be split into two units, each containing 5 models.

FACTION KEYWORDS	IMPERIUM, ADEPTUS ASTARTES, <CHAPTER>
KEYWORDS	INFANTRY, STERNGUARD VETERAN SQUAD

VANGUARD VETERAN SQUAD

7 POWER

NAME	M	WS	BS	S	T	W	A	Ld	Sv
Space Marine Veteran	6"	3+	3+	4	4	1	2	8	3+
Veteran Sergeant	6"	3+	3+	4	4	1	3	9	3+

This unit contains 1 Veteran Sergeant and 4 Space Marine Veterans. It can include up to 5 additional Space Marine Veterans (**Power Rating +7**). Each model is armed with a bolt pistol, chainsword, frag grenades and krak grenades.

WEAPON	RANGE	TYPE	S	AP	D	ABILITIES
Bolt pistol	12"	Pistol 1	4	0	1	-
Chainsword	Melee	Melee	User	0	1	Each time the bearer fights, it can make 1 additional attack with this weapon.
Relic blade	Melee	Melee	+2	-3	D3	-
Frag grenade	6"	Grenade D6	3	0	1	-
Krak grenade	6"	Grenade 1	6	-1	D3	-
Melta bomb	4"	Grenade 1	8	-4	D6	-

WARGEAR OPTIONS	
	• The Veteran Sergeant may replace his bolt pistol and chainsword with two items from the following list: a storm shield, a relic blade, or an item from the *Pistols* or *Melee Weapons* lists. • Any Space Marine Veteran may replace his bolt pistol and chainsword with a storm shield and an item from the *Pistols* or *Melee Weapons* lists, or with two items from the *Pistols* and/or *Melee Weapons* lists. • One model may take melta bombs. • The entire unit may take jump packs (**Power Rating +1** for a 5-strong unit, or **+2** for a 10-strong one). If they do, their Move characteristic is increased to 12" and they gain the **JUMP PACK** and **FLY** keywords.

ABILITIES	
	And They Shall Know No Fear (pg 10) **Combat Squads:** Before any models are deployed at the start of the game, a Vanguard Veteran Squad containing 10 models may be split into two units, each containing 5 models. **Storm Shield:** A model equipped with a storm shield has a 3+ invulnerable save.
	Jump Pack Assault: During deployment, if the entire unit has jump packs, you can set them up high in the skies instead of placing them on the battlefield. At the end of any of your Movement phases this unit can assault from above – set them up anywhere on the battlefield that is more than 9" away from any enemy models.

FACTION KEYWORDS	**IMPERIUM, ADEPTUS ASTARTES, <CHAPTER>**
KEYWORDS	**INFANTRY, VANGUARD VETERAN SQUAD**

Vanguard Veteran Squads strike like a hammer from the heavens, carving through the enemy with matchless skill.

DREADNOUGHT

7 POWER

NAME	M	WS	BS	S	T	W	A	Ld	Sv
Dreadnought	6"	3+	3+	6	7	8	4	8	3+

A Dreadnought is a single model equipped with an assault cannon, a storm bolter and a Dreadnought combat weapon.

WEAPON	RANGE	TYPE	S	AP	D	ABILITIES
Assault cannon	24"	Heavy 6	6	-1	1	-
Heavy flamer	8"	Heavy D6	5	-1	1	This weapon automatically hits its target.
Missile launcher	When attacking with this weapon, choose one of the profiles below.					
- Frag missile	48"	Heavy D6	4	0	1	-
- Krak missile	48"	Heavy 1	8	-2	D6	-
Storm bolter	24"	Rapid Fire 2	4	0	1	-
Twin autocannon	48"	Heavy 4	7	-1	2	-
Dreadnought combat weapon	Melee	Melee	x2	-3	3	-

WARGEAR OPTIONS	• This model may replace its assault cannon with an item from the *Dreadnought Heavy Weapons* list. • This model may replace its Dreadnought combat weapon and storm bolter with a missile launcher or a twin autocannon. • This model may replace its storm bolter with a heavy flamer.

ABILITIES	**Smoke Launchers:** Once per game, instead of shooting any weapons in the Shooting phase, this model can use its smoke launchers; until your next Shooting phase your opponent must subtract 1 from all hit rolls for ranged weapons that target this vehicle.	**Explodes:** If this model is reduced to 0 wounds, roll a D6 before removing the model from the battlefield; on a 6 it explodes, and each unit within 3" suffers D3 mortal wounds.

FACTION KEYWORDS	IMPERIUM, ADEPTUS ASTARTES, <CHAPTER>

KEYWORDS	VEHICLE, DREADNOUGHT

By piloting these walking tanks, severely injured and crippled battle-brothers continue to serve their Chapter.

VENERABLE DREADNOUGHT

8 POWER

NAME	M	WS	BS	S	T	W	A	Ld	Sv
Venerable Dreadnought	6"	2+	2+	6	7	8	4	8	3+

A Venerable Dreadnought is a single model equipped with an assault cannon, a storm bolter and a Dreadnought combat weapon.

WEAPON	RANGE	TYPE	S	AP	D	ABILITIES
Assault cannon	24"	Heavy 6	6	-1	1	-
Heavy flamer	8"	Heavy D6	5	-1	1	This weapon automatically hits its target.
Missile launcher		When attacking with this weapon, choose one of the profiles below.				
- Frag missile	48"	Heavy D6	4	0	1	-
- Krak missile	48"	Heavy 1	8	-2	D6	-
Storm bolter	24"	Rapid Fire 2	4	0	1	-
Twin autocannon	48"	Heavy 4	7	-1	2	-
Dreadnought combat weapon	Melee	Melee	x2	-3	3	-

WARGEAR OPTIONS	• This model may replace its assault cannon with a weapon from the *Dreadnought Heavy Weapons* list. • This model may replace its Dreadnought combat weapon and storm bolter with a missile launcher or a twin autocannon. • This model may replace its storm bolter with a heavy flamer.
ABILITIES	**Unyielding Ancient:** Roll a D6 each time this model loses a wound; on a 6 the damage is ignored and that wound is not lost. **Explodes:** If this model is reduced to 0 wounds, roll a D6 before removing the model from the battlefield; on a 6 it explodes, and each unit within 3" suffers D3 mortal wounds.	**Smoke Launchers:** Once per game, instead of shooting any weapons in the Shooting phase, this model can use its smoke launchers; until your next Shooting phase your opponent must subtract 1 from all hit rolls for ranged weapons that target this vehicle.
FACTION KEYWORDS	IMPERIUM, ADEPTUS ASTARTES, <CHAPTER>
KEYWORDS	VEHICLE, DREADNOUGHT, VENERABLE DREADNOUGHT

CONTEMPTOR DREADNOUGHT

8 POWER

DAMAGE
Some of this model's characteristics change as it suffers damage, as shown below:

REMAINING W	M	BS	WS
6-10+	9"	2+	2+
3-5	6"	3+	3+
1-2	4"	4+	4+

NAME	M	WS	BS	S	T	W	A	Ld	Sv
Contemptor Dreadnought	*	*	*	7	7	10	4	8	3+

A Contemptor Dreadnought is a single model equipped with a multi-melta, a combi-bolter and a Dreadnought combat weapon.

WEAPON	RANGE	TYPE	S	AP	D	ABILITIES
Combi-bolter	24"	Rapid Fire 2	4	0	1	-
Multi-melta	24"	Heavy 1	8	-4	D6	If the target is within half range of this weapon, roll two dice when inflicting damage with it and discard the lowest result.
Kheres pattern assault cannon	24"	Heavy 6	7	-1	1	-
Dreadnought combat weapon	Melee	Melee	x2	-3	3	-

WARGEAR OPTIONS	• This model may replace its multi-melta with a Kheres pattern assault cannon.
ABILITIES	**Atomantic Shielding:** This model has a 5+ invulnerable save. **Explodes:** If this model is reduced to 0 wounds, roll a D6 before removing the model from the battlefield; on a 6 it explodes, and each unit within 6" suffers D3 mortal wounds.
FACTION KEYWORDS	IMPERIUM, ADEPTUS ASTARTES, <CHAPTER>
KEYWORDS	VEHICLE, DREADNOUGHT, CONTEMPTOR DREADNOUGHT

IRONCLAD DREADNOUGHT

10 POWER

NAME	M	WS	BS	S	T	W	A	Ld	Sv
Ironclad Dreadnought	6"	3+	3+	6	8	8	4	8	3+

An Ironclad Dreadnought is a single model equipped with a seismic hammer, a meltagun, a storm bolter and a Dreadnought combat weapon.

WEAPON	RANGE	TYPE	S	AP	D	ABILITIES
Heavy flamer	8"	Heavy D6	5	-1	1	This weapon automatically hits its target.
Hunter-killer missile	48"	Heavy 1	8	-2	D6	A model can only fire each of its hunter-killer missiles once per battle.
Hurricane bolter	24"	Rapid Fire 6	4	0	1	-
Meltagun	12"	Assault 1	8	-4	D6	If the target is within half range of this weapon, roll two dice when inflicting damage with it and discard the lowest result.
Storm bolter	24"	Rapid Fire 2	4	0	1	-
Dreadnought chainfist	Melee	Melee	x2	-4	4	-
Dreadnought combat weapon	Melee	Melee	x2	-3	3	-
Seismic hammer	Melee	Melee	x2	-4	5	When attacking with this weapon, you must subtract 1 from the hit roll.

WARGEAR OPTIONS	
	• This model may replace its seismic hammer with a Dreadnought chainfist.
	• This model may replace its Dreadnought combat weapon and storm bolter with a hurricane bolter.
	• This model may replace its storm bolter with a heavy flamer.
	• This model may replace its meltagun with a heavy flamer.
	• This model may take up to two hunter-killer missiles.
	• This model may take ironclad assault launchers.

ABILITIES	
	Wrecker: You can re-roll hit rolls of 1 for this model if it is equipped with two melee weapons. **Ironclad Assault Launchers:** If this model is equipped with ironclad assault launchers and finishes a charge move within 1" of an enemy unit, roll a D6. On a 4+ that unit suffers D3 mortal wounds.	**Smoke Launchers:** Once per game, instead of shooting any weapons in the Shooting phase, this model can use its smoke launchers; until your next Shooting phase your opponent must subtract 1 from all hit rolls for ranged weapons that target this vehicle. **Explodes:** If this model is reduced to 0 wounds, roll a D6 before removing the model from the battlefield; on a 6 it explodes, and each unit within 3" suffers D3 mortal wounds.

FACTION KEYWORDS	IMPERIUM, ADEPTUS ASTARTES, <CHAPTER>
KEYWORDS	VEHICLE, DREADNOUGHT, IRONCLAD DREADNOUGHT

TERMINATOR SQUAD

13 POWER

NAME	M	WS	BS	S	T	W	A	Ld	Sv
Terminator	5"	3+	3+	4	4	2	2	8	2+
Terminator Sergeant	5"	3+	3+	4	4	2	3	9	2+

This unit contains 1 Terminator Sergeant and 4 Terminators. It can include up to 5 additional Terminators (**Power Rating +13**).
• The Terminator Sergeant is armed with a storm bolter and power sword.
• Each Terminator is armed with a storm bolter and power fist.

WEAPON	RANGE	TYPE	S	AP	D	ABILITIES
Storm bolter	24"	Rapid Fire 2	4	0	1	-
Chainfist	Melee	Melee	x2	-4	2	When attacking with this weapon, you must subtract 1 from the hit roll.
Power fist	Melee	Melee	x2	-3	D3	When attacking with this weapon, you must subtract 1 from the hit roll.
Power sword	Melee	Melee	User	-3	1	-

WARGEAR OPTIONS	
	• For every five models in the unit, one Terminator may replace his storm bolter with a weapon from the *Terminator Heavy Weapons* list. • Any Terminator may replace his power fist with a chainfist. • The unit may take a teleport homer.

ABILITIES	
	And They Shall Know No Fear (pg 10) **Combat Squads:** Before any models are deployed at the start of the game, a Terminator Squad containing 10 models may be split into two units, each containing 5 models. **Teleport Strike:** During deployment, you can set up this unit in a teleportarium chamber instead of placing them on the battlefield. At the end of any of your Movement phases this unit can teleport into battle – set them up anywhere on the battlefield that is more than 9" away from any enemy models.	**Teleport Homer:** If this unit has a teleport homer, place it anywhere in your deployment zone when your army deploys. If an enemy model is ever within 9" of the teleport homer, it is deactivated and removed from the battlefield. Whilst there are any friendly <CHAPTER> teleport homers on the battlefield, this unit can perform an emergency teleport instead of moving in its Movement phase. At the end of the Movement phase, remove this unit and then set it up with all models within 6" of a friendly <CHAPTER> teleport homer. That teleport homer is then removed from the battlefield. **Crux Terminatus:** All models in this unit have a 5+ invulnerable save.

FACTION KEYWORDS	IMPERIUM, ADEPTUS ASTARTES, <CHAPTER>
KEYWORDS	INFANTRY, TERMINATOR, TERMINATOR SQUAD

TERMINATOR ASSAULT SQUAD

NAME	M	WS	BS	S	T	W	A	Ld	Sv
Terminator	5"	3+	3+	4	4	2	2	8	2+
Terminator Sergeant	5"	3+	3+	4	4	2	3	9	2+

This unit contains 1 Terminator Sergeant and 4 Terminators. It can include up to 5 additional Terminators (**Power Rating +13**). Each model is armed with two lightning claws.

WEAPON	RANGE	TYPE	S	AP	D	ABILITIES
Lightning claw	Melee	Melee	User	-2	1	You can re-roll failed wound rolls for this weapon. If a model is armed with two lightning claws, each time it fights it can make 1 additional attack with them.
Thunder hammer	Melee	Melee	x2	-3	3	When attacking with this weapon, you must subtract 1 from the hit roll.

WARGEAR OPTIONS	• Any model may replace its two lightning claws with a thunder hammer and storm shield. • The unit may take a teleport homer.

ABILITIES	**And They Shall Know No Fear** (pg 10) **Combat Squads:** Before any models are deployed at the start of the game, a Terminator Assault Squad containing 10 models may be split into two units, each containing 5 models. **Teleport Strike:** During deployment, you can set up this unit in a teleportarium chamber instead of placing them on the battlefield. At the end of any of your Movement phases this unit can teleport into battle – set them up anywhere on the battlefield that is more than 9" away from any enemy models. **Crux Terminatus:** All models in this unit have a 5+ invulnerable save.	**Storm Shield:** A model with a storm shield has a 3+ invulnerable save. **Teleport Homer:** If this unit has a teleport homer, place it anywhere in your deployment zone when your army deploys. If an enemy model is ever within 9" of the teleport homer, it is deactivated and removed from the battlefield. Whilst there are any friendly <CHAPTER> teleport homers on the battlefield, this unit can perform an emergency teleport instead of moving in its Movement phase. At the end of the Movement phase, remove this unit and then set it up with all models within 6" of a friendly <CHAPTER> teleport homer. That teleport homer is then removed from the battlefield.

FACTION KEYWORDS	IMPERIUM, ADEPTUS ASTARTES, <CHAPTER>
KEYWORDS	INFANTRY, TERMINATOR, TERMINATOR ASSAULT SQUAD

Clad in impervious Tactical Dreadnought Armour, Terminators Squads are walking tanks armed with devastating weaponry.

CATAPHRACTII TERMINATOR SQUAD

13 POWER

NAME	M	WS	BS	S	T	W	A	Ld	Sv
Cataphractii Terminator	4"	3+	3+	4	4	2	2	8	2+
Cataphractii Sergeant	4"	3+	3+	4	4	2	3	9	2+

This unit contains 1 Cataphractii Sergeant and 4 Cataphractii Terminators. It can include up to 5 additional Cataphractii Terminators (**Power Rating +13**).
• The Cataphractii Sergeant is armed with a combi-bolter and power sword.
• Each Cataphractii Terminator is armed with a combi-bolter and power fist.

WEAPON	RANGE	TYPE	S	AP	D	ABILITIES
Combi-bolter	24"	Rapid Fire 2	4	0	1	-
Grenade harness	12"	Assault D6	4	1	1	-
Heavy flamer	8"	Heavy D6	5	-1	1	This weapon automatically hits its target.
Chainfist	Melee	Melee	x2	-4	2	When attacking with this weapon, you must subtract 1 from the hit roll.
Lightning claw	Melee	Melee	User	-2	1	You can re-roll failed wound rolls for this weapon. If a model is armed with two lightning claws, each time it fights it can make 1 additional attack with them.
Power fist	Melee	Melee	x2	-3	D3	When attacking with this weapon, you must subtract 1 from the hit roll.
Power sword	Melee	Melee	User	-3	1	-

WARGEAR OPTIONS	
	• For every five models in the unit, one Cataphractii Terminator may replace his combi-bolter with a heavy flamer.
	• Any model may replace his combi-bolter with a lightning claw.
	• Any Cataphractii Terminator may replace his power fist with a chainfist or a lightning claw.
	• The Cataphractii Sergeant may replace his power sword with a chainfist, a power fist or a lightning claw.
	• The Cataphractii Sergeant may take a grenade harness.

ABILITIES

And They Shall Know No Fear (pg 10)

Combat Squads: Before deployment at the start of the game, a Cataphractii Terminator Squad containing 10 models may be split into two units, each containing 5 models.

Cataphractii Armour: Models in this unit have a 4+ invulnerable save, but you must halve the result of the dice rolled when determining how far this model Advances.

Teleport Strike: During deployment, you can set up this unit in a teleportarium chamber instead of placing them on the battlefield. At the end of any of your Movement phases this unit can teleport into battle – set them up anywhere on the battlefield that is more than 9" away from any enemy models.

FACTION KEYWORDS	IMPERIUM, ADEPTUS ASTARTES, <CHAPTER>
KEYWORDS	INFANTRY, TERMINATOR, CATAPHRACTII TERMINATOR SQUAD

Only the longest-serving veterans of a Chapter still stride to war in this ancient pattern of Terminator armour.

TARTAROS TERMINATOR SQUAD

NAME	M	WS	BS	S	T	W	A	Ld	Sv
Tartaros Terminator	6"	3+	3+	4	4	2	2	8	2+
Tartaros Sergeant	6"	3+	3+	4	4	2	3	9	2+

This unit contains 1 Tartaros Sergeant and 4 Tartaros Terminators. It can include up to 5 additional Tartaros Terminators (**Power Rating +13**).
• The Tartaros Sergeant is armed with a combi-bolter and power sword.
• Each Tartaros Terminator is armed with a combi-bolter and power fist.

WEAPON	RANGE	TYPE	S	AP	D	ABILITIES
Combi-bolter	24"	Rapid Fire 2	4	0	1	-
Grenade harness	12"	Assault D6	4	1	1	-
Heavy flamer	8"	Heavy D6	5	-1	1	This weapon automatically hits its target.
Plasma blaster	When attacking with this weapon, choose one of the profiles below.					
- Standard	18"	Assault 2	7	-3	1	
- Supercharge	18"	Assault 2	8	-3	2	On a hit roll of 1, the bearer is slain after all of this weapon's shots have been resolved.
Reaper autocannon	36"	Heavy 4	7	-1	1	-
Volkite charger	15"	Heavy 2	5	0	2	-
Chainfist	Melee	Melee	x2	-4	2	When attacking with this weapon, you must subtract 1 from the hit roll.
Lightning claw	Melee	Melee	User	-2	1	You can re-roll failed wound rolls for this weapon. If a model is armed with two lightning claws, each time it fights it can make 1 additional attack with them.
Power fist	Melee	Melee	x2	-3	D3	When attacking with this weapon, you must subtract 1 from the hit roll.
Power sword	Melee	Melee	User	-3	1	

WARGEAR OPTIONS	
	• For every five models in the unit, one Cataphractii Terminator may replace his combi-bolter with a heavy flamer or a reaper autocannon. • Any Tartaros Terminator may replace his combi-bolter and power fist with two lightning claws. • The Tartaros Sergeant may replace his combi-bolter and power sword with two lightning claws. • Any Tartaros Terminator may replace his power fist with a chainfist. • The Tartaros Sergeant may replace his power sword with a chainfist or a power fist. • The Tartaros Sergeant may replace his combi-bolter with a plasma blaster or a volkite charger. • For every five models in the unit, one model may take a grenade harness.

ABILITIES		
	And They Shall Know No Fear (pg 10) **Combat Squads:** Before deployment at the start of the game, a Tartaros Terminator Squad containing 10 models may be split into two units, each containing 5 models. **Tartaros Armour:** Models in this unit have a 5+ invulnerable save.	**Teleport Strike:** During deployment, you can set up this unit in a teleportarium chamber instead of placing them on the battlefield. At the end of any of your Movement phases this unit can teleport into battle – set them up anywhere on the battlefield that is more than 9" away from any enemy models.

FACTION KEYWORDS	IMPERIUM, ADEPTUS ASTARTES, <CHAPTER>
KEYWORDS	INFANTRY, TERMINATOR, TARTAROS TERMINATOR SQUAD

⚡ 5 POWER   ASSAULT SQUAD

NAME	M	WS	BS	S	T	W	A	Ld	Sv
Space Marine	6"	3+	3+	4	4	1	1	7	3+
Space Marine Sergeant	6"	3+	3+	4	4	1	2	8	3+

This unit contains 1 Space Marine Sergeant and 4 Space Marines. It can include up to 5 additional Space Marines (**Power Rating +4**). Each model is armed with a bolt pistol, chainsword, frag grenades and krak grenades.

WEAPON	RANGE	TYPE	S	AP	D	ABILITIES
Bolt pistol	12"	Pistol 1	4	0	1	-
Flamer	8"	Assault D6	4	0	1	This weapon automatically hits its target.
Plasma pistol	When attacking with this weapon, choose one of the profiles below.					
- Standard	12"	Pistol 1	7	-3	1	-
- Supercharge	12"	Pistol 1	8	-3	2	On a hit roll of 1, the bearer is slain.
Chainsword	Melee	Melee	User	0	1	Each time the bearer fights, it can make 1 additional attack with this weapon.
Eviscerator	Melee	Melee	x2	-4	D3	When attacking with this weapon, you must subtract 1 from the hit roll.
Frag grenade	6"	Grenade D6	3	0	1	-
Krak grenade	6"	Grenade 1	6	-1	D3	-
Melta bomb	4"	Grenade 1	8	-4	D6	-

WARGEAR OPTIONS
- The Space Marine Sergeant may replace his bolt pistol with an item from the *Melee Weapons* or *Pistols* lists.
- The Space Marine Sergeant may replace his chainsword with an item from the *Melee Weapons* list.
- The Space Marine Sergeant may take a combat shield.
- The Space Marine Sergeant may take melta bombs.
- Up to two Space Marines may replace their bolt pistol and chainsword with a flamer, or with a plasma pistol and a chainsword.
- For every five models in the unit, one model may replace its bolt pistol and chainsword with an eviscerator.
- The entire unit may take jump packs (**Power Rating +1** for a 5-strong unit, or **+2** for a 10-strong one). If they do, their Move characteristic is increased to 12" and they gain the **JUMP PACK** and **FLY** keywords.

ABILITIES

And They Shall Know No Fear (pg 10)

Combat Shield: A model with a combat shield has a 5+ invulnerable save.

Combat Squads: Before any models are deployed at the start of the game, an Assault Squad containing 10 models may be split into two units, each containing 5 models.

Jump Pack Assault: During deployment, if the entire unit has jump packs, you can set them up high in the skies instead of placing them on the battlefield. At the end of any of your Movement phases this unit can assault from above – set them up anywhere on the battlefield that is more than 9" away from any enemy models.

FACTION KEYWORDS	**IMPERIUM, ADEPTUS ASTARTES, \<CHAPTER\>**
KEYWORDS	**INFANTRY, ASSAULT SQUAD**

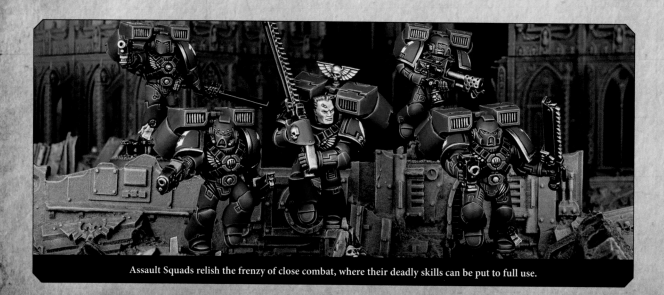

Assault Squads relish the frenzy of close combat, where their deadly skills can be put to full use.

INCEPTOR SQUAD

8 POWER

NAME	M	WS	BS	S	T	W	A	Ld	Sv
Inceptor	10"	3+	3+	4	5	2	2	7	3+
Inceptor Sergeant	10"	3+	3+	4	5	2	3	8	3+

This unit contains 2 Inceptors and 1 Inceptor Sergeant. Each model is equipped with two assault bolters.

WEAPON	RANGE	TYPE	S	AP	D	ABILITIES
Assault bolter	18"	Assault 3	5	-1	1	-

ABILITIES	**And They Shall Know No Fear** (pg 10)
	Crushing Charge: Roll a D6 each time an Inceptor finishes a charge move within 1" of an enemy unit; on a 6, that unit suffers a mortal wound.
	Meteoric Descent: During deployment, you can set up this unit in high orbit instead of placing it on the battlefield. At the end of any of your Movement phases this unit can use a meteoric descent – set it up anywhere on the battlefield that is more than 9" away from any enemy models.

FACTION KEYWORDS	IMPERIUM, ADEPTUS ASTARTES, <CHAPTER>
KEYWORDS	INFANTRY, JUMP PACK, MK X GRAVIS, PRIMARIS, FLY, INCEPTOR SQUAD

SCOUT BIKE SQUAD

5 POWER

NAME	M	WS	BS	S	T	W	A	Ld	Sv
Scout Biker	16"	3+	3+	4	5	2	1	7	4+
Scout Biker Sergeant	16"	3+	3+	4	5	2	2	8	4+

This unit contains 1 Scout Biker Sergeant and 2 Scout Bikers. It can include up to 3 additional Scout Bikers (**Power Rating +4**) or up to 6 additional Scout Bikers (**Power Rating +8**). Each model is equipped with a bolt pistol, an Astartes shotgun, a combat knife, frag grenades and krak grenades. Each of their Scout bikes is equipped with a twin boltgun.

WEAPON	RANGE	TYPE	S	AP	D	ABILITIES
Astartes grenade launcher	When attacking with this weapon, choose one of the profiles below.					
- Frag grenade	24"	Assault D6	3	0	1	-
- Krak grenade	24"	Assault 1	6	-1	D3	-
Astartes shotgun	12"	Assault 2	4	0	1	If the target is within half range, add 1 to this weapon's Strength.
Bolt pistol	12"	Pistol 1	4	0	1	-
Twin boltgun	24"	Rapid Fire 2	4	0	1	-
Combat knife	Melee	Melee	User	0	1	Each time the bearer fights, it can make 1 additional attack with this weapon.
Frag grenade	6"	Grenade D6	3	0	1	-
Krak grenade	6"	Grenade 1	6	-1	D3	-

WARGEAR OPTIONS	• The Scout Biker Sergeant may replace his bolt pistol with an item from the *Sergeant Equipment* list.
	• Up to three Scout Bikers may replace their bike's twin boltgun with an Astartes grenade launcher.

ABILITIES	**And They Shall Know No Fear** (pg 10)
	Combat Squads: Before any models are deployed at the start of the game a Scout Bike Squad containing 6 models may be split into two units, each containing 3 models. A Scout Bike Squad containing 9 models may be split into three units, each containing 3 models.
	Turbo-boost: When this unit Advances, add 6" to its Move characteristic for that Movement phase instead of rolling a dice.

FACTION KEYWORDS	IMPERIUM, ADEPTUS ASTARTES, <CHAPTER>
KEYWORDS	BIKER, SCOUT, SCOUT BIKE SQUAD

BIKE SQUAD

6 POWER

NAME	M	WS	BS	S	T	W	A	Ld	Sv
Space Marine Biker	14"	3+	3+	4	5	2	1	7	3+
Biker Sergeant	14"	3+	3+	4	5	2	2	8	3+
Attack Bike	14"	3+	3+	4	5	4	2	7	3+

This unit contains 1 Biker Sergeant and 2 Space Marine Bikers. It can include up to 3 additional Space Marine Bikers (**Power Rating +5**) or up to 5 additional Space Marine Bikers (**Power Rating +8**). It can also include a single Attack Bike (**Power Rating +3**).
- The Space Marine Bikers and the Biker Sergeant are each equipped with a bolt pistol, frag grenades and krak grenades. Each of their Space Marine bikes is equipped with a twin boltgun.
- The Space Marine Attack Bike is equipped with a twin boltgun and a heavy bolter, and is crewed by two Space Marines armed with bolt pistols, frag grenades and krak grenades.

WEAPON	RANGE	TYPE	S	AP	D	ABILITIES
Bolt pistol	12"	Pistol 1	4	0	1	-
Boltgun	24"	Rapid Fire 1	4	0	1	-
Heavy bolter	36"	Heavy 3	5	-1	1	-
Multi-melta	24"	Heavy 1	8	-4	D6	If the target is within half range of this weapon, roll two dice when inflicting damage with it and discard the lowest result.
Twin boltgun	24"	Rapid Fire 2	4	0	1	-
Chainsword	Melee	Melee	User	0	1	Each time the bearer fights, it can make 1 additional attack with this weapon.
Frag grenade	6"	Grenade D6	3	0	1	-
Krak grenade	6"	Grenade 1	6	-1	D3	-

WARGEAR OPTIONS	• The Space Marine Sergeant may replace his bolt pistol with an item from the *Sergeant Equipment* list. • Any Space Marine Biker may replace his bolt pistol with a chainsword. • Up to two Space Marine Bikers may replace their bolt pistol with an item from the *Special Weapons* list. • The Attack Bike may replace its heavy bolter with a multi-melta.
ABILITIES	**And They Shall Know No Fear** (pg 10) **Combat Squads:** Before any models are deployed at the start of the game a Bike Squad containing 6 models may be split into two units, each containing 3 models. A Bike Squad containing 9 models may be split into two units, one of which has 4 models including the Attack Bike. **Turbo-boost:** When this unit Advances, add 6" to its Move characteristic for that Movement phase instead of rolling a dice.
FACTION KEYWORDS	**IMPERIUM, ADEPTUS ASTARTES, <CHAPTER>**
KEYWORDS	**BIKER, BIKE SQUAD**

Space Marine Bikers weave and jink through a hail of fire, outflanking and encircling their helpless prey.

ATTACK BIKE SQUAD

3 POWER

NAME	M	WS	BS	S	T	W	A	Ld	Sv
Attack Bike	14"	3+	3+	4	5	4	2	7	3+

This unit contains 1 Attack Bike. It can include 1 additional Attack Bike (**Power Rating +3**) or 2 additional Attack Bikes (**Power Rating +6**). Each model is equipped with a twin boltgun and a heavy bolter, and is crewed by two Space Marines armed with bolt pistols, frag grenades and krak grenades.

WEAPON	RANGE	TYPE	S	AP	D	ABILITIES
Bolt pistol	12"	Pistol 1	4	0	1	-
Heavy bolter	36"	Heavy 3	5	-1	1	-
Multi-melta	24"	Heavy 1	8	-4	D6	If the target is within half range of this weapon, roll two dice when inflicting damage with it and discard the lowest result.
Twin boltgun	24"	Rapid Fire 2	4	0	1	-
Frag grenade	6"	Grenade D6	3	0	1	-
Krak grenade	6"	Grenade 1	6	-1	D3	-

WARGEAR OPTIONS	• Any model may replace its heavy bolter with a multi-melta.
ABILITIES	**And They Shall Know No Fear** (pg 10) **Turbo-boost:** When this unit Advances, add 6" to its Move characteristic for that Movement phase instead of rolling a dice.
FACTION KEYWORDS	**IMPERIUM, ADEPTUS ASTARTES, <CHAPTER>**
KEYWORDS	**BIKER, ATTACK BIKE SQUAD**

LAND SPEEDER STORM

5 POWER

NAME	M	WS	BS	S	T	W	A	Ld	Sv
Land Speeder Storm	18"	3+	3+	4	5	7	2	7	4+

A Land Speeder Storm is a single model equipped with a heavy bolter and a cerberus launcher.

WEAPON	RANGE	TYPE	S	AP	D	ABILITIES
Assault cannon	24"	Heavy 6	6	-1	1	-
Cerberus launcher	18"	Heavy D6	4	0	1	-
Heavy bolter	36"	Heavy 3	5	-1	1	-
Heavy flamer	8"	Heavy D6	5	-1	1	This weapon automatically hits its target.
Multi-melta	24"	Heavy 1	8	-4	D6	If the target is within half range of this weapon, roll two dice when inflicting damage with it and discard the lowest result.

WARGEAR OPTIONS	• This model may replace its heavy bolter with a multi-melta, a heavy flamer or an assault cannon.
ABILITIES	**Open-topped:** Models embarked on this vehicle can shoot in their Shooting phase. They measure range and draw line of sight from any point on the vehicle. When they do so, any restrictions or modifiers that apply to this model also apply to its passengers; for example, the passengers cannot shoot if this model has Fallen Back in the same turn, cannot shoot (except with Pistols) if this model is within 1" of an enemy unit, and so on. Note that the passengers cannot shoot if this model Falls Back, even though the Land Speeder Storm itself can. **Explodes:** If this model is reduced to 0 wounds, roll a D6 before removing it from the battlefield and before any embarked models disembark. On a 6 it explodes, and each unit within 3" suffers a mortal wound.
TRANSPORT	This model can transport 5 **<CHAPTER> SCOUT INFANTRY** models.
FACTION KEYWORDS	**IMPERIUM, ADEPTUS ASTARTES, <CHAPTER>**
KEYWORDS	**VEHICLE, TRANSPORT, LAND SPEEDER, SCOUT, FLY, LAND SPEEDER STORM**

6 POWER — LAND SPEEDERS

NAME	M	WS	BS	S	T	W	A	Ld	Sv
Land Speeder	16"	3+	3+	4	5	6	2	7	3+

This unit contains 1 Land Speeder. It can include up to 2 additional Land Speeders (**Power Rating +6 per model**). Each model is equipped with a heavy bolter.

WEAPON	RANGE	TYPE	S	AP	D	ABILITIES
Assault cannon	24"	Heavy 6	6	-1	1	-
Heavy bolter	36"	Heavy 3	5	-1	1	-
Heavy flamer	8"	Heavy D6	5	-1	1	This weapon automatically hits its target.
Multi-melta	24"	Heavy 1	8	-4	D6	If the target is within half range of this weapon, roll two dice when inflicting damage with it and discard the lowest result.
Typhoon missile launcher	When attacking with this weapon, choose one of the profiles below.					
- Frag missile	48"	Heavy 2D6	4	0	1	-
- Krak missile	48"	Heavy 2	8	-2	D6	-

WARGEAR OPTIONS
- Any model may replace its heavy bolter with a multi-melta or a heavy flamer.
- Any model may take an assault cannon, a heavy flamer, a typhoon missile launcher, a heavy bolter or a multi-melta.

ABILITIES

And They Shall Know No Fear (pg 10)

Anti-grav Upwash: Models in this unit have a Move characteristic of 20", instead of 16", whilst the unit contains 3 models.

Explodes: If a model in this unit is reduced to 0 wounds, roll a D6 before removing it from the battlefield. On a 6 it explodes, and each unit within 3" suffers a mortal wound.

FACTION KEYWORDS IMPERIUM, ADEPTUS ASTARTES, <CHAPTER>

KEYWORDS VEHICLE, FLY, LAND SPEEDERS

---

4 POWER — RHINO

NAME	M	WS	BS	S	T	W	A	Ld	Sv
Rhino	*	6+	*	6	7	10	*	8	3+

DAMAGE

Some of this model's characteristics change as it suffers damage, as shown below:

REMAINING W	M	BS	A
6-10+	12"	3+	3
3-5	6"	4+	D3
1-2	3"	5+	1

A Rhino is a single model equipped with a storm bolter.

WEAPON	RANGE	TYPE	S	AP	D	ABILITIES
Hunter-killer missile	48"	Heavy 1	8	-2	D6	This weapon can only be fired once per battle.
Storm bolter	24"	Rapid Fire 2	4	0	1	-

WARGEAR OPTIONS
- This model may take a hunter-killer missile.
- This model may take an additional storm bolter.

ABILITIES

Self-Repair: Roll a D6 at the start of each of your turns; on a 6, this model regains one lost wound.

Smoke Launchers: Once per game, instead of shooting any weapons in the Shooting phase, this model can use its smoke launchers; until your next Shooting phase your opponent must subtract 1 from all hit rolls for ranged weapons that target this vehicle.

Explodes: If this model is reduced to 0 wounds, roll a D6 before removing it from the battlefield and before any embarked models disembark. On a 6 it explodes, and each unit within 6" suffers D3 mortal wounds.

TRANSPORT This model can transport 10 <CHAPTER> INFANTRY models. It cannot transport JUMP PACK, TERMINATOR, PRIMARIS or CENTURION models.

FACTION KEYWORDS IMPERIUM, ADEPTUS ASTARTES, <CHAPTER>

KEYWORDS VEHICLE, TRANSPORT, RHINO

RHINO PRIMARIS

9 POWER

DAMAGE
Some of this model's characteristics change as it suffers damage, as shown below:

REMAINING W	M	BS	A
6-10+	12"	3+	3
3-5	6"	4+	D3
1-2	3"	5+	1

NAME	M	WS	BS	S	T	W	A	Ld	Sv
Rhino Primaris	*	6+	*	6	7	10	*	8	3+

A Rhino Primaris is a single model equipped with a twin plasma gun and an orbital array.

WEAPON	RANGE	TYPE	S	AP	D	ABILITIES
Hunter-killer missile	48"	Heavy 1	8	-2	D6	This weapon can only be fired once per battle.
Orbital array	72"	Heavy D3	10	-4	D6	This weapon can only be fired once per battle. This weapon can target units that are not visible to the bearer. When targeting units with 10 or more models, change this weapon's Type to Heavy D6.
Twin plasma gun	When attacking with this weapon, choose one of the profiles below.					
- Standard	24"	Rapid Fire 2	7	-3	1	
- Supercharge	24"	Rapid Fire 2	8	-3	2	On a hit roll of 1, the bearer is slain after all of this weapon's shots have been resolved.

WARGEAR OPTIONS	• This model may take a hunter-killer missile.
ABILITIES	**Self-Repair:** Roll a D6 at the start of each of your turns; on a 6, this model regains one lost wound. **Smoke Launchers:** Once per game, instead of shooting any weapons in the Shooting phase, this model can use its smoke launchers; until your next Shooting phase your opponent must subtract 1 from all hit rolls for ranged weapons that target this vehicle. **Explodes:** If this model is reduced to 0 wounds, roll a D6 before removing it from the battlefield and before any embarked models disembark. On a 6 it explodes, and each unit within 6" suffers D3 mortal wounds. **Servo-skull Hub:** In each of your Shooting phases, choose one of the following effects: *Targeting Data Skull:* Add 1 to hit rolls made for a single friendly <Chapter> unit within 12" of this model until the end of the phase. *Repair Skull:* Choose a single <Chapter> Vehicle within 12" of this model. That model regains 1 lost wound. *Vox Skull:* Subtract 1 from Morale tests taken for friendly <Chapter> units within 12" of this model until your next Shooting phase.
TRANSPORT	This model can transport 6 <Chapter> Infantry models. It cannot transport Jump Pack, Primaris, Terminator or Centurion models.
FACTION KEYWORDS	Imperium, Adeptus Astartes, <Chapter>
KEYWORDS	Vehicle, Transport, Rhino Primaris

RAZORBACK

NAME	M	WS	BS	S	T	W	A	Ld	Sv
Razorback	*	6+	*	6	7	10	*	8	3+

DAMAGE
Some of this model's characteristics change as it suffers damage, as shown below:

REMAINING W	M	BS	A
6-10+	12"	3+	3
3-5	6"	4+	D3
1-2	3"	5+	1

A Razorback is a single model equipped with a twin heavy bolter.

WEAPON	RANGE	TYPE	S	AP	D	ABILITIES
Hunter-killer missile	48"	Heavy 1	8	-2	D6	This weapon can only be fired once per battle.
Lascannon	48"	Heavy 1	9	-3	D6	-
Storm bolter	24"	Rapid Fire 2	4	0	1	-
Twin assault cannon	24"	Heavy 12	6	-1	1	-
Twin heavy bolter	36"	Heavy 6	5	-1	1	-
Twin lascannon	48"	Heavy 2	9	-3	D6	-
Twin heavy flamer	8"	Assault 2D6	5	-1	1	This weapon automatically hits its target.
Twin plasma gun	When attacking with this weapon, choose one of the profiles below.					
- Standard	24"	Rapid Fire 2	7	-3	1	
- Supercharge	24"	Rapid Fire 2	8	-3	2	On a hit roll of 1, the bearer is slain after all of this weapon's shots have been resolved.

WARGEAR OPTIONS	• This model may replace its twin heavy bolter with a twin lascannon, twin assault cannon, twin heavy flamer or a lascannon and twin plasma gun. • This model may take a hunter-killer missile. • This model may take a storm bolter.
ABILITIES	**Explodes:** If this model is reduced to 0 wounds, roll a D6 before removing it from the battlefield and before any embarked models disembark. On a 6 it explodes, and each unit within 6" suffers D3 mortal wounds.	**Smoke Launchers:** Once per game, instead of shooting any weapons in the Shooting phase, this model can use its smoke launchers; until your next Shooting phase your opponent must subtract 1 from all hit rolls for ranged weapons that target this vehicle.
TRANSPORT	This model can transport 6 <CHAPTER> INFANTRY models. It cannot transport JUMP PACK, TERMINATOR, PRIMARIS or CENTURION models.
FACTION KEYWORDS	IMPERIUM, ADEPTUS ASTARTES, <CHAPTER>
KEYWORDS	VEHICLE, TRANSPORT, RAZORBACK

DROP POD

NAME	M	WS	BS	S	T	W	A	Ld	Sv
Drop Pod	0"	-	3+	6	6	8	0	8	3+

A Drop Pod is a single model equipped with a storm bolter.

WEAPON	RANGE	TYPE	S	AP	D	ABILITIES
Deathwind launcher	12"	Assault D6	5	0	1	-
Storm bolter	24"	Rapid Fire 2	4	0	1	-

WARGEAR OPTIONS	• This model may replace its storm bolter with a deathwind launcher.
ABILITIES	**Drop Pod Assault:** During deployment, you can set up this model, along with any units embarked within it, in orbit instead of placing it on the battlefield. At the end of any of your Movement phases this model can perform a drop pod assault – set it up anywhere on the battlefield that is more than 9" away from any enemy models. Any models embarked inside must immediately disembark, but they must be set up more than 9" away from any enemy models. Any models that cannot be set up because there is not enough room are slain. **Immobile:** After this model has been set up on the battlefield it cannot move for any reason, and no units can embark upon it.
TRANSPORT	This model can transport 10 <CHAPTER> INFANTRY models. It cannot transport JUMP PACK, TERMINATOR, PRIMARIS or CENTURION models.
FACTION KEYWORDS	IMPERIUM, ADEPTUS ASTARTES, <CHAPTER>
KEYWORDS	VEHICLE, TRANSPORT, DROP POD

STORMHAWK INTERCEPTOR

9 POWER

NAME	M	WS	BS	S	T	W	A	Ld	Sv
Stormhawk Interceptor	*	6+	*	6	7	10	*	8	3+

DAMAGE
Some of this model's characteristics change as it suffers damage, as shown below:

REMAINING W	M	BS	A
6-10+	20-60"	3+	3
3-5	20-40"	4+	D3
1-2	20-25"	5+	1

A Stormhawk Interceptor is a single model equipped with two assault cannons, two heavy bolters and an Icarus stormcannon.

WEAPON	RANGE	TYPE	S	AP	D	ABILITIES
Assault cannon	24"	Heavy 6	6	-1	1	-
Heavy bolter	36"	Heavy 3	5	-1	1	-
Icarus stormcannon	48"	Heavy 3	7	-1	2	Add 1 to all hit rolls made for this weapon against targets that can **FLY**. Subtract 1 from the hit rolls made for this weapon against all other targets.
Las-talon	24"	Heavy 2	9	-3	D6	-
Skyhammer missile launcher	60"	Heavy 3	7	-1	D3	Add 1 to all hit rolls made for this weapon against targets that can **FLY**. Subtract 1 from the hit rolls made for this weapon against all other targets.
Typhoon missile launcher	When attacking with this weapon, choose one of the profiles below.					
- Frag missile	48"	Heavy 2D6	4	0	1	-
- Krak missile	48"	Heavy 2	8	-2	D6	-

WARGEAR OPTIONS	• This model may replace its two heavy bolters with a skyhammer missile launcher or a typhoon missile launcher. • This model may replace its Icarus stormcannon with a las-talon.

ABILITIES	**Airborne:** This model cannot charge, can only be charged by units that can **FLY**, and can only attack or be attacked in the Fight phase by units that can **FLY**. **Crash and Burn:** If this model is reduced to 0 wounds, roll a D6 before removing the model from the battlefield; on a 6 it crashes and explodes, and each unit within 6" suffers D3 mortal wounds. **Infernum Halo-launcher:** You can re-roll save rolls of 1 for this model.	**Supersonic:** Each time this model moves, first pivot it on the spot up to 90° (this does not contribute to how far the model moves), and then move the model straight forwards. Note that it cannot pivot again after the initial pivot. When this model Advances, increase its Move characteristic by 20" until the end of the phase – do not roll a dice. **Hard to Hit:** Your opponent must subtract 1 from hit rolls for attacks that target this model in the Shooting phase. **Interceptor:** You can add 1 to hit rolls for this model when targeting an enemy in the Shooting phase that can **FLY**.

FACTION KEYWORDS	IMPERIUM, ADEPTUS ASTARTES, <CHAPTER>

KEYWORDS	VEHICLE, FLY, STORMHAWK INTERCEPTOR

Stormhawk Interceptors are deadly air superiority craft; swift, agile and bristling with weaponry.

STORMTALON GUNSHIP

9 POWER

NAME	M	WS	BS	S	T	W	A	Ld	Sv
Stormtalon Gunship	*	6+	*	6	6	10	*	8	3+

A Stormtalon Gunship is a single model equipped with a twin assault cannon and two heavy bolters.

DAMAGE

Some of this model's characteristics change as it suffers damage, as shown below:

REMAINING W	M	BS	A
6-10+	20-50"	3+	3
3-5	20-35"	4+	D3
1-2	20"	5+	1

WEAPON	RANGE	TYPE	S	AP	D	ABILITIES
Heavy bolter	36"	Heavy 3	5	-1	1	-
Lascannon	48"	Heavy 1	9	-3	D6	-
Skyhammer missile launcher	60"	Heavy 3	7	-1	D3	Add 1 to all hit rolls made for this weapon against targets that can **FLY**. Subtract 1 from the hit rolls made for this weapon against all other targets.
Twin assault cannon	24"	Heavy 12	6	-1	1	-
Typhoon missile launcher	When attacking with this weapon, choose one of the profiles below.					
- Frag missile	48"	Heavy 2D6	4	0	1	-
- Krak missile	48"	Heavy 2	8	-2	D6	-

WARGEAR OPTIONS	• This model may replace its two heavy bolters with two lascannons, a skyhammer missile launcher or a typhoon missile launcher.

ABILITIES	**Airborne:** This model cannot charge, can only be charged by units that can **FLY**, and can only attack or be attacked in the Fight phase by units that can **FLY**. **Supersonic:** Each time this model moves, first pivot it on the spot up to 90° (this does not contribute to how far the model moves), and then move the model straight forwards. Note that it cannot pivot again after the initial pivot. When this model Advances, increase its Move characteristic by 20" until the end of the phase – do not roll a dice. **Hard to Hit:** Your opponent must subtract 1 from hit rolls for attacks that target this model in the Shooting phase.	**Interceptor:** You can add 1 to hit rolls for this model when targeting an enemy in the Shooting phase that cannot **FLY**. **Hover Jet:** Before this model moves in your Movement phase, you can declare it will hover. Its Move characteristic becomes 20" until the end of the phase, and it loses the Airborne, Hard to Hit and Supersonic abilities until the beginning of your next Movement phase. **Crash and Burn:** If this model is reduced to 0 wounds, roll a D6 before removing the model from the battlefield; on a 6 it crashes and explodes, and each unit within 6" suffers D3 mortal wounds.

FACTION KEYWORDS	IMPERIUM, ADEPTUS ASTARTES, <CHAPTER>
KEYWORDS	VEHICLE, FLY, STORMTALON GUNSHIP

Stormtalons engage their thruster engines to hover above the battlefield before unleashing devastating salvoes at ground targets.

DEVASTATOR SQUAD

NAME	M	WS	BS	S	T	W	A	Ld	Sv
Space Marine	6"	3+	3+	4	4	1	1	7	3+
Space Marine Sergeant	6"	3+	3+	4	4	1	2	8	3+
Armorium Cherub	6"	6+	-	2	4	1	1	3	6+

This unit contains 1 Space Marine Sergeant and 4 Space Marines. It can include up to 5 additional Space Marines (**Power Rating +4**). Each model is armed with a boltgun, bolt pistol, frag grenades and krak grenades. The unit may be accompanied by an Armorium Cherub, which is not armed with any weapons.

WEAPON	RANGE	TYPE	S	AP	D	ABILITIES
Bolt pistol	12"	Pistol 1	4	0	1	-
Boltgun	24"	Rapid Fire 1	4	0	1	-
Frag grenade	6"	Grenade D6	3	0	1	-
Krak grenade	6"	Grenade 1	6	-1	D3	-

WARGEAR OPTIONS	• The Space Marine Sergeant may replace his boltgun with items from the *Sergeant Equipment* list. • Up to four Space Marines may replace their boltguns with an item from the *Heavy Weapons* list.

ABILITIES	**And They Shall Know No Fear** (pg 10) **Combat Squads:** Before any models are deployed at the start of the game, a Devastator Squad containing 10 models may be split into two units, each containing 5 models. **Signum:** Before this unit shoots in the Shooting phase, you can choose one model from this unit that is within 3" of its Sergeant; you can add 1 to hit rolls made for your chosen model's weapons this phase.	**Armorium Cherub:** Once per game, after a model in this unit has fired, an Armorium Cherub can reload that model's weapons. When it does so, remove the Armorium Cherub and that model can immediately shoot again. The removal of an Armorium Cherub (for any reason) is ignored for the purposes of morale.

FACTION KEYWORDS	IMPERIUM, ADEPTUS ASTARTES, <CHAPTER>
KEYWORDS	INFANTRY, DEVASTATOR SQUAD

Devastator Squads overwhelm their targets in an earth-shattering barrage of heavy weapons fire.

CENTURION DEVASTATOR SQUAD

17 POWER

NAME	M	WS	BS	S	T	W	A	Ld	Sv
Centurion	4"	3+	3+	5	5	3	2	7	2+
Centurion Sergeant	4"	3+	3+	5	5	3	3	8	2+

This unit contains 1 Centurion Sergeant and 2 Centurions. It can include up to 3 additional Centurions (**Power Rating +17**). Each model is armed with two heavy bolters and a hurricane bolter.

WEAPON	RANGE	TYPE	S	AP	D	ABILITIES
Centurion missile launcher	36"	Assault D3	8	-2	D3	-
Grav-cannon and grav-amp	24"	Heavy 4	5	-3	1	If the target has a Save characteristic of 3+ or better, this weapon has a Damage characteristic of D3.
Heavy bolter	36"	Heavy 3	5	-1	1	-
Hurricane bolter	24"	Rapid Fire 6	4	0	1	-
Lascannon	48"	Heavy 1	9	-3	D6	-

WARGEAR OPTIONS	
	• Any model may replace his hurricane bolter with a Centurion missile launcher.
	• Any model may replace his two heavy bolters with either two lascannons, or a grav-cannon and grav-amp.

ABILITIES

And They Shall Know No Fear (pg 10)

Combat Squads: Before any models are deployed at the start of the game, a Centurion Devastator Squad containing 6 models may be split into two units, each containing 3 models.

Decimator Protocols: Models in this unit do not suffer the penalty to hit rolls for moving and firing Heavy weapons.

Omniscope: Enemy units do not receive the benefit to their saving throws for being in cover against attacks made by a unit that includes a Centurion Sergeant.

FACTION KEYWORDS	IMPERIUM, ADEPTUS ASTARTES, <CHAPTER>
KEYWORDS	INFANTRY, CENTURION, CENTURION DEVASTATOR SQUAD

HELLBLASTER SQUAD

12 POWER

NAME	M	WS	BS	S	T	W	A	Ld	Sv
Hellblaster	6"	3+	3+	4	4	2	2	7	3+
Hellblaster Sergeant	6"	3+	3+	4	4	2	3	8	3+

This unit contains 1 Hellblaster Sergeant and 4 Hellblasters. Each model is armed with a plasma incinerator, a bolt pistol, frag grenades and krak grenades.

WEAPON	RANGE	TYPE	S	AP	D	ABILITIES
Bolt pistol	12"	Pistol 1	4	0	1	-
Plasma incinerator	When attacking with this weapon, choose one of the profiles below.					
- Standard	30"	Rapid Fire 1	7	-4	1	-
- Supercharge	30"	Rapid Fire 1	8	-4	2	On a hit roll of 1, the bearer is slain after all of this weapon's shots have been resolved.
Frag grenade	6"	Grenade D6	3	0	1	-
Krak grenade	6"	Grenade 1	6	-1	D3	-

ABILITIES	And They Shall Know No Fear (pg 10)
FACTION KEYWORDS	IMPERIUM, ADEPTUS ASTARTES, <CHAPTER>
KEYWORDS	INFANTRY, PRIMARIS, HELLBLASTER SQUAD

THUNDERFIRE CANNON

NAME	M	WS	BS	S	T	W	A	Ld	Sv
Thunderfire Cannon	3"	6+	3+	3	6	4	1	8	3+
Techmarine Gunner	6"	3+	2+	4	4	2	3	8	2+

This unit contains 1 Thunderfire Cannon and 1 Techmarine Gunner.
- The Thunderfire Cannon shoots using the thunderfire cannon profile below.
- The Techmarine Gunner is armed with two servo-arms, a bolt pistol, a plasma cutter and a flamer.

WEAPON	RANGE	TYPE	S	AP	D	ABILITIES
Bolt pistol	12"	Pistol 1	4	0	1	-
Flamer	8"	Assault D6	4	0	1	This weapon automatically hits its target.
Plasma cutter	When attacking with this weapon, choose one of the profiles below.					
- Standard	12"	Assault 1	7	-3	1	-
- Supercharge	12"	Assault 1	8	-3	2	On a hit roll of 1, the bearer is slain.
Thunderfire cannon	60"	Heavy 4D3	5	0	1	This weapon can target units that are not visible to the firing model.
Servo-arm	Melee	Melee	x2	-2	3	Each servo-arm can only be used to make one attack each time this model fights. When a model attacks with this weapon, you must subtract 1 from the hit roll.

ABILITIES	**And They Shall Know No Fear** (pg 10) **Artillery:** A Thunderfire Cannon can only fire its ranged weapon if a friendly <CHAPTER> Techmarine Gunner is within 3". A single Techmarine Gunner cannot operate multiple Thunderfire Cannons in this way in a single turn. If, at any point, there are no Techmarine Gunners within 6" of a Thunderfire Cannon, it immediately shuts down and is removed from play.	**Techmarine Gunner:** A Thunderfire Cannon and its Techmarine Gunner must be deployed as a single group with each model within 3" of the one other. From that point on the Thunderfire Cannon and the Techmarine Gunner act as separate units. **Blessing of the Omnissiah:** At the end of your Movement phase a Techmarine Gunner can repair a single <CHAPTER> VEHICLE within 1". That model regains D3 lost wounds.
FACTION KEYWORDS	IMPERIUM, ADEPTUS ASTARTES, <CHAPTER>	
KEYWORDS (THUNDERFIRE CANNON)	VEHICLE, ARTILLERY, THUNDERFIRE CANNON	
KEYWORDS (TECHMARINE GUNNER)	CHARACTER, INFANTRY, TECHMARINE	

The Thunderfire Cannon is a quad-barrelled artillery piece that hurls high-explosive ordnance at the enemy.

PREDATOR

9 POWER

NAME	M	WS	BS	S	T	W	A	Ld	Sv
Predator	*	6+	*	6	7	11	*	8	3+

DAMAGE
Some of this model's characteristics change as it suffers damage, as shown below:

REMAINING W	M	BS	A
6-11+	12"	3+	3
3-5	6"	4+	D3
1-2	3"	5+	1

A Predator is a single model equipped with a Predator autocannon.

WEAPON	RANGE	TYPE	S	AP	D	ABILITIES
Heavy bolter	36"	Heavy 3	5	-1	1	-
Hunter-killer missile	48"	Heavy 1	8	-2	D6	This weapon can only be fired once per battle.
Lascannon	48"	Heavy 1	9	-3	D6	-
Predator autocannon	48"	Heavy 2D3	7	-1	3	-
Storm bolter	24"	Rapid Fire 2	4	0	1	-
Twin lascannon	48"	Heavy 2	9	-3	D6	-

WARGEAR OPTIONS	• This model may replace its Predator autocannon with a twin lascannon. • This model may take two heavy bolters or two lascannons. • This model may take a hunter-killer missile. • This model may take a storm bolter.
ABILITIES	**Smoke Launchers:** Once per game, instead of shooting any weapons in the Shooting phase, this model can use its smoke launchers; until your next Shooting phase your opponent must subtract 1 from all hit rolls for ranged weapons that target this vehicle. **Explodes:** If this model is reduced to 0 wounds, roll a D6 before removing the model from the battlefield; on a 6 it explodes, and each unit within 6" suffers D3 mortal wounds.
FACTION KEYWORDS	IMPERIUM, ADEPTUS ASTARTES, <CHAPTER>
KEYWORDS	VEHICLE, PREDATOR

WHIRLWIND

6 POWER

NAME	M	WS	BS	S	T	W	A	Ld	Sv
Whirlwind	*	6+	*	6	7	11	*	8	3+

DAMAGE
Some of this model's characteristics change as it suffers damage, as shown below:

REMAINING W	M	BS	A
6-11+	12"	3+	3
3-5	6"	4+	D3
1-2	3"	5+	1

A Whirlwind is a single model equipped with a Whirlwind vengeance launcher.

WEAPON	RANGE	TYPE	S	AP	D	ABILITIES
Hunter-killer missile	48"	Heavy 1	8	-2	D6	This weapon can only be fired once per battle.
Storm bolter	24"	Rapid Fire 2	4	0	1	-
Whirlwind castellan launcher	72"	Heavy 2D6	6	0	1	This weapon can target units that are not visible to the firing model.
Whirlwind vengeance launcher	72"	Heavy 2D3	7	-1	2	This weapon can target units that are not visible to the firing model.

WARGEAR OPTIONS	• This model may replace its Whirlwind vengeance launcher with a Whirlwind castellan launcher. • This model may take a hunter-killer missile. • This model may take a storm bolter.
ABILITIES	**Smoke Launchers:** Once per game, instead of shooting any weapons in the Shooting phase, this model can use its smoke launchers; until your next Shooting phase your opponent must subtract 1 from all hit rolls for ranged weapons that target this vehicle. **Explodes:** If this model is reduced to 0 wounds, roll a D6 before removing the model from the battlefield; on a 6 it explodes, and each unit within 6" suffers D3 mortal wounds.
FACTION KEYWORDS	IMPERIUM, ADEPTUS ASTARTES, <CHAPTER>
KEYWORDS	VEHICLE, WHIRLWIND

VINDICATOR

NAME	M	WS	BS	S	T	W	A	Ld	Sv
Vindicator	✱	6+	✱	6	8	11	✱	8	3+

DAMAGE
Some of this model's characteristics change as it suffers damage, as shown below:

REMAINING W	M	BS	A
6-11+	10"	3+	3
3-5	5"	4+	D3
1-2	3"	5+	1

A Vindicator is a single model equipped with a demolisher cannon.

WEAPON	RANGE	TYPE	S	AP	D	ABILITIES
Demolisher cannon	24"	Heavy D3	10	-3	D6	When attacking units with 5 or more models, change this weapon's Type to Heavy D6.
Hunter-killer missile	48"	Heavy 1	8	-2	D6	This weapon can only be fired once per battle.
Storm bolter	24"	Rapid Fire 2	4	0	1	-

WARGEAR OPTIONS	• This model may take a hunter-killer missile. • This model may take a storm bolter.
ABILITIES	**Smoke Launchers:** Once per game, instead of shooting any weapons in the Shooting phase, this model can use its smoke launchers; until your next Shooting phase your opponent must subtract 1 from all hit rolls for ranged weapons that target this vehicle. **Explodes:** If this model is reduced to 0 wounds, roll a D6 before removing the model from the battlefield; on a 6 it explodes, and each unit within 6" suffers D3 mortal wounds.
FACTION KEYWORDS	IMPERIUM, ADEPTUS ASTARTES, <CHAPTER>
KEYWORDS	VEHICLE, VINDICATOR

HUNTER

NAME	M	WS	BS	S	T	W	A	Ld	Sv
Hunter	✱	6+	✱	6	8	11	✱	8	3+

DAMAGE
Some of this model's characteristics change as it suffers damage, as shown below:

REMAINING W	M	BS	A
6-11+	10"	3+	3
3-5	5"	4+	D3
1-2	3"	5+	1

A Hunter is a single model equipped with a skyspear missile launcher.

WEAPON	RANGE	TYPE	S	AP	D	ABILITIES
Hunter-killer missile	48"	Heavy 1	8	-2	D6	This weapon can only be fired once per battle.
Skyspear missile launcher	60"	Heavy 1	9	-3	D6	Add 1 to all hit rolls made for this weapon against targets that can **FLY**. You can re-roll failed hit rolls for this weapon.
Storm bolter	24"	Rapid Fire 2	4	0	1	-

WARGEAR OPTIONS	• This model may take a hunter-killer missile. • This model may take a storm bolter.
ABILITIES	**Smoke Launchers:** Once per game, instead of shooting any weapons in the Shooting phase, this model can use its smoke launchers; until your next Shooting phase your opponent must subtract 1 from all hit rolls for ranged weapons that target this vehicle. **Explodes:** If this model is reduced to 0 wounds, roll a D6 before removing the model from the battlefield; on a 6 it explodes, and each unit within 6" suffers D3 mortal wounds.
FACTION KEYWORDS	IMPERIUM, ADEPTUS ASTARTES, <CHAPTER>
KEYWORDS	VEHICLE, HUNTER

STALKER

NAME	M	WS	BS	S	T	W	A	Ld	Sv
Stalker	*	6+	*	6	8	11	*	8	3+

DAMAGE

Some of this model's characteristics change as it suffers damage, as shown below:

REMAINING W	M	BS	A
6-11+	10"	3+	3
3-5	5"	4+	D3
1-6	3"	5+	1

A Stalker is a single model equipped with two Icarus stormcannons.

WEAPON	RANGE	TYPE	S	AP	D	ABILITIES
Hunter-killer missile	48"	Heavy 1	8	-2	D6	This weapon can only be fired once per battle.
Icarus stormcannon	48"	Heavy 3	7	-1	2	Add 1 to all hit rolls made for this weapon against targets that can **FLY**. Subtract 1 from the hit rolls made for this weapon against all other targets.
Storm bolter	24"	Rapid Fire 2	4	0	1	-

WARGEAR OPTIONS	• This model may take a hunter-killer missile. • This model may take a storm bolter.
ABILITIES	**Smoke Launchers:** Once per game, instead of shooting any weapons in the Shooting phase, this model can use its smoke launchers; until your next Shooting phase your opponent must subtract 1 from all hit rolls for ranged weapons that target this vehicle. **Explodes:** If this model is reduced to 0 wounds, roll a D6 before removing the model from the battlefield; on a 6 it explodes, and each unit within 6" suffers D3 mortal wounds.
FACTION KEYWORDS	**IMPERIUM, ADEPTUS ASTARTES, <CHAPTER>**
KEYWORDS	**VEHICLE, STALKER**

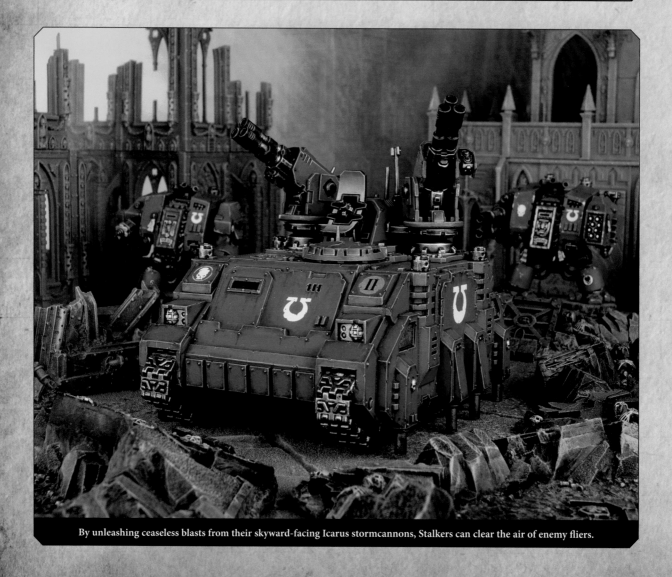

By unleashing ceaseless blasts from their skyward-facing Icarus stormcannons, Stalkers can clear the air of enemy fliers.

STORMRAVEN GUNSHIP

15 POWER

NAME	M	WS	BS	S	T	W	A	Ld	Sv
Stormraven Gunship	*	6+	*	8	7	14	*	9	3+

A Stormraven Gunship is a single model equipped with a twin assault cannon, a twin heavy bolter and two stormstrike missile launchers.

DAMAGE

Some of this model's characteristics change as it suffers damage, as shown below:

REMAINING W	M	BS	A
8-14+	20-45"	3+	3
4-7	20-30"	4+	D3
1-3	20"	5+	1

WEAPON	RANGE	TYPE	S	AP	D	ABILITIES
Hurricane bolter	24"	Rapid Fire 6	4	0	1	-
Stormstrike missile launcher	72"	Heavy 1	8	-3	3	-
Twin assault cannon	24"	Heavy 12	6	-1	1	-
Twin heavy bolter	36"	Heavy 6	5	-1	1	-
Twin heavy plasma cannon	When attacking with this weapon, choose one of the profiles below.					
- Standard	36"	Heavy 2D3	7	-3	1	-
- Supercharge	36"	Heavy 2D3	8	-3	2	For each hit roll of 1, the bearer suffers 1 mortal wound after all of this weapon's shots have been resolved.
Twin lascannon	48"	Heavy 2	9	-3	D6	-
Twin multi-melta	24"	Heavy 2	8	-4	D6	If the target is within half range of this weapon, roll two dice when inflicting damage with it and discard the lowest result.
Typhoon missile launcher	When attacking with this weapon, choose one of the profiles below.					
- Frag missile	48"	Heavy 2D6	4	0	1	-
- Krak missile	48"	Heavy 2	8	-2	D6	-

WARGEAR OPTIONS	• This model may replace its twin assault cannon with a twin lascannon or a twin heavy plasma cannon. • This model may replace its twin heavy bolter with a twin multi-melta or a typhoon missile launcher. • This model may take two hurricane bolters.

ABILITIES	**Airborne:** This model cannot charge, can only be charged by units that can **FLY**, and can only attack or be attacked in the Fight phase by units that can **FLY**. **Supersonic:** Each time this model moves, first pivot it on the spot up to 90° (this does not contribute to how far the model moves), and then move the model straight forwards. Note that it cannot pivot again after the initial pivot. When this model Advances, increase its Move characteristic by 20" until the end of the phase – do not roll a dice. **Hard to Hit:** Your opponent must subtract 1 from hit rolls for attacks that target this model in the Shooting phase.	**Hover Jet:** Before this model moves in your Movement phase, you can declare it will hover. Its Move characteristic becomes 20" until the end of the phase, and it loses the Airborne, Hard to Hit and Supersonic abilities until the beginning of your next Movement phase. **Crash and Burn:** If this model is reduced to 0 wounds, roll a D6 before removing the model from the battlefield and before any embarked models disembark. On a 6 it crashes and explodes, and each unit within 6" suffers D3 mortal wounds. **Power of the Machine Spirit:** This model does not suffer the penalty to hit rolls for moving and firing Heavy weapons.

TRANSPORT	This model can transport 12 <CHAPTER> INFANTRY models and 1 <CHAPTER> DREADNOUGHT. Each JUMP PACK or TERMINATOR model takes the space of two other infantry models and each CENTURION takes the space of 3 other infantry models. It cannot transport PRIMARIS models.
FACTION KEYWORDS	IMPERIUM, ADEPTUS ASTARTES, <CHAPTER>
KEYWORDS	VEHICLE, TRANSPORT, FLY, STORMRAVEN GUNSHIP

LAND RAIDER

19 POWER

NAME	M	WS	BS	S	T	W	A	Ld	Sv
Land Raider	*	6+	*	8	8	16	*	9	2+

A Land Raider is a single model equipped with a twin heavy bolter and two twin lascannons.

DAMAGE
Some of this model's characteristics change as it suffers damage, as shown below:

REMAINING W	M	BS	A
9-16+	10"	3+	6
5-8	5"	4+	D6
1-4	3"	5+	1

WEAPON	RANGE	TYPE	S	AP	D	ABILITIES
Hunter-killer missile	48"	Heavy 1	8	-2	D6	This weapon can only be fired once per battle.
Multi-melta	24"	Heavy 1	8	-4	D6	If the target is within half range of this weapon, roll two dice when inflicting damage with it and discard the lowest result.
Storm bolter	24"	Rapid Fire 2	4	0	1	-
Twin heavy bolter	36"	Heavy 6	5	-1	1	-
Twin lascannon	48"	Heavy 2	9	-3	D6	-

WARGEAR OPTIONS	• This model may take a hunter-killer missile. • This model may take a storm bolter. • This model may take a multi-melta.

ABILITIES

Explodes: If this model is reduced to 0 wounds, roll a D6 before removing it from the battlefield and before any embarked models disembark. On a 6 it explodes, and each unit within 6" suffers D6 mortal wounds.

Power of the Machine Spirit: This model does not suffer the penalty to hit rolls for moving and firing Heavy weapons.

Smoke Launchers: Once per game, instead of shooting any weapons in the Shooting phase, this model can use its smoke launchers; until your next Shooting phase your opponent must subtract 1 from all hit rolls for ranged weapons that target this vehicle.

TRANSPORT

This model can transport 10 <CHAPTER> INFANTRY models. Each JUMP PACK or TERMINATOR model takes the space of two other models and each CENTURION takes the space of three other models. It cannot transport PRIMARIS models.

FACTION KEYWORDS

IMPERIUM, ADEPTUS ASTARTES, <CHAPTER>

KEYWORDS

VEHICLE, TRANSPORT, LAND RAIDER

The Land Raider is a mobile fortress, a monstrous armoured behemoth that carries Space Marines to war.

LAND RAIDER CRUSADER

DAMAGE
Some of this model's characteristics change as it suffers damage, as shown below:

REMAINING W	M	BS	A
9-16+	10"	3+	6
5-8	5"	4+	D6
1-4	3"	5+	1

NAME	M	WS	BS	S	T	W	A	Ld	Sv
Land Raider Crusader	*	6+	*	8	8	16	*	9	2+

A Land Raider Crusader is a single model equipped with a twin assault cannon and two hurricane bolters.

WEAPON	RANGE	TYPE	S	AP	D	ABILITIES
Hunter-killer missile	48"	Heavy 1	8	-2	D6	This weapon can only be fired once per battle.
Hurricane bolter	24"	Rapid Fire 6	4	0	1	-
Multi-melta	24"	Heavy 1	8	-4	D6	If the target is within half range of this weapon, roll two dice when inflicting damage with it and discard the lowest result.
Storm bolter	24"	Rapid Fire 2	4	0	1	-
Twin assault cannon	24"	Heavy 12	6	-1	1	-

WARGEAR OPTIONS	
	• This model may take a hunter-killer missile.
	• This model may take a storm bolter.
	• This model may take a multi-melta.

ABILITIES	
	Smoke Launchers: Once per game, instead of shooting any weapons in the Shooting phase, this model can use its smoke launchers; until your next Shooting phase your opponent must subtract 1 from all hit rolls for ranged weapons that target this vehicle. **Frag Assault Launchers:** Roll a D6 each time this model finishes a charge move within 1" of an enemy unit; on a 4+ that unit suffers D3 mortal wounds.	**Power of the Machine Spirit:** This model does not suffer the penalty to hit rolls for moving and firing Heavy weapons. **Explodes:** If this model is reduced to 0 wounds, roll a D6 before removing it from the battlefield and before any embarked models disembark. On a 6 it explodes, and each unit within 6" suffers D6 mortal wounds.

TRANSPORT	
	This model can transport 16 <CHAPTER> INFANTRY models. Each JUMP PACK or TERMINATOR model takes the space of two other models and each CENTURION takes the space of three other models. It cannot transport PRIMARIS models.

FACTION KEYWORDS	
	IMPERIUM, ADEPTUS ASTARTES, <CHAPTER>

KEYWORDS	
	VEHICLE, TRANSPORT, LAND RAIDER, LAND RAIDER CRUSADER

The Crusader-pattern Land Raider has an expanded hold, allowing it to transport more warriors to the heart of the battle.

LAND RAIDER REDEEMER

DAMAGE
Some of this model's characteristics change as it suffers damage, as shown below:

REMAINING W	M	BS	A
9-16+	10"	3+	6
5-8	5"	4+	D6
1-4	3"	5+	1

NAME	M	WS	BS	S	T	W	A	Ld	Sv
Land Raider Redeemer	*	6+	*	8	8	16	*	9	2+

A Land Raider Redeemer is a single model equipped with a twin assault cannon and two flamestorm cannons.

WEAPON	RANGE	TYPE	S	AP	D	ABILITIES
Flamestorm cannon	8"	Heavy D6	6	-2	2	This weapon automatically hits its target.
Hunter-killer missile	48"	Heavy 1	8	-2	D6	This weapon can only be fired once per battle.
Multi-melta	24"	Heavy 1	8	-4	D6	If the target is within half range of this weapon, roll two dice when inflicting damage with it and discard the lowest result.
Storm bolter	24"	Rapid Fire 2	4	0	1	-
Twin assault cannon	24"	Heavy 12	6	-1	1	-

WARGEAR OPTIONS	• This model may take a hunter-killer missile. • This model may take a storm bolter. • This model may take a multi-melta.
ABILITIES	**Smoke Launchers:** Once per game, instead of shooting any weapons in the Shooting phase, this model can use its smoke launchers; until your next Shooting phase your opponent must subtract 1 from all hit rolls for ranged weapons that target this vehicle. **Frag Assault Launchers:** Roll a D6 each time this model finishes a charge move within 1" of an enemy unit; on a 4+ that unit suffers D3 mortal wounds.	**Power of the Machine Spirit:** This model does not suffer the penalty to hit rolls for moving and firing Heavy weapons. **Explodes:** If this model is reduced to 0 wounds, roll a D6 before removing it from the battlefield and before any embarked models disembark. On a 6 it explodes, and each unit within 6" suffers D6 mortal wounds.
TRANSPORT	This model can transport 12 <Chapter> Infantry models. Each Jump Pack or Terminator model takes the space of two other models and each Centurion takes the space of three other models. It cannot transport Primaris models.
FACTION KEYWORDS	Imperium, Adeptus Astartes, <Chapter>
KEYWORDS	Vehicle, Transport, Land Raider, Land Raider Redeemer

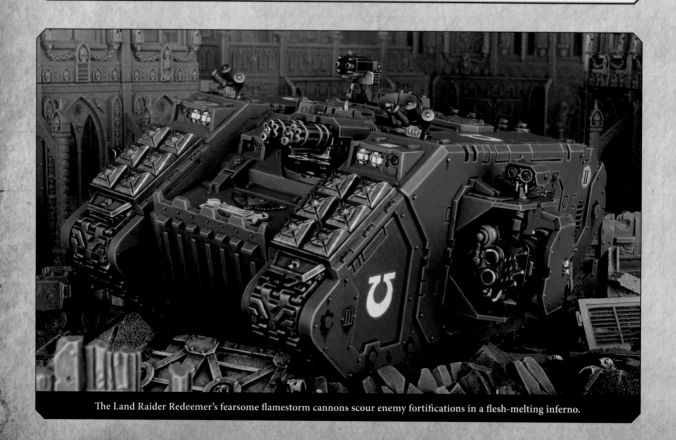

The Land Raider Redeemer's fearsome flamestorm cannons scour enemy fortifications in a flesh-melting inferno.

LAND RAIDER EXCELSIOR

NAME	M	WS	BS	S	T	W	A	Ld	Sv
Land Raider Excelsior	*	6+	*	8	8	16	*	9	2+

DAMAGE
Some of this model's characteristics change as it suffers damage, as shown below:

REMAINING W	M	BS	A
9-16+	10"	3+	6
5-8	5"	4+	D6
1-4	3"	5+	1

This unit contains one Land Raider Excelsior. It is equipped with two twin lascannons and a grav-cannon and grav-amp.

WEAPON	RANGE	TYPE	S	AP	D	ABILITIES
Combi-plasma	When attacking with this weapon, choose one or both of the profiles below. If you choose both, subtract 1 from all hit rolls for this weapon.					
- Boltgun	24"	Rapid Fire 1	4	0	1	-
- Plasma gun	24"	Rapid Fire 1	7	-3	1	This weapon can be supercharged by the bearer before firing. If they do so, increase the Strength and Damage of the weapon by 1 this turn. On any hit rolls of 1 when firing supercharge, the bearer is slain after all of the weapon's shots have been resolved.
Grav-cannon and grav-amp	24"	Heavy 4	5	-3	1	If the target has a Save characteristic of 3+ or better, this weapon has a Damage characteristic of D3.
Hunter-killer missile	48"	Heavy 1	8	-2	D6	A model can only fire each of its hunter-killer missiles once per battle.
Storm bolter	24"	Rapid Fire 2	4	0	1	-
Twin lascannon	48"	Heavy 2	9	-3	D6	-

WARGEAR OPTIONS	
	• This model may take a hunter-killer missile. • This model may take a storm bolter. • This model may take a multi-melta. • This model may take a combi-plasma.

ABILITIES	
	Aquila Aegis Field: This model has a 5+ invulnerable save. **Data Augurs:** While this model is within 24" of any friendly <Chapter> Rhinos Primaris, add 1 to its hit rolls for shooting attacks. **Smoke Launchers:** Once per game, instead of shooting any weapons in the Shooting phase, this model can use its smoke launchers; until your next Shooting phase your opponent must subtract 1 from all hit rolls for ranged weapons that target this vehicle.	**Rites of Battle:** You can re-roll hit rolls of 1 made for friendly <Chapter> units within 6" of this model. **Power of the Machine Spirit:** This model does not suffer the penalty to hit rolls for moving and firing Heavy weapons. **Explodes:** If this model is reduced to 0 wounds, roll a D6 before removing it from the battlefield and before any embarked models disembark. On a 6 it explodes, and each unit within 6" suffers D6 mortal wounds.

TRANSPORT	This model can transport 10 <Chapter> Infantry models. Each **Jump Pack** or **Terminator** model takes the space of two other models and each **Centurion** takes the space of three other models. It cannot transport **Primaris** models.

FACTION KEYWORDS	Imperium, Adeptus Astartes, <Chapter>

KEYWORDS	Character, Vehicle, Land Raider, Transport, Land Raider Excelsior

ULTRAMARINES

Strategic masterminds and warriors of boundless courage, the Ultramarines are true paragons of what it means to be a Space Marine. At last reunited with their lost Primarch, the legendary tactician Roboute Guilliman, the Chapter will see the enemies of Humanity scoured from the galaxy and the Imperium endure the encroaching darkness at any cost.

The Ultramarines have always been the largest and most exemplary force amongst the Adeptus Astartes. During the days of the Great Crusade, the XIII Legion reclaimed untold worlds in the name of the Emperor, their Primarch Roboute Guilliman inspiring his sons to ever greater feats of bravery and tactical brilliance. Yet for all his might in battle, Guilliman was as much a statesman as he was a warrior. Recognising his gifts for diplomacy and command, the Emperor granted him dominion over the stellar empire of Ultramar, and under the Primarch's guidance this sector was transformed into a beacon of order and civilisation, a glimpse of Mankind's glorious destiny. Ultramar has survived through the carnage of the Horus Heresy, the rebirth of its beloved Primarch and countless xenos invasions, and still stands proud and defiant against the fresh horrors unleashed by the Great Rift.

The Ultramarines rigidly adhere to the tenets of the Codex Astartes that Guilliman himself authored in the wake of the Horus Heresy, codifying the manner in which Space Marines Chapters should prosecute war. Thus, they are often seen as the quintessential fighting Chapter of the Adeptus Astartes. Tactical Squads form the unbreakable backbone of their Battle Companies, advancing with sure precision under the cover of merciless fusillades from fire support units. Around this central core, specialist vehicles and troops are deployed in order to best counter the enemy's tactics. The Ultramarines are peerless masters of battlefield strategy, able to pivot and adjust in the midst of battle with astonishing speed. Where the likes of the Space Wolves revel in their individuality, the Sons of Guilliman prize rigid discipline and order above all. They fight with efficient cohesion, each warrior aware of his place in the order of combat, guided always by the words of the hallowed Codex. There is, after all, no foe that cannot be defeated with the correct battle plan.

Unlike the majority of the Adeptus Astartes, the Ultramarines do not recruit from a single world. They seek neophyte warriors from all across the Realm of Ultramar, and as a result can train new recruits and replace casualties at a far more rapid rate than most of their fellow Chapters. This allows the Ultramarines to simultaneously prosecute many different campaigns across the galaxy, while also dedicating their Reserve Companies to the task of training recruits and defending the borders of their domain. Additionally, in the wake of Roboute Guilliman's miraculous return and the subsequent Ultima Founding, the Chapter finds itself bolstered by the might of Primaris reinforcements.

All of the Ultramarines' martial skill, courage and tactical expertise will be required in the days to come, as the raw corruption of Chaos bleeds out across the galaxy and the legions of the Dark Powers seep forth to defile and destroy. Against the innumerable hostile forces that threaten to tear the Imperium apart, the Sons of Guilliman stand taller than ever before, ready to follow their beloved Primarch into the very fires of damnation.

RESURRECTION OF A PRIMARCH

For a hundred centuries, Roboute Guilliman, Primarch of the Ultramarines and Lord Commander of the Imperium, was held in stasis in a shrine within the Fortress of Hera upon the Chapter's home world of Macragge. Wounded grievously by the traitor Primarch Fulgrim's Chaos-tainted blades, there seemed little hope that the Avenging Son would ever rise from this temporal coma.

Yet the mysterious Aeldari Yvraine, prophet of the newly risen God of the Dead, saw the Ultramarines Primarch's resurrection as part of a grand plan that would see Chaos eternally defeated, her deity ascendant and her race saved from the doom that has long awaited it. Allying with the enigmatic Archmagos Dominus Belisarius Cawl of Mars – who was moving towards the same goal as part of the newly declared Celestinian Crusade – Yvraine and her allies fought their way past the forces of the Dark Powers until they reached Macragge and the Shrine of Guilliman.

The specifics of what followed remain known only to a very few, but in a miracle that shook the Imperium to its core, Guilliman emerged from his throne room, an ancient demi-god walking amongst his people once more. The Avenging Son did not indulge himself long in mourning his lost years or the desperate state in which he found his beloved Imperium. Armoured in a suit of regenerative war-plate and wielding his fallen father's flaming sword, Guilliman led the Primaris Marines created by Cawl on a grand campaign across the galaxy. The so-called Indomitus Crusade would mark the first significant Imperial offensive against the forces spilling forth from the Great Rift.

ROBOUTE GUILLIMAN

NAME	M	WS	BS	S	T	W	A	Ld	Sv
Roboute Guilliman	8"	2+	2+	6	6	9	6	10	2+

Roboute Guilliman is a single model armed with the Emperor's Sword and the Hand of Dominion. Only one of this model may be included in your army.

WEAPON	RANGE	TYPE	S	AP	D	ABILITIES
Hand of Dominion (shooting)	24"	Rapid Fire 3	6	-1	2	-
The Emperor's Sword	Melee	Melee	+2	-4	3	If you roll a wound roll of 6+ for this weapon, it inflicts D3 mortal wounds in addition to its normal damage.
Hand of Dominion (melee)	Melee	Melee	x2	-3	3	-

ABILITIES	
	And They Shall Know No Fear (pg 10)
	Armour of Fate: Roboute Guilliman has a 3+ invulnerable save. In addition, the first time Roboute Guilliman is reduced to 0 wounds, roll a D6. On a 4+ set him up again at the end of the phase, as close as possible to his previous position and more than 1" from any enemies, with D6 wounds remaining.
	Author of the Codex: If your army is Battle-forged, you receive an additional 3 Command Points if Roboute Guilliman is your Warlord.
	Master of Battle: You can add 1 to Advance and charge rolls for friendly IMPERIUM units within 12" of Roboute Guilliman, and re-roll hit rolls of 1 and failed Morale tests for these units.
	XIII Primarch: You can re-roll any failed hit and wound rolls for friendly ULTRAMARINES units within 6" of Roboute Guilliman.
FACTION KEYWORDS	IMPERIUM, ADEPTUS ASTARTES, ULTRAMARINES
KEYWORDS	CHARACTER, MONSTER, PRIMARCH, ROBOUTE GUILLIMAN

Roboute Guilliman leads the Ultramarines, a living legend and a figure of desperate hope in a darkening galaxy.

MARNEUS CALGAR

13 POWER

NAME	M	WS	BS	S	T	W	A	Ld	Sv
Marneus Calgar	5"	2+	2+	4	4	7	5	9	2+

Marneus Calgar is a single model armed with the Gauntlets of Ultramar and a relic blade. Only one **MARNEUS CALGAR** may be included in your army.

WEAPON	RANGE	TYPE	S	AP	D	ABILITIES
Gauntlets of Ultramar (shooting)	24"	Rapid Fire 2	4	-1	2	-
Gauntlets of Ultramar (melee)	Melee	Melee	x2	-3	D3	-
Relic blade	Melee	Melee	+2	-3	D3	-

ABILITIES	
And They Shall Know No Fear (pg 10) **Armour of Antilochus:** Marneus Calgar has a 4+ invulnerable save. In addition, all damage suffered by Marneus Calgar is halved (rounding up). **Chapter Master:** You can re-roll failed hit rolls for friendly **ULTRAMARINES** units within 6" of Marneus Calgar.	**Master Tactician:** If your army is Battle-forged, you receive an additional 2 Command Points if Marneus Calgar is your Warlord. **Teleport Strike:** During deployment, you can set up Marneus Calgar in a teleportarium chamber instead of placing him on the battlefield. At the end of any of your Movement phases Marneus Calgar can teleport into battle – set him up anywhere on the battlefield that is more than 9" away from any enemy models.

FACTION KEYWORDS	IMPERIUM, ADEPTUS ASTARTES, ULTRAMARINES
KEYWORDS	CHARACTER, INFANTRY, CHAPTER MASTER, TERMINATOR, MARNEUS CALGAR

MARNEUS CALGAR
IN ARTIFICER ARMOUR

12 POWER

NAME	M	WS	BS	S	T	W	A	Ld	Sv
Marneus Calgar in Artificer Armour	6"	2+	2+	4	4	6	5	9	2+

Marneus Calgar in Artificer Armour is a single model armed with the Gauntlets of Ultramar and a relic blade. Only one **MARNEUS CALGAR** may be included in your army.

WEAPON	RANGE	TYPE	S	AP	D	ABILITIES
Gauntlets of Ultramar (shooting)	24"	Rapid Fire 2	4	-1	2	-
Gauntlets of Ultramar (melee)	Melee	Melee	x2	-3	D3	-
Relic blade	Melee	Melee	+2	-3	D3	-

ABILITIES	
And They Shall Know No Fear (pg 10) **Chapter Master:** You can re-roll any failed hit rolls for friendly **ULTRAMARINES** units within 6" of Marneus Calgar.	**Iron Halo:** Marneus Calgar in Artificer Armour has a 4+ invulnerable save. **Master Tactician:** If your army is Battle-forged, you receive an additional 2 Command Points if Marneus Calgar is your Warlord.

FACTION KEYWORDS	IMPERIUM, ADEPTUS ASTARTES, ULTRAMARINES
KEYWORDS	CHARACTER, INFANTRY, CHAPTER MASTER, MARNEUS CALGAR

CAPTAIN SICARIUS

7 POWER

NAME	M	WS	BS	S	T	W	A	Ld	Sv
Captain Sicarius	6"	2+	2+	4	4	5	4	9	2+

Captain Sicarius is a single model armed with the Talassarian Tempest Blade, a plasma pistol, frag grenades and krak grenades. Only one of this model may be included in your army.

WEAPON	RANGE	TYPE	S	AP	D	ABILITIES
Plasma pistol	When attacking with this weapon, choose one of the profiles below.					
- Standard	12"	Pistol 1	7	-3	1	-
- Supercharge	12"	Pistol 1	8	-3	2	On a hit roll of 1, the bearer is slain.
Talassarian Tempest Blade	Melee	Melee	User	-3	D3	Any wound rolls of 6+ made for this weapon cause D3 mortal wounds instead of the normal damage.
Frag grenade	6"	Grenade D6	3	0	1	-
Krak grenade	6"	Grenade 1	6	-1	D3	-

ABILITIES	
	And They Shall Know No Fear (pg 10)
	Iron Halo: Captain Sicarius has a 4+ invulnerable save.
	Rites of Battle: You can re-roll hit rolls of 1 made for **Ultramarines** units within 6" of Captain Sicarius.
	Battle-forged Heroes: Friendly **Ultramarines** Tactical Squads within 6" of Captain Sicarius can always fight first in the Fight phase, even if they didn't charge. If the enemy has units that have charged, or that have a similar ability, then alternate choosing units to fight with, starting with the player whose turn is taking place.
FACTION KEYWORDS	**Imperium, Adeptus Astartes, Ultramarines**
KEYWORDS	**Character, Infantry, Captain, Sicarius**

CHIEF LIBRARIAN TIGURIUS

7 POWER

NAME	M	WS	BS	S	T	W	A	Ld	Sv
Chief Librarian Tigurius	6"	3+	3+	4	4	4	3	9	3+

Chief Librarian Tigurius is a single model armed with the Rod of Tigurius, a bolt pistol, frag grenades and krak grenades. Only one of this model may be included in your army.

WEAPON	RANGE	TYPE	S	AP	D	ABILITIES
Bolt pistol	12"	Pistol 1	4	0	1	-
Rod of Tigurius	Melee	Melee	+3	-1	D3	-
Frag grenade	6"	Grenade D6	3	0	1	-
Krak grenade	6"	Grenade 1	6	-1	D3	-

ABILITIES	
	And They Shall Know No Fear (pg 10)
	Hood of Hellfire: You can add 1 to Deny the Witch tests you take for Chief Librarian Tigurius against enemy **Psykers** within 12". In addition, you can re-roll failed Psychic tests taken for Chief Librarian Tigurius.
	Master of Prescience: Your opponent must subtract 1 from hit rolls for attacks that target Chief Librarian Tigurius.
PSYKER	Chief Librarian Tigurius can attempt to manifest two psychic powers in each friendly Psychic phase, and attempt to deny two psychic powers in each enemy Psychic phase. He knows the *Smite* power and three psychic powers from the Librarius discipline (pg 10).
FACTION KEYWORDS	**Imperium, Adeptus Astartes, Ultramarines**
KEYWORDS	**Character, Infantry, Librarian, Psyker, Tigurius**

CHAPLAIN CASSIUS

7 POWER

NAME	M	WS	BS	S	T	W	A	Ld	Sv
Chaplain Cassius	6"	2+	3+	4	5	4	3	9	3+

Chaplain Cassius is a single model armed with Infernus, a bolt pistol, a crozius arcanum, frag grenades and krak grenades. Only one of this model may be included in your army.

WEAPON	RANGE	TYPE	S	AP	D	ABILITIES
Bolt pistol	12"	Pistol 1	4	0	1	-
Infernus		When attacking with this weapon, choose one or both of the profiles below. If you choose both, subtract 1 from all hit rolls for this weapon.				
- Flamer	8"	Assault D6	4	0	1	This weapon automatically hits its target.
- Master-crafted boltgun	24"	Rapid Fire 1	4	-1	2	-
Crozius arcanum	Melee	Melee	+1	-1	2	-
Frag grenade	6"	Grenade D6	3	0	1	-
Krak grenade	6"	Grenade 1	6	-1	D3	-

ABILITIES	And They Shall Know No Fear (pg 10)	**Litanies of Hate:** You can re-roll failed hit rolls in the Fight phase for friendly **ULTRAMARINES** units within 6" of Chaplain Cassius.
	Rosarius: Chaplain Cassius has a 4+ invulnerable save.	
	Inspired Retribution: Roll a dice each time a friendly **ULTRAMARINES** model within 6" of Chaplain Cassius is slain in the Fight phase. On a 6, the unit that made that attack suffers a mortal wound after it has finished making its attacks.	**Spiritual Leader:** All friendly **ULTRAMARINES** units that are within 6" of Chaplain Cassius in the Morale phase can use his Leadership instead of their own.

FACTION KEYWORDS	IMPERIUM, ADEPTUS ASTARTES, ULTRAMARINES
KEYWORDS	CHARACTER, INFANTRY, CHAPLAIN, CASSIUS

SERGEANT TELION

5 POWER

NAME	M	WS	BS	S	T	W	A	Ld	Sv
Sergeant Telion	7"	3+	2+	4	4	4	2	8	4+

Sergeant Telion is a single model armed with Quietus, a bolt pistol, frag grenades and krak grenades. Only one of this model may be included in your army.

WEAPON	RANGE	TYPE	S	AP	D	ABILITIES
Bolt pistol	12"	Pistol 1	4	0	1	
Quietus	36"	Heavy 2	4	-1	D3	When Sergeant Telion fires this weapon he may target an enemy **CHARACTER** even if it is not the closest enemy unit.
Frag grenade	6"	Grenade D6	3	0	1	-
Krak grenade	6"	Grenade 1	6	-1	D3	-

ABILITIES	And They Shall Know No Fear (pg 10)	**Infiltrator:** When you set up Sergeant Telion during deployment, he can set up anywhere on the battlefield that is more than 9" from the enemy deployment zone.
	Voice of Experience: In each of your Shooting phases, you can add 1 to all hit rolls made for a single friendly **ULTRAMARINES SCOUT** unit within 3" of Sergeant Telion.	**Camo Cloak:** You can add 2 to saving throws made for Sergeant Telion when he receives the benefits of cover, instead of 1.

FACTION KEYWORDS	IMPERIUM, ADEPTUS ASTARTES, ULTRAMARINES
KEYWORDS	CHARACTER, INFANTRY, SCOUT, TELION

SERGEANT CHRONUS

☠ +3 POWER

NAME	M	WS	BS	S	T	W	A	Ld	Sv
Sergeant Chronus (Tank Commander)	As vehicle		2+		As vehicle				
Sergeant Chronus (Infantry)	6"	3+	2+	4	4	4	2	8	3+

A single **ULTRAMARINES** Rhino, Razorback, Predator, Vindicator, Whirlwind, Hunter, Stalker, Land Raider, Land Raider Crusader or Land Raider Redeemer in your army can take Sergeant Chronus as an upgrade. Your army may only include one Sergeant Chronus.

WEAPON	RANGE	TYPE	S	AP	D	ABILITIES
Bolt pistol	12"	Pistol 1	4	0	1	-
Servo-arm	Melee	Melee	x2	-2	3	Each servo-arm can only be used to make one attack each time this model fights. When a model attacks with this weapon, you must subtract 1 from the hit roll.
Frag grenade	6"	Grenade D6	3	0	1	-
Krak grenade	6"	Grenade 1	6	-1	D3	-

ABILITIES	And They Shall Know No Fear (pg 10)
	Tank Commander: Sergeant Chronus always begins the game commanding a vehicle (see above). Whilst commanding the vehicle, use that vehicle's normal profile, weapons, abilities, keywords and characteristics, with the exception of its Ballistic Skill – use Sergeant Chronus' Ballistic Skill of 2+ when firing with the vehicle instead. If Sergeant Chronus is commanding a vehicle at the start of your turn, he can restore one lost wound it has suffered.

If Sergeant Chronus' vehicle has been reduced to 0 wounds, set him up within 3" before removing the vehicle from the battlefield. He is treated as a passenger disembarking from a destroyed transport. Assuming he survives, Sergeant Chronus then uses the Infantry profile above and the keywords below. He is equipped with a bolt pistol, servo-arm, and frag and krak grenades. |
| FACTION KEYWORDS | **IMPERIUM, ADEPTUS ASTARTES, ULTRAMARINES** |
| KEYWORDS | **CHARACTER, INFANTRY, CHRONUS** |

TYRANNIC WAR VETERANS

✠ 5 POWER

NAME	M	WS	BS	S	T	W	A	Ld	Sv
Tyrannic War Veteran	6"	3+	3+	4	4	1	2	8	3+
Veteran Sergeant	6"	3+	3+	4	4	1	3	9	3+

This unit contains 1 Veteran Sergeant and 3 Tyrannic War Veterans. It can include up to 6 additional Tyrannic War Veterans (**Power Rating +6**). Each model is equipped with a special issue boltgun, a bolt pistol, frag grenades and krak grenades.

WEAPON	RANGE	TYPE	S	AP	D	ABILITIES
Bolt pistol	12"	Pistol 1	4	0	1	-
Special issue boltgun	30"	Rapid Fire 1	4	-2	1	-
Frag grenade	6"	Grenade D6	3	0	1	-
Krak grenade	6"	Grenade 1	6	-1	D3	-

ABILITIES	And They Shall Know No Fear (pg 10)
	Combat Squads: Before any models are deployed at the start of the game, a unit of Tyrannic War Veterans containing 10 models may be split into two units, each containing 5 models.

Avenge the Fallen 1st: You can re-roll failed hit and wound rolls for attacks made by this unit that target **TYRANIDS**. |
| FACTION KEYWORDS | **IMPERIUM, ADEPTUS ASTARTES, ULTRAMARINES** |
| KEYWORDS | **INFANTRY, TYRANNIC WAR VETERANS** |

TERMINUS ULTRA

NAME	M	WS	BS	S	T	W	A	Ld	Sv
Terminus Ultra	＊	6+	＊	8	8	16	＊	9	2+

DAMAGE

Some of this model's characteristics change as it suffers damage, as shown below:

REMAINING W	M	BS	A
9-16+	10"	3+	6
5-8	5"	4+	D6
1-4	3"	5+	1

A Terminus Ultra is a single model equipped with three twin lascannons and two lascannons.

WEAPON	RANGE	TYPE	S	AP	D	ABILITIES
Hunter-killer missile	48"	Heavy 1	8	-2	D6	This weapon can only be fired once per battle.
Lascannon	48"	Heavy 1	9	-3	D6	-
Multi-melta	24"	Heavy 1	8	-4	D6	If the target is within half range of this weapon, roll two dice when inflicting damage with it and discard the lowest result.
Storm bolter	24"	Rapid Fire 2	4	0	1	-
Twin lascannon	48"	Heavy 2	9	-3	D6	-

WARGEAR OPTIONS	• This model may take a hunter-killer missile. • This model may take a storm bolter. • This model may take a multi-melta.

ABILITIES	**Smoke Launchers:** Once per game, instead of shooting any weapons in the Shooting phase, this model can use its smoke launchers; until your next Shooting phase your opponent must subtract 1 from all hit rolls for ranged weapons that target this vehicle. **Power of the Machine Spirit:** This model does not suffer the penalty to hit rolls for moving and firing Heavy weapons.	**Power Overload:** If you roll three or more hit rolls of 1 for this model's lascannons or twin lascannons in the same phase, it experiences a power overload and suffers 6 mortal wounds. **Explodes:** If this model is reduced to 0 wounds, roll a D6 before removing it from the battlefield; on a 6 it explodes, and each unit within 6" suffers D6 mortal wounds.

FACTION KEYWORDS	**IMPERIUM, ADEPTUS ASTARTES, ULTRAMARINES**
KEYWORDS	**VEHICLE, LAND RAIDER, TERMINUS ULTRA**

IMPERIAL FISTS

The Sons of Dorn are masters of siege warfare and constructing fortifications, an implacable and utterly unyielding Chapter who have defended the Imperium for long millennia. They are the indefatigable protectors of Mankind and the guardians of Holy Terra itself, and are ever prepared to pay the ultimate price to secure victory.

The Imperial Fists earned their reputation for resolute determination and stubborn refusal to accede defeat during the glorious Great Crusade. During this grand endeavour, their unrivalled skill at siege warfare was utilised to earn the compliance of countless worlds. Under the command of Rogal Dorn, their stoic and unshakeable Primarch, the Fists earned accolade after accolade, and were chosen by the Emperor to be the praetorians of Terra, the cradle of Humanity and the centre of his power. When the Primarch Horus rose up in rebellion against his father, the Fists were one of the few loyalist Chapters not to suffer hideous loss of life in the opening exchanges of the Heresy. As reports filtered through to Dorn regarding the true horror of the civil war that was now engulfing the Imperium, the Fists began to oversee the fortification of Terra, knowing full well that the Arch-Traitor's fleets and armies would cleave a bloody path through the galaxy with the ultimate goal of assaulting the throneworld.

The Siege of Terra was undoubtedly the Imperial Fists' finest hour, and though their eventual victory came at appalling cost, it perfectly showcased the fighting style of these resolute warriors. When afforded the time to construct their own fortifications and lace their kill-zones with mines, trip-wires and overlapping fields of fire, the Imperial Fists can hold their ground against a force many times their size. Where other Chapters specialise in the lightning assault, the Fists prefer to pin the enemy in place with artillery bombardments and heavy weapon fusillades, before dispatching any survivors with a punishing storm of precision bolter fire.

Imperial Fists do not seek adulation or glory for their countless battle honours. To the Sons of Dorn, the true worth is to be found in the performance of such deeds, not in their recounting. Pride is a dangerous thing, and in the past the Chapter has suffered terribly due to the innate stubbornness inherited from their Primarch, and their utter refusal to retreat. The Fists face a constant battle of will to overcome this psychological flaw, and it is a testament to their stoicism that several times in their history they have recovered from losses that would have destroyed any other Chapter. Indeed, their sheer obstinacy has led to many astonishing victories against seemingly impossible odds.

> 'We stand against the rising tide of Chaos. None shall move us, or lay us low. Our foes shall batter themselves bloody against the fortress of our contempt, and grind their bones to powder upon the ramparts of our disdain. And when they are naught but dust upon the wind, we will remain.'
>
> - Captain Lydoro, Imperial Fists 4th Company

CAPTAIN LYSANDER

NAME	M	WS	BS	S	T	W	A	Ld	Sv
Captain Lysander	5"	2+	2+	4	4	6	4	9	2+

Captain Lysander is a single model armed with the Fist of Dorn. Only one of this model may be included in your army.

WEAPON	RANGE	TYPE	S	AP	D	ABILITIES
Fist of Dorn	Melee	Melee	+6	-3	3	-

ABILITIES	And They Shall Know No Fear (pg 10)
	Iron Halo and Storm Shield: Captain Lysander has a 3+ invulnerable save.
	Rites of Battle: You can re-roll hit rolls of 1 made for friendly **IMPERIAL FISTS** units within 6" of Captain Lysander.
	Teleport Strike: During deployment, you can set up Captain Lysander in a teleportarium chamber instead of placing him on the battlefield. At the end of any of your Movement phases Captain Lysander can teleport into battle – set him up anywhere on the battlefield that is more than 9" away from any enemy models.
	Icon of Obstinacy: Add 1 to the Leadership of all friendly **IMPERIAL FISTS** units within 6" of Captain Lysander.
FACTION KEYWORDS	**IMPERIUM, ADEPTUS ASTARTES, IMPERIAL FISTS**
KEYWORDS	**CHARACTER, INFANTRY, CAPTAIN, TERMINATOR, LYSANDER**

Captain Darnath Lysander has smashed the life from countless Chaos champions with the artefact weapon known as the Fist of Dorn.

CRIMSON FISTS

A successor Chapter of the Imperial Fists, the Crimson Fists have inherited their progenitor's grim resolve and unwillingness to admit defeat. Despite suffering a tragedy that crippled their Chapter's strength, these warriors have clawed their way back from the abyss, and continue to fight on in the name of the Emperor.

The Crimson Fists Chapter was formed during the Second Founding, as the galaxy recovered from the trauma of the Horus Heresy. During the years of reunification and reparation that followed, they proved themselves true descendants of the Primarch Rogal Dorn, fighting in dozens of campaign across the galaxy. Such was their zeal and rigid adherence to the Codex Astartes that they became highly trusted agents of the Imperium, and were often tasked with missions of particular importance.

It was many years later, when the Ork horde of Waaagh! Snagrod fell upon their home planet of Rynn's World, that the Crimson Fists would face their greatest test. As the greenskin armies descended upon their fortress-cities, the Chapter unleashed its full might, fighting with a furious determination and courage that would have stirred the heart of Dorn himself. Led by their legendary Chapter Master Pedro Kantor, the Crimson Fists slaughtered the Orks by the thousand, and it seemed that this would be another glorious victory to be recorded in the Chapter's histories. It was at this moment of apparent triumph that tragedy struck. A malfunctioning plasma warhead struck the primary munitions magazine of the Crimson Fists' fortress monastery. The resulting detonation was cataclysmic, a billowing explosion of white-hot fire that annihilated six entire companies of Crimson Fists in an instant.

It was only due to the Chapter's innate refusal to give in and the charismatic leadership of Pedro Kantor that this disaster did not become the crux point of the Crimson Fists' defeat. Instead they rallied, gathering the remnants of their brotherhood alongside Rynn's World's surviving militia regiments, and staging a heroic defence. This resistance lasted for eighteen months of bitter fighting. Finally, the Crimson Fists emerged triumphant, though their numbers were tragically few. Yet self-pity and defeatism is not in the nature of the descendants of Rogal Dorn. The Chapter has risen from the ashes of the disaster at Rynn's World, slowly rebuilding their numbers and embarking upon new campaigns of conquest and xenocide. This display of stoicism and willpower has earned the Chapter much respect within the Adeptus Astartes. The furious hatred that the Crimson Fists bear towards the greenskins that laid them low will always burn hot, and Pedro Kantor has used the fire of that hatred to forge his Chapter anew.

> 'Let the Orks come by the thousand, or by the tens of thousands; we shall be ready for them. This world is the Emperor's, not theirs, and we shall wash it clean with their blood.'
> - Pedro Kantor, Chapter Master of the Crimson Fists

PEDRO KANTOR

NAME	M	WS	BS	S	T	W	A	Ld	Sv
Pedro Kantor	6"	2+	2+	4	4	6	4	9	2+

Pedro Kantor is a single model armed with Dorn's Arrow, a power fist, frag grenades and krak grenades. Only one of this model may be included in your army.

WEAPON	RANGE	TYPE	S	AP	D	ABILITIES
Dorn's Arrow	24"	Assault 4	4	-1	1	-
Power fist	Melee	Melee	x2	-3	D3	When attacking with this weapon, you must subtract 1 from the hit roll.
Frag grenade	6"	Grenade D6	3	0	1	-
Krak grenade	6"	Grenade 1	6	-1	D3	-

ABILITIES	And They Shall Know No Fear (pg 10)
	Iron Halo: Pedro Kantor has a 4+ invulnerable save.
	Chapter Master: You can re-roll any failed hit rolls for friendly **CRIMSON FISTS** units within 6" of Pedro Kantor.
	Oath of Rynn: All friendly **CRIMSON FISTS** models add 1 to their Attacks characteristic whilst they are within 6" of Pedro Kantor.
FACTION KEYWORDS	**IMPERIUM, ADEPTUS ASTARTES, CRIMSON FISTS**
KEYWORDS	**CHARACTER, INFANTRY, CHAPTER MASTER, PEDRO KANTOR**

Chapter Master Pedro Kantor's stubborn determination dragged the Crimson Fists back from the brink of oblivion.

BLACK TEMPLARS

Driven ever onward to righteous battle, the zealous warriors of the Black Templars launch crusades of conquest and destruction deep into enemy territory. Unlike their fellow Adeptus Astartes brotherhoods, the Templars maintain an absolute belief in the God-Emperor as a divine being.

The Black Templars were one of the Imperial Fists' original successor Chapters. While the majority of the Adeptus Astartes accepted the limitations and demands of the Codex Astartes, the first High Marshal of the Black Templars – the legendary Sigismund – saw the document as a slight against the Primarch Rogal Dorn's teachings. Refusing to adhere to its demands, Sigismund led his warriors into the depths of space, taking the war directly to the enemies of Mankind.

In the centuries since their founding, the Black Templars have drifted ever further from the core tenets of Guilliman's grand work. Their fanatical devotion to the cult of the God-Emperor lends them an iron will and ferocious strength, but also alienates them from their fellow Space Marines, many of whom find their zealotry distasteful. That the Black Templars venerate the Emperor as a literal deity is seen by many other Chapters as a blinkered and dangerous ideology.

Rather than maintaining a single home world from which they recruit and operate, the Black Templars are a fleet-based Chapter. Refusing to adhere to the limit of one thousand active Space Marines as demanded by the Codex Astartes, each Black Templars battle-fleet contains thousands of warriors. These scattered navies embark upon dozens of bloody crusades across the galaxy. Though the current High Marshal, Helbrecht, retains overall authority from his Battle Barge, the *Eternal Crusader*, the Chapter rarely gathers as one – instead, the individual Marshals in charge of each crusade are granted leave to carry out the Templars' divine purge of the xenos and the witch. The Black Templars bear a particular hatred for rogue and alien psykers, whose corrupted power can potentially drag entire planetary systems away from the Emperor's light.

Following the example of High Marshal Sigismund, an unmatched swordsman and the former First Captain of the Imperial Fists Legion, the Black Templars specialise in close combat. Unlike the majority of Space Marine Chapters, they maintain no Scout Company. Instead, their Neophytes are each assigned to an Initiate battle-brother, who trains his apprentice in the art of the sword. By the time these Neophytes are ready to join the Chapter's battleline squads, they wield their blades as an extension of their bodies. True masters of the form who have proved themselves upon hundreds of battlefields are granted ascension to the Marshal's Sword Brethren, elite warriors who are deployed to the most viciously contested zones upon a battlefield.

The Black Templars fight with a merciless, focused aggression, launching themselves upon the foe while bellowing their battle-oaths and prayers to the divine Emperor. The Chapter's single-minded fanaticism has granted them strong ties with the Ecclesiarchy, and it is common to see marching ranks of Black Templars battle-brothers accompanied by frenzied flagellant warriors and mad-eyed priests spitting creeds of eternal hatred against the heretic and the alien.

> *'Trust in your hatred for the mutant and the heretic, brothers. Embrace the vengeful wrath you feel within your hearts. In the fires of war we shall honour the divine Emperor, praise be his name.'*
>
> *- Marshal Montfort, Excorius Crusade*

HIGH MARSHAL HELBRECHT

9 POWER

NAME	M	WS	BS	S	T	W	A	Ld	Sv
High Marshal Helbrecht	6"	2+	2+	4	4	6	4	9	2+

High Marshal Helbrecht is a single model armed with the Sword of the High Marshals, a combi-melta, frag grenades and krak grenades. Only one of this model may be included in your army.

WEAPON	RANGE	TYPE	S	AP	D	ABILITIES
Combi-melta	When attacking with this weapon, choose one or both of the profiles below. If you choose both, subtract 1 from all hit rolls for this weapon.					
- Boltgun	24"	Rapid Fire 1	4	0	1	-
- Meltagun	12"	Assault 1	8	-4	D6	If the target is within half range of this weapon, roll two dice when inflicting damage with it and discard the lowest result.
Sword of the High Marshals	Melee	Melee	+1	-3	D3	Helbrecht can make D3 additional attacks with this weapon if he charged in his turn.
Frag grenade	6"	Grenade D6	3	0	1	-
Krak grenade	6"	Grenade 1	6	-1	D3	-

ABILITIES	And They Shall Know No Fear (pg 10)	**Crusade of Wrath:** All friendly **BLACK TEMPLARS** models add 1 to their Strength characteristic whilst they are within 6" of High Marshal Helbrecht.
	Chapter Master: You can re-roll any failed hit rolls for friendly **BLACK TEMPLARS** units within 6" of High Marshal Helbrecht.	**Iron Halo:** High Marshal Helbrecht has a 4+ invulnerable save.

FACTION KEYWORDS	IMPERIUM, ADEPTUS ASTARTES, BLACK TEMPLARS
KEYWORDS	CHARACTER, INFANTRY, CHAPTER MASTER, HIGH MARSHAL HELBRECHT

THE EMPEROR'S CHAMPION

6 POWER

NAME	M	WS	BS	S	T	W	A	Ld	Sv
The Emperor's Champion	6"	2+	3+	4	4	4	4	8	2+

The Emperor's Champion is a single model armed with a Black Sword, a bolt pistol, frag grenades and krak grenades. Only one of this model may be included in your army.

WEAPON	RANGE	TYPE	S	AP	D	ABILITIES
Bolt pistol	12"	Pistol 1	4	0	1	-
Black Sword	Melee	Melee	+2	-3	D3	You can re-roll any failed wound rolls when attacking with this weapon if the target is a **CHARACTER** or a **MONSTER**.
Frag grenade	6"	Grenade D6	3	0	1	-
Krak grenade	6"	Grenade 1	6	-1	D3	-

ABILITIES	And They Shall Know No Fear (pg 10)	**Slayer of Champions:** You can re-roll any failed hit rolls made for this model in the Fight phase when attacking enemy **CHARACTERS**.
	Sigismund's Honour: Add 1 to the Emperor's Champion's Strength and Attacks characteristics whilst he is within 1" of any enemy **CHARACTERS**.	**Armour of Faith:** The Emperor's Champion has a 4+ invulnerable save.

FACTION KEYWORDS	IMPERIUM, ADEPTUS ASTARTES, BLACK TEMPLARS
KEYWORDS	CHARACTER, INFANTRY, EMPEROR'S CHAMPION

CHAPLAIN GRIMALDUS

6 POWER

NAME	M	WS	BS	S	T	W	A	Ld	Sv
Chaplain Grimaldus	6"	2+	3+	4	4	4	3	9	3+

Chaplain Grimaldus is a single model armed with a crozius arcanum, plasma pistol, frag grenades and krak grenades. Only one of this model may be included in your army.

WEAPON	RANGE	TYPE	S	AP	D	ABILITIES
Plasma pistol	When attacking with this weapon, choose one of the profiles below.					
- Standard	12"	Pistol 1	7	-3	1	-
- Supercharge	12"	Pistol 1	8	-3	2	On a hit roll of 1, the bearer is slain.
Crozius arcanum	Melee	Melee	+1	-1	2	-
Frag grenade	6"	Grenade D6	3	0	1	-
Krak grenade	6"	Grenade 1	6	-1	D3	-

ABILITIES	And They Shall Know No Fear (pg 10)	Rosarius: Chaplain Grimaldus has a 4+ invulnerable save.
	Litanies of Hate: You can re-roll any failed hit rolls in the Fight phase for any friendly **BLACK TEMPLARS** units within 6" of Chaplain Grimaldus.	**Unmatched Zeal:** If you roll a hit roll of 6+ in the Fight phase for a friendly **BLACK TEMPLARS** unit within 6" of Chaplain Grimaldus, you can immediately make 1 additional attack with that model. These bonus attacks do not themselves generate further bonus attacks.
	Spiritual Leader: All friendly **BLACK TEMPLARS** units that are within 6" of Chaplain Grimaldus in the Morale phase can use his Leadership instead of their own.	

FACTION KEYWORDS	IMPERIUM, ADEPTUS ASTARTES, BLACK TEMPLARS
KEYWORDS	CHARACTER, INFANTRY, CHAPLAIN, GRIMALDUS

CENOBYTE SERVITORS

1 POWER

NAME	M	WS	BS	S	T	W	A	Ld	Sv
Cenobyte Servitor	5"	5+	5+	3	3	1	1	6	4+

This unit contains 3 Cenobyte Servitors. Each model is armed with a close combat weapon. Only one unit of Cenobyte Servitors may be included in your army.

WEAPON	RANGE	TYPE	S	AP	D	ABILITIES
Close combat weapon	Melee	Melee	User	0	1	-

ABILITIES	**Mindwiped:** Cenobyte Servitors improve their Weapon Skill to 4+ and their Leadership to 9, whilst they are within 6" of Chaplain Grimaldus.	**Relic of Helsreach:** Friendly **BLACK TEMPLARS** units automatically pass Morale tests whilst they are within 12" of any models from this unit.

FACTION KEYWORDS	IMPERIUM, ADEPTUS ASTARTES, BLACK TEMPLARS
KEYWORDS	INFANTRY, SERVITORS, CENOBYTE SERVITORS

CRUSADER SQUAD

NAME	M	WS	BS	S	T	W	A	Ld	Sv
Initiate	6"	3+	3+	4	4	1	1	7	3+
Neophyte	6"	3+	3+	4	4	1	1	6	4+
Sword Brother	6"	3+	3+	4	4	1	2	8	3+

This unit contains 5 Initiates. It can include up to 5 additional Initiates (**Power Rating +4**). It can also include up to 5 Neophytes (**Power Rating +3**) or up to 10 Neophytes (**Power Rating +6**). A Sword Brother can take the place of one Initiate. Each model is armed with a boltgun, bolt pistol, frag grenades and krak grenades.

WEAPON	RANGE	TYPE	S	AP	D	ABILITIES
Astartes shotgun	12"	Assault 2	4	0	1	If the target is within half range, add 1 to this weapon's Strength.
Bolt pistol	12"	Pistol 1	4	0	1	-
Boltgun	24"	Rapid Fire 1	4	0	1	-
Chainsword	Melee	Melee	User	0	1	Each time the bearer fights, it can make 1 additional attack with this weapon.
Combat knife	Melee	Melee	User	0	1	Each time the bearer fights, it can make 1 additional attack with this weapon.
Power axe	Melee	Melee	+1	-2	1	-
Power fist	Melee	Melee	x2	-3	D3	When attacking with this weapon, you must subtract 1 from the hit roll.
Power maul	Melee	Melee	+2	-1	1	-
Power sword	Melee	Melee	User	-3	1	-
Frag grenade	6"	Grenade D6	3	0	1	-
Krak grenade	6"	Grenade 1	6	-1	D3	-

WARGEAR OPTIONS	• A Sword Brother may replace his bolt pistol and boltgun with items from the *Sergeant Equipment* list. • Any Initiate may replace his boltgun with a chainsword. • One Initiate may replace his boltgun with an item from the *Special Weapons* list. • One Initiate may replace his boltgun with an item from the *Heavy Weapons* list, or a power sword, power axe, power maul or power fist. • Any Neophyte may replace his boltgun with an Astartes shotgun or a combat knife.
ABILITIES	And They Shall Know No Fear (pg 10)
FACTION KEYWORDS	IMPERIUM, ADEPTUS ASTARTES, BLACK TEMPLARS
KEYWORDS	INFANTRY, CRUSADER SQUAD

High Marshal Helbrecht embodies the uncompromising resolve and martial might of the Black Templars.

RAVEN GUARD

The Raven Guard are a solemn brotherhood of patient hunters, true masters of the sudden ambush. They launch their stealth strikes from the shadows with a speed and grace that should be impossible for those clad in full battle-plate.

Though for the most part they adhere to the Codex Astartes, the Raven Guard have always remained distant from their fellow Adeptus Astartes. They are by nature a cold and aloof breed. This reserved attitude often draws suspicion from more bellicose Chapters, but the Raven Guard care little. Their keen minds are ever fixed upon their next mission. They watch and they wait, as patient and lethal as death itself, seizing upon the slightest opening in their enemy's defence before falling upon them in a swift, explosive assault.

Raven Guard warriors inherit the pale skin and coal-black hair of their Primarch, the enigmatic Corvus Corax. Where the majority of his brothers sought the most glorious victories and prestigious deeds to impress their gene-father the Emperor, Corax put his unique talents to use in the field of covert operations and subterfuge. Whilst his father's favoured sons – Guilliman, Sanguinius and Horus – were showered with accolades, Corax went about his grim business in the shadows without complaint. Without his Legion's bloody work, numerous wars of compliance would have stalled in their tracks, and countless billions of Imperial lives would have been lost.

To this day the Sons of Corax continue to fight from the shadows, launching lightning assaults upon the enemies of the Imperium.

To better suit this style of warfare, Raven Guard detachments contain large numbers of scouts, jump troops and aircraft – units with the speed and manoeuvrability to quickly encircle and overwhelm the foe. Under the command of one of the Chapter's fiercely independent Shadow Captains – such as the fabled Kayvaan Shrike, recently promoted to Chapter Master after the death of his predecessor during the Damocles Crusade – a Raven Guard company can harry and misdirect a far larger force, striking relentlessly from all sides and inflicting horrific casualties before fading into the shadows once more. Not for the Raven Guard is a drawn-out war of attrition. They pluck the eyes from their enemy, cripple its supply lines and leave it stranded and vulnerable. Only then will the final assault be unleashed, and the prey eliminated with cold fury.

> *'I never imagined something so huge could move so fast. One moment that T'au machine was blasting us to hell, and the next it was in pieces, great gouges torn through its torso. All I saw was a blur of raven-black, like the shadows themselves had taken up arms against the xenos. We didn't lose another soul that day.'*
>
> *- Guardsman Heibler, 37th Verdane Sabres*

KAYVAAN SHRIKE

8 POWER

NAME	M	WS	BS	S	T	W	A	Ld	Sv
Kayvaan Shrike	12"	2+	2+	4	4	5	5	9	3+

Kayvaan Shrike is a single model armed with the Raven's Talons, a bolt pistol, frag grenades and krak grenades. Only one of this model may be included in your army.

WEAPON	RANGE	TYPE	S	AP	D	ABILITIES
Bolt pistol	12"	Pistol 1	4	0	1	-
Raven's Talons	Melee	Melee	User	-3	D3	You can re-roll failed wound rolls for this weapon.
Frag grenade	6"	Grenade D6	3	0	1	-
Krak grenade	6"	Grenade 1	6	-1	D3	-

ABILITIES	**And They Shall Know No Fear** (pg 10) **Chapter Master:** You can re-roll failed hit rolls for friendly **RAVEN GUARD** units within 6" of Kayvaan Shrike. **Winged Deliverance:** You can re-roll failed charge rolls for friendly **RAVEN GUARD JUMP PACK** units within 6" of Kayvaan Shrike.	**Jump Pack Assault:** During deployment, you may set up Kayvaan Shrike high in the skies instead of placing him on the battlefield. At the end of any of your Movement phases, he can make a sudden assault to arrive on the battlefield; set him up anywhere that is more than 9" from any enemy models. **Iron Halo:** Kayvaan Shrike has a 4+ invulnerable save.

FACTION KEYWORDS	**IMPERIUM, ADEPTUS ASTARTES, RAVEN GUARD**
KEYWORDS	**CHARACTER, INFANTRY, CHAPTER MASTER, JUMP PACK, FLY, SHRIKE**

Chapter Master Kayvaan Shrike is a legendary figure – a hero to the Imperium and a harbinger of swift death to its enemies.

SALAMANDERS

The Salamanders are masters in the crafting of destruction upon the battlefield, and experts in the arts of the forge. Their dedication to destroying the Imperium's enemies is only outmatched by their commitment to protect those who reside within it, giving them a reputation for heroism that is very much at odds with their intimidating appearance.

The Salamanders believe that their endless war against the darkness is a test of mettle and endurance. Each battle is a crucible within which they are tempered, made true, and quenched by the blood of the enemy. They hold true to the tenets of their founder, the Primarch Vulkan, whose immortal legacy of valour and selfless courage is borne with pride.

In a galaxy populated with murderous butchers and dangerous madmen, even amongst the ranks of Humanity, the Salamanders shine out as a beacons of virtue. Yet even the common citizens they save from disaster view these armoured saviours with suspicion and fear. The constant fires and radioactive sun of their home world, Nocturne, have reacted with their gene-seed to give the Salamanders coal-black skin and strange red eyes. They wear the scaled skins of the draconic lizards and saurian mega-predators that prowl the mountains of Nocturne, and – having a legendary affinity with fire – stride undaunted through fierce conflagrations as they mow down their enemies. To the ill-educated and superstitious peoples of the Imperium, the appearance of the Salamanders makes them appear as abyssal fiends. If anything, the opposite is true. These warriors may be Angels of Death, but they live only to ensure Humanity's survival in whatever way they can.

The Salamanders Chapter is organised into seven warrior houses, for they were given dispensation by Roboute Guilliman in the aftermath of the Heresy to maintain their traditional organisational structure. First amongst them are the legendary battle-brothers known as the Firedrakes, whose deeds are high points in the Imperium's military history. Every Salamander is trained in the ways of the smith, the better to create and maintain the works of art that are their favoured weapons. Needless to say, the exceptionally well-crafted tools of war used by the most experienced Salamanders are deadly in the extreme. Many an enemy battle line has melted away to boiling slurry and molten bone under the fire and fury of an assault from the Sons of Vulkan.

THE LEGACY OF THE PRIMARCH

The treasured relics detailed in the Tome of Fire were forged by Vulkan himself. It is said that should the Salamanders prove skilled enough to find them all and gather them in one place, the Primarch will return to them. As a result, the Chapter has sought them out across the galaxy on a series of epic endeavours that have seen traitor worlds burnt to cinders and alien enclaves reduced to ash. The former Captain of the 4th Company, Forgefather He'stan, wields the Gauntlet of the Forge and the Spear of Vulkan, and wears upon his back the scaled cloak known as Kesare's Mantle. Dogged and indefatigable, he will not cease in his crusade of retrieval until the rest of the Primarch's ancestral artefacts have been torn from the usurpers who claimed them and reunited with their rightful owners.

VULKAN HE'STAN

NAME	M	WS	BS	S	T	W	A	Ld	Sv
Vulkan He'stan	6"	2+	2+	4	4	5	4	9	2+

Vulkan He'stan is a single model armed with the Gauntlet of the Forge, the Spear of Vulkan, a bolt pistol, frag grenades and krak grenades. Only one of this model may be included in your army.

WEAPON	RANGE	TYPE	S	AP	D	ABILITIES
Bolt pistol	12"	Pistol 1	4	0	1	-
Gauntlet of the Forge	8"	Assault D6	5	-1	1	This weapon automatically hits its target.
Spear of Vulkan	Melee	Melee	+2	-2	D3	-
Frag grenade	6"	Grenade D6	3	0	1	-
Krak grenade	6"	Grenade 1	6	-1	D3	-

ABILITIES	And They Shall Know No Fear (pg 10)	**Forgefather:** You can re-roll failed hit and wound rolls for friendly **SALAMANDERS** models within 6" of Vulkan He'stan that are firing melta or flame weapons. For the purposes of this ability, a melta weapon is any weapon profile whose name includes the word 'melta' (e.g. meltagun, multi-melta etc.) and a flame weapon is any weapon profile whose name includes the word 'flame' (e.g. flamer, heavy flamer, flamestorm cannon, flamestorm gauntlet etc.). Vulkan He'stan's Gauntlet of the Forge is also a flame weapon.
	Rites of Battle: You can re-roll hit rolls of 1 made for friendly **SALAMANDERS** units within 6" of Vulkan He'stan.	
	Kesare's Mantle: Vulkan He'stan has a 3+ invulnerable save.	

FACTION KEYWORDS	**IMPERIUM, ADEPTUS ASTARTES, SALAMANDERS**
KEYWORDS	**CHARACTER, INFANTRY, CAPTAIN, VULKAN HE'STAN**

Forgefather Vulkan He'stan has scorched entire worlds to ashes in his quest to recover the treasures of his lost Primarch.

WHITE SCARS

Fierce of aspect but noble to the core, the White Scars are huntsmen beyond compare. They run their quarry to the ground with lightning charges, relishing the thrill of the chase and the feeling of the wind on their weather-beaten skin. They bear their wounds with pride, for they hail from a warrior culture that prizes bravery and joy in battle most highly.

The White Scars are recruited from the tribal nomads of Chogoris. Though they are a Codex-adherent Chapter that willingly embraced Guilliman's teachings after the Horus Heresy, they value mounted warfare more than any other. The vast majority will go to battle upon fast-moving but rugged vehicles that bear dents and gouges from many centuries of conflict. It is said the White Scars are born in the saddle, and that they are never truly content unless fighting in a high-octane running battle.

White Scars have a singular appearance. Their armour of white ceramite is emblazoned with stylised scars that echo those carved into their flesh upon inception. When they remove their helms to better savour the sensations of the battlefield, long topknots whip out from shaved scalps as their triumphant laughter is carried on the wind. Those who have heard of their legendary reputation cower in fear at the sight of white armour glinting in the dawn light, for it usually means they are already encircled and as good as dead.

Though the White Scars are ferocious on the attack, they use their natural flair for lightning assault as a precision tool. They are experts in fieldcraft and the use of the environment against the foe. When they level their well-honed blow it is not as a reckless berserker, but as a master predator entirely focused on the kill.

Just as a Chogorian tribesman forms a bond of mutual respect with his war stallion, a White Scars rider will find a kinship with the machine spirit of his bike. This gives him an innate knowledge of how and when to push his vehicle to the limit. The mounted warriors of the White Scars are famous for truly impressive feats of heroism and skill. A White Scars battle-brother might ride his bike through a promethium inferno to emerge as a blazing herald of death, or veer up the side of a half-shattered tank to soar, bolters blazing, through the air before slamming down with bone-crushing force into the enemies skulking behind it. These warriors take fierce pleasure in their Emperor-given task of slaughter, singing tribal battle chants and revelling in the heat of war as they plough on in search of fresh prey.

Should a company of White Scars declare a Great Hunt against a particularly dangerous foe, it will cross the length of the galaxy in order to claim their adversaries' heads. They take great pains to ensure the enemy's first sight of them is also his last, striking with the speed of a lightning bolt to blast the enemy apart before a retaliatory strike can be levelled in return. In doing so they honour the teachings of their Primarch, Jaghatai Khan.

Though the first and only true master of Chogoris has long since disappeared into the mists of history, the Great Khan's legend is indelibly etched into the annals of the White Scars. It influences their every thought and deed to this day. They organise their companies as brotherhoods, and their Captains are known as Khans, each driven to the heights of excellence by the rivalry that has long thrived between them. When the Chapter musters in strength the night before war is to commence, these leaders engage in contests of martial prowess or physical strength to determine who has the honour of leading the charge at the dawn of battle. Once the enemy has been bested, the decapitated heads of their champions will be stripped of flesh, dipped in molten silver, and returned to the grand bastions of their fortress monastery – known as Quan Zhou – there to rot in silence upon the spiked walls as a warning for all to see.

Beneath the barbaric practices of these battle-scarred Space Marines lies a rigid code of honour. They give their all to the singular duty of protecting the Imperium; should the need arise, they will pursue their enemy through the most hostile war zones for years on end, and charge without fear into the teeth of the enemy guns.

> 'Surround yourself with the greatest warriors at your command, or cower in the deepest darkest hole you can find. It matters not. I shall take your head for the Great Khan and the Emperor.'
>
> *- Kor'sarro Khan, White Scars Master of the Hunt*

6 POWER — KOR'SARRO KHAN

NAME	M	WS	BS	S	T	W	A	Ld	Sv
Kor'sarro Khan	6"	2+	2+	4	4	5	4	9	3+

Kor'sarro Khan is a single model armed with Moonfang, a bolt pistol, frag grenades and krak grenades. Only one KOR'SARRO KHAN may be included in your army.

WEAPON	RANGE	TYPE	S	AP	D	ABILITIES
Bolt pistol	12"	Pistol 1	4	0	1	-
Moonfang	Melee	Melee	User	-3	D3	This weapon has Strength x2 if the target is a CHARACTER.
Frag grenade	6"	Grenade D6	3	0	1	-
Krak grenade	6"	Grenade 1	6	-1	D3	-

ABILITIES

And They Shall Know No Fear (pg 10)

Rites of Battle: You can re-roll hit rolls of 1 made for friendly WHITE SCARS units within 6" of Kor'sarro Khan.

For the Khan!: Add 1 to the Strength of friendly WHITE SCARS units within 6" of Kor'sarro Khan when they attack in the Fight phase if they charged that turn.

Iron Halo: Kor'sarro Khan has a 4+ invulnerable save.

FACTION KEYWORDS IMPERIUM, ADEPTUS ASTARTES, WHITE SCARS

KEYWORDS CHARACTER, INFANTRY, CAPTAIN, KOR'SARRO KHAN

7 POWER — KOR'SARRO KHAN ON MOONDRAKKAN

NAME	M	WS	BS	S	T	W	A	Ld	Sv
Kor'sarro Khan on Moondrakkan	14"	2+	2+	4	5	6	4	9	3+

Kor'sarro Khan on Moondrakkan is a single model armed with Moonfang, a bolt pistol, frag grenades and krak grenades. His Space Marine bike, Moondrakkan, is equipped with a twin boltgun. Only one KOR'SARRO KHAN may be included in your army.

WEAPONS	RANGE	TYPE	S	AP	D	ABILITIES
Bolt pistol	12"	Pistol 1	4	0	1	-
Twin boltgun	24"	Rapid Fire 2	4	0	1	-
Moonfang	Melee	Melee	User	-3	D3	This weapon has Strength x2 if the target is a CHARACTER.
Frag grenade	6"	Grenade D6	3	0	1	-
Krak grenade	6"	Grenade 1	6	-1	D3	-

ABILITIES

And They Shall Know No Fear (pg 10)

Rites of Battle: You can re-roll hit rolls of 1 made for friendly WHITE SCARS units within 6" of Kor'sarro Khan.

Turbo-boost: When Kor'sarro Khan on Moondrakkan Advances, add 6" to his Move characteristic for that Movement phase instead of rolling a dice.

For the Khan!: Add 1 to the Strength of friendly WHITE SCARS units within 6" of Kor'sarro Khan when they attack in the Fight phase if they charged that turn.

Iron Halo: Kor'sarro Khan has a 4+ invulnerable save.

FACTION KEYWORDS IMPERIUM, ADEPTUS ASTARTES, WHITE SCARS

KEYWORDS BIKER, CHARACTER, CAPTAIN, KOR'SARRO KHAN

LEGION OF THE DAMNED

As if from nowhere they appear, skull-helmed figures wreathed in ethereal flames, their bolters spitting ectoplasmic fire that melts through thick stone and metal with ease, blasting enemies who have taken cover to ash. On battlefields uncounted these spectral warriors have intervened to reverse the course of battle for the Imperium, only to disappear without a trace.

Over the millennia of war since the end of the Horus Heresy, strange reports have filtered in from across the vast expanse of the Imperium. Multiple accounts have been recorded of silent, ghostly Space Marines emerging from the mists, bolters spitting white-hot fusillades of death into the enemies of the Imperium. Each of these warriors' armour is covered with bleached bones and flame motifs, the macabre iconography of the angry dead, and they inspire a potent terror in those heretics and xenos against whom they march. This eldritch force appears only when all hope seems lost, and though they do not speak a word, the hearts of all who witness their righteous fury are emboldened with a heady mix of dread fear and fresh hope. Those who whisper such tales name these phantasmal saviours the Legion of the Damned.

Countless inquests into these strange warriors have been launched by the Inquisition, but while they have generated dozens of different theories, none have ever been proven. Some believe the Legion are a psychic phenomenon summoned into being by the collective faith of Humanity; others insist that they are the spirits of those loyalist Astartes slain during the Horus Heresy, drawn forth from beyond the veil of death to wreak retribution on their ancient foes. Whatever the truth may be, it cannot be denied that the Legion of the Damned has prevented countless costly defeats for Imperial forces by virtue of their inspiring presence and merciless attacks, and their wraith-light has brought illumination to the blackest of circumstances.

Due to their shrouded origins and mysterious nature, it is impossible to ascertain much about the organisational structure of the Legion, if indeed it even has one; the Legionnaires make no sound at all in battle, and have never communicated in any conventional way with those they have rescued. They simply march forth in the traditional gun lines of the Adeptus Astartes, ignoring the volleys of enemy fire that pass harmlessly through their armour, and unleashing an apocalyptic thunderstorm of bolt rounds in return. When the killing is done and the armies of the Emperor are victorious, the Legion of the Damned depart as mysteriously as they arrived. The scattered, charred bodies of the dead and the tales of wild-eyed survivors are the only clues that they were ever there.

DAMNED LEGIONNAIRES

NAME	M	WS	BS	S	T	W	A	Ld	Sv
Legionnaire	5"	3+	3+	4	4	1	2	10	3+
Legionnaire Sergeant	5"	3+	3+	4	4	1	3	10	3+

This unit contains 1 Legionnaire Sergeant and 4 Legionnaires. It can include up to 5 additional Legionnaires (**Power Rating +7**). Each model is armed with a boltgun, bolt pistol, frag grenades and krak grenades.

WEAPON	RANGE	TYPE	S	AP	D	ABILITIES
Bolt pistol	12"	Pistol 1	4	0	1	-
Boltgun	24"	Rapid Fire 1	4	0	1	-
Flamer	8"	Assault D6	4	0	1	This weapon automatically hits its target.
Heavy flamer	8"	Heavy D6	5	-1	1	This weapon automatically hits its target.
Meltagun	12"	Assault 1	8	-4	D6	If the target is within half range of this weapon, roll two dice when inflicting damage with it and discard the lowest result.
Multi-melta	24"	Heavy 1	8	-4	D6	If the target is within half range of this weapon, roll two dice when inflicting damage with it and discard the lowest result.
Plasma gun	When attacking with this weapon, choose one of the profiles below.					
- Standard	24"	Rapid Fire 1	7	-3	1	-
- Supercharge	24"	Rapid Fire 1	8	-3	2	On a hit roll of 1, the bearer is slain after all of this weapon's shots have been resolved.
Plasma pistol	When attacking with this weapon, choose one of the profiles below.					
- Standard	12"	Pistol 1	7	-3	1	-
- Supercharge	12"	Pistol 1	8	-3	2	On a hit roll of 1, the bearer is slain.
Storm bolter	24"	Rapid Fire 2	4	0	1	-
Chainsword	Melee	Melee	User	0	1	Each time the bearer fights, it can make 1 additional attack with this weapon.
Power axe	Melee	Melee	+1	-2	1	-
Power fist	Melee	Melee	x2	-3	D3	When attacking with this weapon, you must subtract 1 from the hit roll.
Power maul	Melee	Melee	+2	-1	1	-
Power sword	Melee	Melee	User	-3	1	-
Frag grenade	6"	Grenade D6	3	0	1	-
Krak grenade	6"	Grenade 1	6	-1	D3	-

WARGEAR OPTIONS	• One Legionnaire may replace his boltgun with a flamer, meltagun or plasma gun. • One Legionnaire may replace his boltgun with a heavy flamer or multi-melta. • The Legionnaire Sergeant may replace his boltgun with a chainsword, power fist, power axe, power sword or power maul. • The Legionnaire Sergeant may replace his bolt pistol with a plasma pistol or storm bolter.
ABILITIES	**And They Shall Know No Fear** (pg 10) **Aid Unlooked For:** During deployment, you can set up this unit in the aether instead of placing it on the battlefield. At the end of any of your Movement phases this unit can materialise – set it up anywhere on the battlefield that is more than 9" away from any enemy models. **Flaming Projectiles:** Enemy units do not gain any bonus to their saving throws for being in cover when targeted by shooting attacks made by this unit. **Unyielding Spectres:** All models in this unit have a 3+ invulnerable save.
FACTION KEYWORDS	IMPERIUM, ADEPTUS ASTARTES, LEGION OF THE DAMNED
KEYWORDS	INFANTRY, DAMNED LEGIONNAIRES

BLOOD ANGELS

Nobility. Sacrifice. Glory. These are the hallmarks of all Adeptus Astartes, and no Chapter embodies these ideals with greater zeal than the Blood Angels. Swift and sure, they are the Emperor's blade, and they strike without mercy. Yet for all their accomplishments and deeds of heroism since the Great Crusade, the Blood Angels suffer from a fatal flaw.

Since the dawn of the Imperium the Blood Angels have fought at the vanguard of the Emperor's armies. Again and again they have led from the front, proving themselves exemplars of everything Space Marines should be. These fast-striking elite forces can launch coordinated attacks to sweep away foes, regardless of ground or atmospheric conditions, and seize victory even when vastly outnumbered. Despite having won many laurels, the Blood Angels continue to strive for perfection, ever eager to win further renown. In this, they take after their Primarch, the legendary Sanguinius. Angel-winged and beautiful, Sanguinius was arguably the greatest of his father's sons. A mighty warrior and inspiring leader, Sanguinius' glory was that of a demi-god, and the Legion sired from his blood followed him with unquestioning devotion.

It was during the epic battles at the close of the Horus Heresy that Sanguinius fell, slain by his brother Primarch, the Warmaster Horus. Sanguinius and the Space Marines made from his gene-seed shared a special bond. His tragic death to the Archenemy left a mental scar upon the Chapter, a fugue that continues to mar their glory. A flaw in the gene-seed that is passed down from the Primarch to each new generation of Blood Angels causes the warriors to struggle constantly with the excessive rage that dwells within them. The Blood Angels were always aggressive, for to attack was their nature, but this propensity goes beyond bold assaults into berserk frenzies. It is a mark of shame to give in to this Red Thirst, as it is known, in any but the most dire circumstances. Only with rigid discipline can the Blood Angels keep themselves in check. Yet for some not even their mental fortitude is enough to prevent the next stage of their decline – the Black Rage.

Despite the best efforts of luminaries such as Brother Corbulo and Chaplain Lemartes, there is no escaping the curse that haunts Sanguinius' sons. Those Blood Angels that succumb to the Black Rage are quarantined off into their own company, known as the Death Company, and carefully guided by Chaplains. A warrior overcome with the Black Rage becomes mad with fury, slurring the past into the present so that he no longer recognizes his own comrades. Instead, those afflicted often believe they are Sanguinius himself upon the eve of his destruction, with the bloody battles of the Horus Heresy raging all around. These damned souls are gathered and their armour painted black before a Chaplain leads them into battle one final time. In a berserk rage the Death Company storms the deadliest part of the battlefield, each member shrugging off mortal blows to continue the fight until every last drop of their strength is gone.

Every Blood Angel knows it is better to die gloriously in battle than face that decline into bestial madness. And so, to this day, each of those Space Marines tied to Sanguinius' bloodline seek the very boldest of deeds in the hope of leaving behind a shining legacy of sacrifice.

After the devastation of their home world of Baal by an overwhelming invasion of Tyranids from Hive Fleet Leviathan, the Blood Angels have rebuilt their Chapter swiftly with the aid of the Ultramarines Primarch, Roboute Guilliman. In the organisation of their battle-brothers, the Blood Angels largely follow the dictates of Guilliman's text, the Codex Astartes – with a few modifications. They have many more jump pack-equipped warriors than a standard Chapter, as befits their aggressive style of war, and the legendary Baal Predator tank is fitted with turbo-charged engines that enable it to speed after the angelic assault.

Blood Angels Apothecaries are known as Sanguinary Priests, and are adept at handling the unique gene-seed of the Chapter, while Blood Angels Chaplains are trusted not only with the spiritual well-being of their battle-brothers, but also the fate of the Death Company, whom they guide into battle. So respected are these offices that should a Chapter Master fall to the Black Rage, temporary joint command of the Chapter will often be undertaken by the Sanguinary High Priest and the High Chaplain.

Resplendent in their winged armour, the Sanguinary Guard serve as an honour detail, each one a direct descendent of those who once guarded Sanguinius himself. To see them in battle is to glimpse the glory that has maintained the Blood Angels' prominent place in the Imperium for ten thousand years.

Although doomed by their own tragic legacy, the Sons of Sanguinius remain steadfastly loyal in their service to the Emperor. They remain hopeful that one day a cure will be found for their affliction. Until that day they will continue to fight at the vanguard of the Imperium's most deadly battles, ever striving to be remembered in honour rather than disgrace.

ABILITIES
The following abilities are common to several Blood Angels units:

And They Shall Know No Fear
You can re-roll failed Morale tests for this unit.

Black Rage
You can add 1 to this unit's Attacks characteristic in the Fight phase if it charged in the preceding Charge phase. In addition, roll a D6 each time this unit loses a wound. On a roll of 6 the damage is ignored.

Jump Pack Assault
During deployment, if this model has a jump pack, you can set it up high in the skies instead of placing it on the battlefield. At the end of any of your Movement phases this model can assault from above – set it up anywhere on the battlefield that is more than 9" away from any enemy models.

BLOOD ANGELS CHAPTER

The following Space Marines datasheets can be from the Blood Angels Chapter. Those that are replace the <CHAPTER> keyword on their datasheet in all instances with BLOOD ANGELS. If a Space Marines unit does not appear on the list below, it cannot be from the Blood Angels Chapter, and so cannot have the BLOOD ANGELS Faction keyword. BLOOD ANGELS PSYKERS generate their psychic powers from the Sanguinary discipline (below) instead of the Librarius discipline.

- Assault Squad (pg 42)
- Attack Bike Squad (pg 45)
- Bike Squad (pg 44)
- Captain (pg 12)
- Captain in Gravis Armour (pg 13)
- Captain in Terminator Armour (pg 12)
- Captain on Bike (pg 14)
- Chaplain (pg 19)
- Chaplain in Terminator Armour (pg 20)
- Chaplain on Bike (pg 20)
- Company Ancient [1] (pg 23)
- Company Champion [1] (pg 24)
- Company Veterans [1] (pg 26)
- Devastator Squad (pg 51)
- Dreadnought (pg 35)
- Drop Pod (pg 48)
- Hellblaster Squad (pg 52)
- Imperial Space Marine (pg 30)
- Inceptor Squad (pg 43)
- Intercessor Squad (pg 30)
- Land Raider (pg 58)
- Land Raider Crusader (pg 59)
- Land Raider Excelsior (pg 61)
- Land Raider Redeemer (pg 60)
- Land Speeders (pg 46)
- Librarian (pg 14)
- Librarian in Terminator Armour (pg 15)
- Librarian on Bike (pg 15)
- Predator (pg 54)

- Primaris Ancient (pg 24)
- Primaris Lieutenants (pg 22)
- Razorback (pg 48)
- Rhino (pg 46)
- Rhino Primaris (pg 47)
- Sanguinary Novitiate – use the Apothecary [1] datasheet (pg 21)
- Scout Bike Squad (pg 43)
- Scout Squad (pg 29)
- Servitors (pg 16)
- Sternguard Veteran Squad (pg 33)
- Stormraven Gunship (pg 57)
- Tactical Squad (pg 28)
- Techmarine [1] (pg 16)
- Techmarine on Bike (pg 17)
- Terminator Assault Squad (pg 39)
- Terminator Squad (pg 38)
- Vanguard Veteran Squad (pg 34)
- Vindicator (pg 55)
- Whirlwind (pg 54)

[1] These units may take jump packs (**Power Rating +1**). If they do so, their Move characteristic is increased to 12" and they gain the **JUMP PACK** and **FLY** keywords, and the Jump Pack Assault ability (pg 88). A Techmarine that takes a jump pack no longer has a servo-arm.

SANGUINARY DISCIPLINE

Before the battle, generate the psychic powers for PSYKERS that can use powers from the Sanguinary discipline using the table below. You can either roll a D3 to generate their powers randomly (re-roll any duplicate results), or you can select the psychic powers you wish the psyker to have.

SANGUINARY DISCIPLINE	
D3	**PSYCHIC POWER**
1	**Blood Boil** *Blood Boil* has a warp charge value of 5. If manifested, select a visible enemy unit within 18" of the psyker and roll three dice. The target suffers a mortal wound for each result that equals or exceeds its Toughness characteristic.
2	**Shield of Sanguinius** *Shield of Sanguinius* has a warp charge value of 6. If manifested, select a friendly BLOOD ANGELS unit within 12" of the psyker. Until the start of your next Psychic phase, that unit has a 4+ invulnerable save.
3	**Unleash Rage** *Unleash Rage* has a warp charge value of 6. If manifested, select a friendly BLOOD ANGELS unit within 12" of the psyker. Until the start of your next Psychic phase, that unit has +1 Attack.

WARGEAR

Many of the units you will find on the following pages reference one or more wargear lists. When this is the case, the unit may take any item from the appropriate list on pg 11, with the following amendments.

The Blood Angels favour different weapons to other Space Marine Chapters. Add the following weapons to the *Pistols* and *Sergeant Equipment* lists when equipping Blood Angels units:

- Inferno pistol
- Hand flamer

Add the following weapon to the *Heavy Weapons* list when equipping Blood Angels units:

- Heavy flamer

The profiles for the weapons in these lists can be found in the appendix (pg 207 and 213).

BLOOD ANGELS SUCCESSOR CHAPTERS

There are many proud Space Marine Chapters that trace their origins to the gene-seed of the Blood Angels. From the frenzied Flesh Tearers to the brooding Angels Vermillion, all share the martial prowess and fiery blood-lust of their forefather Sanguinius. If you wish to theme your army as a Blood Angels successor Chapter, use the rules presented in this section but substitute the BLOOD ANGELS keyword in all instances on the datasheets and rules presented in this section with the name of your Blood Angels successor Chapter. Note, however, that named characters that can only be included in your army once cannot be from any other Chapter – Commander Dante is the Chapter Master of the Blood Angels Chapter, and not any successor Chapter.

COMMANDER DANTE

11 POWER

NAME	M	WS	BS	S	T	W	A	Ld	Sv
Commander Dante	12"	2+	2+	4	4	6	6	9	2+

Commander Dante is a single model armed with the Axe Mortalis, an inferno pistol, frag grenades and krak grenades. Only one of this model may be included in your army.

WEAPON	RANGE	TYPE	S	AP	D	ABILITIES
Inferno pistol	6"	Pistol 1	8	-4	D6	If the target is within half range of this weapon, roll two dice when inflicting damage with it and discard the lowest result.
The Axe Mortalis	Melee	Melee	+2	-3	D3	You can re-roll failed wound rolls for this weapon if the target is a **Character**.
Frag grenade	6"	Grenade D6	3	0	1	-
Krak grenade	6"	Grenade 1	6	-1	D3	-

ABILITIES	
And They Shall Know No Fear (pg 88) **Chapter Master:** You can re-roll failed hit rolls for friendly **Blood Angels** within 6" of Commander Dante. **Jump Pack Assault:** During deployment, you can set up Commander Dante high in the skies instead of placing him on the battlefield. At the end of any of your Movement phases Commander Dante can assault from above – set him up anywhere on the battlefield that is more than 9" away from any enemy models.	**Death Mask:** Enemy units suffer a -1 modifier to their Leadership while they are within 3" of any models wearing a death mask. **Iron Halo:** Commander Dante has a 4+ invulnerable save.

FACTION KEYWORDS	IMPERIUM, ADEPTUS ASTARTES, BLOOD ANGELS
KEYWORDS	CHARACTER, INFANTRY, CHAPTER MASTER, JUMP PACK, FLY, COMMANDER DANTE

CAPTAIN TYCHO

5 POWER

NAME	M	WS	BS	S	T	W	A	Ld	Sv
Captain Tycho	6"	2+	2+	4	4	5	4	9	2+

Captain Tycho is a single model armed with Blood Song, a bolt pistol, frag grenades and krak grenades. Only one **Tycho** may be included in your army.

WEAPON	RANGE	TYPE	S	AP	D	ABILITIES
Blood Song	When attacking with this weapon, choose one or both of the profiles below. If you choose both, subtract 1 from all hit rolls for this weapon.					
- Master-crafted boltgun	24"	Rapid Fire 1	4	-1	2	-
- Meltagun	12"	Assault 1	8	-4	D6	If the target is within half range of this weapon, roll two dice when inflicting damage with it and discard the lowest result.
Bolt pistol	12"	Pistol 1	4	0	1	-
Frag grenade	6"	Grenade D6	3	0	1	-
Krak grenade	6"	Grenade 1	6	-1	D3	-

ABILITIES	
And They Shall Know No Fear (pg 88) **Rites of Battle:** You can re-roll hit rolls of 1 made for friendly **Blood Angels** units within 6" of Captain Tycho.	**Abhor the Beast:** Captain Tycho may make D3 additional close combat attacks if he is within 1" of any enemy **Orks** after he has piled in during the Fight phase. **Iron Halo:** Captain Tycho has a 4+ invulnerable save.

FACTION KEYWORDS	IMPERIUM, ADEPTUS ASTARTES, BLOOD ANGELS
KEYWORDS	CHARACTER, INFANTRY, CAPTAIN, TYCHO

TYCHO THE LOST

4 POWER

NAME	M	WS	BS	S	T	W	A	Ld	Sv
Tycho the Lost	6"	2+	2+	4	4	5	4	9	2+

Tycho the Lost is a single model armed with Blood Song, a bolt pistol, frag grenades, krak grenades and an iron halo. Only one **TYCHO** may be included in your army.

WEAPON	RANGE	TYPE	S	AP	D	ABILITIES
Blood Song	When attacking with this weapon, choose one or both of the profiles below. If you choose both, subtract 1 from all hit rolls for this weapon.					
- Master-crafted boltgun	24"	Rapid Fire 1	4	-1	2	-
- Meltagun	12"	Assault 1	8	-4	D6	If the target is within half range of this weapon, roll two dice when inflicting damage with it and discard the lowest result.
Bolt pistol	12"	Pistol 1	4	0	1	-
Frag grenade	6"	Grenade D6	3	0	1	-
Krak grenade	6"	Grenade 1	6	-1	D3	-
ABILITIES	**And They Shall Know No Fear, Black Rage** (pg 88) **Iron Halo:** Tycho the Lost has a 4+ invulnerable save.					**Abhor the Beast:** Tycho the Lost may make D3 additional close combat attacks if he is within 1" of any enemy **ORKS** after he has piled in during the Fight phase.
FACTION KEYWORDS	**IMPERIUM, ADEPTUS ASTARTES, BLOOD ANGELS, DEATH COMPANY**					
KEYWORDS	**CHARACTER, INFANTRY, TYCHO**					

LIBRARIAN DREADNOUGHT

10 POWER

NAME	M	WS	BS	S	T	W	A	Ld	Sv
Librarian Dreadnought	6"	2+	3+	6	7	8	3	9	3+

A Librarian Dreadnought is a single model armed with a Furioso force halberd, a Furioso fist and a storm bolter.

WEAPON	RANGE	TYPE	S	AP	D	ABILITIES
Storm bolter	24"	Rapid Fire 2	4	0	1	-
Heavy flamer	8"	Heavy D6	5	-1	1	This weapon automatically hits its target.
Meltagun	12"	Assault 1	8	-4	D6	If the target is within half range of this weapon, roll two dice when inflicting damage with it and discard the lowest result.
Furioso fist	Melee	Melee	x2	-3	3	-
Furioso force halberd	Melee	Melee	+4	-4	3	-
WARGEAR OPTIONS	• This model may replace its storm bolter with a heavy flamer or a meltagun.					
ABILITIES	**Psychic Hood:** You can add 1 to Deny the Witch tests you take for this model against enemy **PSYKERS** within 12". **Explodes:** If this model is reduced to 0 wounds, roll a D6 before removing the model from the battlefield; on a 6 it explodes, and each unit within 3" suffers D3 mortal wounds.					**Smoke Launchers:** Once per battle, instead of shooting any weapons in the Shooting phase, this model can use its smoke launchers; until your next Shooting phase your opponent must subtract 1 from all hit rolls for ranged weapons that target this vehicle.
PSYKER	This model can attempt to manifest two psychic powers in each friendly Psychic phase, and attempt to deny one psychic power in each enemy Psychic phase. It knows the *Smite* psychic power and two psychic powers from the Sanguinary discipline (pg 89).					
FACTION KEYWORDS	**IMPERIUM, ADEPTUS ASTARTES, BLOOD ANGELS**					
KEYWORDS	**CHARACTER, VEHICLE, DREADNOUGHT, LIBRARIAN, PSYKER, LIBRARIAN DREADNOUGHT**					

CHIEF LIBRARIAN MEPHISTON

8 POWER

NAME	M	WS	BS	S	T	W	A	Ld	Sv
Chief Librarian Mephiston	7"	2+	2+	5	5	5	4	9	2+

Chief Librarian Mephiston is a single model armed with a plasma pistol, the Sanguine Sword, frag grenades and krak grenades. Only one of this model may be included in your army.

WEAPON	RANGE	TYPE	S	AP	D	ABILITIES
Plasma pistol	When attacking with this weapon, choose one of the profiles below.					
- Standard	12"	Pistol 1	7	-3	1	-
- Supercharge	12"	Pistol 1	8	-3	2	On a hit roll of 1, the bearer is slain.
The Sanguine Sword	Melee	Melee	x2	-3	D3	-
Frag grenade	6"	Grenade D6	3	0	1	-
Krak grenade	6"	Grenade 1	6	-1	D3	-

ABILITIES	And They Shall Know No Fear (pg 88) **Lord of Death:** Each time Chief Librarian Mephiston suffers an unsaved wound or a mortal wound roll a D6. On a 5+ the damage is ignored. **Psychic Hood:** You can add 1 to Deny the Witch tests you take for Chief Librarian Mephiston against enemy **PSYKERS** within 12".
PSYKER	Chief Librarian Mephiston can attempt to manifest two psychic powers in each friendly Psychic phase, and attempt to deny two psychic powers in each enemy Psychic phase. He knows the *Smite* psychic power and three psychic powers from the Sanguinary discipline (pg 89).
FACTION KEYWORDS	IMPERIUM, ADEPTUS ASTARTES, BLOOD ANGELS
KEYWORDS	CHARACTER, INFANTRY, LIBRARIAN, PSYKER, CHIEF LIBRARIAN MEPHISTON

THE SANGUINOR

9 POWER

NAME	M	WS	BS	S	T	W	A	Ld	Sv
The Sanguinor	12"	2+	2+	4	4	5	5	9	2+

The Sanguinor is a single model armed with an encarmine broadsword, frag grenades and krak grenades. Only one of this model may be included in your army.

WEAPON	RANGE	TYPE	S	AP	D	ABILITIES
Encarmine broadsword	Melee	Melee	+2	-4	D3	-
Frag grenade	6"	Grenade D6	3	0	1	-
Krak grenade	6"	Grenade 1	6	-1	D3	-

ABILITIES	And They Shall Know No Fear (pg 88) **Aura of Fervour:** You can add 1 to the Attacks characteristic of friendly **BLOOD ANGELS INFANTRY** units within 6" of the Sanguinor. **Avenging Angel:** The Sanguinor can charge even if he Fell Back in the preceding Movement phase.	**Death Mask:** Enemy units suffer a -1 modifier to their Leadership while they are within 3" of any models wearing a death mask. **Iron Halo:** The Sanguinor has a 4+ invulnerable save. **Jump Pack Assault:** During deployment, you can set up the Sanguinor high in the skies instead of placing him on the battlefield. At the end of any of your Movement phases the Sanguinor can assault from above – set him up anywhere on the battlefield that is more than 9" away from any enemy models.
FACTION KEYWORDS	IMPERIUM, ADEPTUS ASTARTES, BLOOD ANGELS	
KEYWORDS	CHARACTER, INFANTRY, JUMP PACK, FLY, THE SANGUINOR	

ASTORATH

8 POWER

NAME	M	WS	BS	S	T	W	A	Ld	Sv
Astorath	12"	2+	2+	4	4	5	4	9	2+

Astorath is a single model armed with the Executioner's Axe, a bolt pistol, frag grenades and krak grenades. Only one of this model may be included in your army.

WEAPON	RANGE	TYPE	S	AP	D	ABILITIES
Bolt pistol	12"	Pistol 1	4	0	1	-
The Executioner's Axe	Melee	Melee	+1	-3	D3	Each time you roll a wound roll of 6+ for this weapon it causes 3 damage instead of D3.
Frag grenade	6"	Grenade D6	3	0	1	-
Krak grenade	6"	Grenade 1	6	-1	D3	-

ABILITIES	
	And They Shall Know No Fear (pg 88) **Redeemer of the Lost:** All friendly **BLOOD ANGELS** units within 6" of Astorath can use his Leadership instead of their own. In addition, friendly **DEATH COMPANY** units automatically pass Morale tests if they are within 6" of Astorath. **Jump Pack Assault:** During deployment, you can set up Astorath high in the skies instead of placing him on the battlefield. At the end of any of your Movement phases Astorath can assault from above – set him up anywhere on the battlefield that is more than 9" away from any enemy models. **Litanies of Hate:** You can re-roll failed hit rolls in the Fight phase for friendly **BLOOD ANGELS** units within 6" of Astorath.	**Mass of Doom:** Once per battle, at the start of your Movement phase, Astorath may chant the Mass of Doom. Roll a D6 for each friendly **BLOOD ANGELS INFANTRY** unit within 6" of Astorath and apply the result below: **D6 Result** 1 **Frenzied Death Throes:** The unit suffers a mortal wound. 2-5 **Dark Wrath:** You can add 1 to hit rolls made for this unit in the Fight phase until the end of your turn. 6 **Vessel of Sanguinius:** You can add 1 to hit rolls made for this unit in the Fight phase until the end of your turn. In addition, the unit has a 4+ invulnerable save until the end of your turn. **Rosarius:** This model has a 4+ invulnerable save.

FACTION KEYWORDS	**IMPERIUM, ADEPTUS ASTARTES, BLOOD ANGELS**
KEYWORDS	**CHARACTER, INFANTRY, CHAPLAIN, JUMP PACK, FLY, ASTORATH**

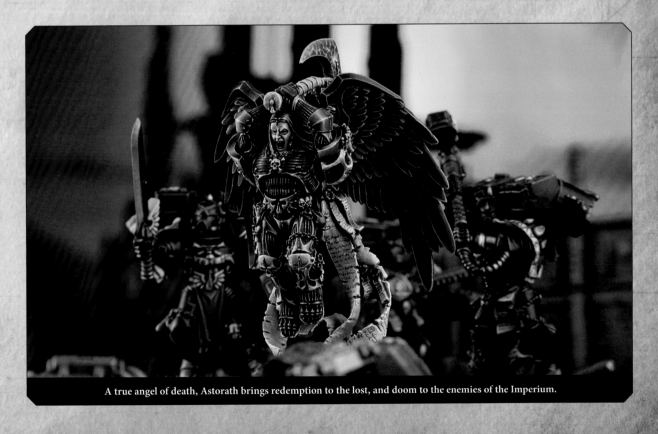

A true angel of death, Astorath brings redemption to the lost, and doom to the enemies of the Imperium.

SANGUINARY PRIEST

4 POWER

NAME	M	WS	BS	S	T	W	A	Ld	Sv
Sanguinary Priest	6"	2+	3+	4	4	4	3	9	3+

A Sanguinary Priest is a single model armed with a bolt pistol, a chainsword, frag grenades and krak grenades.

WEAPON	RANGE	TYPE	S	AP	D	ABILITIES
Bolt pistol	12"	Pistol 1	4	0	1	-
Boltgun	24"	Rapid Fire 1	4	0	1	-
Chainsword	Melee	Melee	User	0	1	Each time the bearer fights, it can make 1 additional attack with this weapon.
Frag grenade	6"	Grenade D6	3	0	1	-
Krak grenade	6"	Grenade 1	6	-1	D3	-

WARGEAR OPTIONS	
	• This model may replace his bolt pistol with a boltgun or an item from the *Pistols* or *Combi-weapons* list.
	• This model may replace his chainsword with an item from the *Melee Weapons* list.
	• This model may replace his bolt pistol with an item from the *Melee Weapons* list.
	• This model may take a jump pack (**Power Rating +1**). If it does, its Move characteristic is increased to 12" and it gains the **Jump Pack** and **Fly** keywords.

ABILITIES	
	And They Shall Know No Fear (pg 88)
	Blood Chalice: Friendly **Blood Angels Infantry** and **Biker** units increase their Strength characteristic by 1 whilst they are within 6" of any **Sanguinary Priests**.
	Narthecium: At the end of any of your Movement phases, the Sanguinary Priest can attempt to heal or revive a single model. Select a friendly **Blood Angels Infantry** or **Biker** unit within 3" of the Sanguinary Priest. If that unit contains a wounded model, it immediately regains D3 lost wounds. If the chosen unit contains no wounded models but one or more of its models have been slain during the battle, roll a D6. On a 4+ a single slain model is returned to the unit with 1 wound remaining. If a Sanguinary Priest fails to revive a model in this manner he can do nothing else for the remainder of the turn (shoot, charge, fight etc.) as he recovers the gene-seed of the fallen warrior. A unit can only be the target of the Narthecium ability once in each turn.
	Jump Pack Assault: During deployment, if this model has a jump pack, you can set it up high in the skies instead of placing it on the battlefield. At the end of any of your Movement phases this model can assault from above – set it up anywhere on the battlefield that is more than 9" away from any enemy models.

FACTION KEYWORDS	**Imperium, Adeptus Astartes, Blood Angels**
KEYWORDS	**Character, Infantry, Sanguinary Priest**

Sanguinary Priests are the preservers of their Chapter's gene-seed and the bearers of the sacred blood chalices.

SANGUINARY PRIEST
ON BIKE

NAME	M	WS	BS	S	T	W	A	Ld	Sv
Sanguinary Priest on Bike	14"	2+	3+	4	5	5	3	9	3+

A Sanguinary Priest on Bike is a single model armed with a bolt pistol, a chainsword, frag grenades, krak grenades, a blood chalice and a narthecium. His Space Marine bike is equipped with a twin boltgun.

WEAPON	RANGE	TYPE	S	AP	D	ABILITIES
Bolt pistol	12"	Pistol 1	4	0	1	-
Boltgun	24"	Rapid Fire 1	4	0	1	-
Twin boltgun	24"	Rapid Fire 2	4	0	1	-
Chainsword	Melee	Melee	User	0	1	Each time the bearer fights, it can make 1 additional attack with this weapon.
Frag grenade	6"	Grenade D6	3	0	1	-
Krak grenade	6"	Grenade 1	6	-1	D3	-

WARGEAR OPTIONS	• This model may replace his bolt pistol with a boltgun or an item from the *Melee*, *Pistols* or *Combi-weapons* list. • This model may replace his chainsword with an item from the *Melee Weapons* list.
ABILITIES	**And They Shall Know No Fear** (pg 88) **Blood Chalice:** Friendly **Blood Angels Infantry** and **Biker** units increase their Strength characteristic by 1 whilst they are within 6" of any **Sanguinary Priests**. **Narthecium:** At the end of any of your Movement phases, the Sanguinary Priest on Bike can attempt to heal or revive a single model. Select a friendly **Blood Angels Infantry** or **Biker** unit within 3" of the Sanguinary Priest on Bike. If that unit contains a wounded model, it immediately regains D3 lost wounds. If the chosen unit contains no wounded models but one or more of its models have been slain during the battle, roll a D6. On a 4+ a single slain model is returned to the unit with 1 wound remaining. If a Sanguinary Priest on Bike fails to revive a model in this manner he can do nothing else for the remainder of the turn (shoot, charge, fight etc.) as he recovers the gene-seed of the fallen warrior. A unit can only be the target of the Narthecium ability once in each turn.
FACTION KEYWORDS	**IMPERIUM, ADEPTUS ASTARTES, BLOOD ANGELS**
KEYWORDS	**BIKER, CHARACTER, SANGUINARY PRIEST**

BROTHER CORBULO

5 POWER

NAME	M	WS	BS	S	T	W	A	Ld	Sv
Brother Corbulo	6"	2+	2+	4	4	5	4	9	3+

Brother Corbulo is a single model armed with Heaven's Teeth, a bolt pistol, frag grenades and krak grenades. Only one of this model may be included in your army.

WEAPON	RANGE	TYPE	S	AP	D	ABILITIES
Bolt pistol	12"	Pistol 1	4	0	1	-
Heaven's Teeth	Melee	Melee	+1	-1	1	-
Frag grenade	6"	Grenade D6	3	0	1	-
Krak grenade	6"	Grenade 1	6	-1	D3	-

ABILITIES	
	And They Shall Know No Fear (pg 88)

Far-Seeing Eye: Once per turn you can re-roll a single dice roll made for Brother Corbulo.

The Red Grail: Friendly **BLOOD ANGELS INFANTRY** and **BIKER** units increase their Strength characteristic by 1 whilst they are within 6" of any **SANGUINARY PRIESTS**. In addition, each time you make a hit roll of 6+ in the Fight phase for a friendly **BLOOD ANGELS** unit within 6" of Brother Corbulo, that unit may immediately make another close combat attack using the same weapons. These bonus attacks cannot themselves generate any additional close combat attacks.

Nartecium: At the end of any of your Movement phases, Brother Corbulo can attempt to heal or revive a single model. Select a friendly **BLOOD ANGELS INFANTRY** or **BIKER** unit within 3" of Brother Corbulo. If that unit contains a wounded model, it immediately regains D3 lost wounds. If the chosen unit contains no wounded models but one or more of its models have been slain during the battle, roll a D6. On a 4+ a single slain model is returned to the unit with 1 wound remaining. If Brother Corbulo fails to revive a model in this manner he can do nothing else for the remainder of the turn (shoot, charge, fight etc.) as he recovers the gene-seed of the fallen warrior. A unit can only be the target of the Nartecium ability once in each turn.

FACTION KEYWORDS	IMPERIUM, ADEPTUS ASTARTES, BLOOD ANGELS
KEYWORDS	CHARACTER, INFANTRY, SANGUINARY PRIEST, BROTHER CORBULO

No other Blood Angel embodies the wisdom and character of Sanguinius more than the Keeper of the Red Grail.

SANGUINARY GUARD ANCIENT

6 POWER

NAME	M	WS	BS	S	T	W	A	Ld	Sv
Sanguinary Guard Ancient	12"	3+	3+	4	4	4	3	9	2+

A Sanguinary Guard Ancient is a single model armed with an angelus boltgun, an encarmine sword, frag grenades and krak grenades.

WEAPON	RANGE	TYPE	S	AP	D	ABILITIES
Angelus boltgun	12"	Assault 2	4	-1	1	-
Inferno pistol	6"	Pistol 1	8	-4	D6	If the target is within half range of this weapon, roll two dice when inflicting damage with it and discard the lowest result.
Plasma pistol	When attacking with this weapon, choose one of the profiles below.					
- Standard	12"	Pistol 1	7	-3	1	-
- Supercharge	12"	Pistol 1	8	-3	2	On a hit roll of 1, the bearer is slain.
Encarmine axe	Melee	Melee	+1	-2	D3	-
Encarmine sword	Melee	Melee	User	-3	D3	-
Power fist	Melee	Melee	x2	-3	D3	When attacking with this weapon, you must subtract 1 from the hit roll.
Frag grenade	6"	Grenade D6	3	0	1	-
Krak grenade	6"	Grenade 1	6	-1	D3	-

WARGEAR OPTIONS	• This model may take a death mask. • This model may replace his angelus boltgun with an inferno pistol or a plasma pistol. • This model may replace his encarmine sword with an encarmine axe or a power fist.

ABILITIES	**And They Shall Know No Fear** (pg 88) **Blood Angels Chapter Banner:** Friendly **BLOOD ANGELS** units within 6" of a Blood Angels Chapter banner do not need to take Morale tests and re-roll wound rolls of 1 in the Fight phase. **Jump Pack Assault:** During deployment, you can set up this model high in the skies instead of placing it on the battlefield. At the end of any of your Movement phases this model can assault from above – set it up anywhere on the battlefield that is more than 9" away from any enemy models.	**Death Mask:** Enemy units suffer a -1 modifier to their Leadership while they are within 3" of any models wearing a death mask. **Heirs of Azkaellon:** You can re-roll failed hit rolls for this model if it is within 6" of a **BLOOD ANGELS** Warlord.

FACTION KEYWORDS	**IMPERIUM, ADEPTUS ASTARTES, BLOOD ANGELS**
KEYWORDS	**CHARACTER, INFANTRY, ANCIENT, JUMP PACK, FLY, SANGUINARY GUARD**

TERMINATOR ANCIENT

NAME	M	WS	BS	S	T	W	A	Ld	Sv
Terminator Ancient	5"	3+	3+	4	4	5	3	8	2+

A Terminator Ancient is a single model armed with a lightning claw.

WEAPON	RANGE	TYPE	S	AP	D	ABILITIES
Lightning claw	Melee	Melee	User	-2	1	You can re-roll failed wound rolls for this weapon.
Thunder hammer	Melee	Melee	x2	-3	3	When attacking with this weapon, you must subtract 1 from the hit roll.

WARGEAR OPTIONS	• This model may replace his lightning claw with a thunder hammer.

ABILITIES	**And They Shall Know No Fear** (pg 88) **Teleport Strike:** During deployment, you can set up this unit in a teleportarium chamber instead of placing it on the battlefield. At the end of any of your Movement phases this unit can teleport into battle – set it up anywhere on the battlefield that is more than 9" away from any enemy models.	**Terminator Armour:** This model has a 5+ invulnerable save. **Archangel Standard:** Friendly **BLOOD ANGELS** units within 6" of an Archangel standard add 1 to their Leadership characteristic, and you can re-roll failed hit rolls for them in the Fight phase.

FACTION KEYWORDS	**IMPERIUM, ADEPTUS ASTARTES, BLOOD ANGELS**
KEYWORDS	**CHARACTER, INFANTRY, ANCIENT, TERMINATOR**

DEATH COMPANY

NAME	M	WS	BS	S	T	W	A	Ld	Sv
Death Company Marine	6"	3+	3+	4	4	1	2	7	3+

This unit contains 5 Death Company Marines. It may include up to 5 additional Death Company Marines (**Power Rating +9**) or up to 10 additional Death Company Marines (**Power Rating +18**). Each model is armed with a bolt pistol, a chainsword, frag grenades and krak grenades.

WEAPON	RANGE	TYPE	S	AP	D	ABILITIES
Bolt pistol	12"	Pistol 1	4	0	1	-
Boltgun	24"	Rapid Fire 1	4	0	1	-
Hand flamer	6"	Pistol D3	3	0	1	This weapon automatically hits its target.
Inferno pistol	6"	Pistol 1	8	-4	D6	If the target is within half range of this weapon, roll two dice when inflicting damage with it and discard the lowest result.
Plasma pistol	When attacking with this weapon, choose one of the profiles below.					
- Standard	12"	Pistol 1	7	-3	1	-
- Supercharge	12"	Pistol 1	8	-3	2	On a hit roll of 1, the bearer is slain.
Chainsword	Melee	Melee	User	0	1	Each time the bearer fights, it can make 1 additional attack with this weapon.
Power axe	Melee	Melee	+1	-2	1	-
Power maul	Melee	Melee	+2	-1	1	-
Power sword	Melee	Melee	User	-3	1	-
Thunder hammer	Melee	Melee	x2	-3	3	When attacking with this weapon, you must subtract 1 from the hit roll.
Frag grenade	6"	Grenade D6	3	0	1	-
Krak grenade	6"	Grenade 1	6	-1	D3	-

WARGEAR OPTIONS	• Any model may replace his bolt pistol with a boltgun, hand flamer, inferno pistol, plasma pistol, power axe, power fist, power maul or power sword. • Any model may replace his chainsword with a power axe, power fist, power maul or power sword. • Any model may replace his chainsword and bolt pistol with a thunder hammer. • The entire unit may take jump packs (**Power Rating +1 per 5 models**). If they do, their Move characteristic is increased to 12" and they gain the **JUMP PACK** and **FLY** keywords.
ABILITIES	**And They Shall Know No Fear, Black Rage** (pg 88) **Jump Pack Assault:** During deployment, if the entire unit has jump packs, you can set them up high in the skies instead of placing them on the battlefield. At the end of any of your Movement phases this unit can assault from above – set them up anywhere on the battlefield that is more than 9" away from any enemy models.
FACTION KEYWORDS	**IMPERIUM, ADEPTUS ASTARTES, BLOOD ANGELS, DEATH COMPANY**
KEYWORDS	**INFANTRY**

LEMARTES

NAME	M	WS	BS	S	T	W	A	Ld	Sv
Lemartes	12"	2+	3+	4	4	4	5	9	3+

Lemartes is a single model armed with the Blood Crozius, a bolt pistol, frag grenades and krak grenades. Only one of this model may be included in your army.

WEAPON	RANGE	TYPE	S	AP	D	ABILITIES
Bolt pistol	12"	Pistol 1	4	0	1	-
The Blood Crozius	Melee	Melee	+2	-2	D3	-
Frag grenade	6"	Grenade D6	3	0	1	-
Krak grenade	6"	Grenade 1	6	-1	D3	-

ABILITIES	And They Shall Know No Fear, Black Rage (pg 88) **Fury Unbound:** You can re-roll failed charge rolls and failed hit rolls in the Fight phase for friendly **DEATH COMPANY** units within 6" of Lemartes. **Guardian of the Lost:** All friendly **DEATH COMPANY** units within 6" of Lemartes can use his Leadership instead of their own.	**Jump Pack Assault:** During deployment, you can set up Lemartes high in the skies instead of placing him on the battlefield. At the end of any of your Movement phases Lemartes can assault from above – set him up anywhere on the battlefield that is more than 9" away from any enemy models. **Rosarius:** Lemartes has a 4+ invulnerable save.
FACTION KEYWORDS	**IMPERIUM, ADEPTUS ASTARTES, BLOOD ANGELS, DEATH COMPANY**	
KEYWORDS	**CHARACTER, INFANTRY, CHAPLAIN, JUMP PACK, FLY, LEMARTES**	

As warden of the Death Company, Lemartes' grim litanies provide guidance for the Lost Brethren.

SANGUINARY GUARD

10 POWER

NAME	M	WS	BS	S	T	W	A	Ld	Sv
Sanguinary Guard	12"	3+	3+	4	4	2	2	8	2+

This unit contains 4 Sanguinary Guard. It may contain up to 6 additional Sanguinary Guard (**Power Rating +12**). Each Sanguinary Guard is armed with an angelus boltgun, encarmine sword, frag grenades and krak grenades.

WEAPON	RANGE	TYPE	S	AP	D	ABILITIES
Angelus boltgun	12"	Assault 2	4	-1	1	-
Inferno pistol	6"	Pistol 1	8	-4	D6	If the target is within half range of this weapon, roll two dice when inflicting damage with it and discard the lowest result.
Plasma pistol	When attacking with this weapon, choose one of the profiles below.					
- Standard	12"	Pistol 1	7	-3	1	-
- Supercharge	12"	Pistol 1	8	-3	2	On a hit roll of 1, the bearer is slain.
Encarmine axe	Melee	Melee	+1	-2	D3	-
Encarmine sword	Melee	Melee	User	-3	D3	-
Power fist	Melee	Melee	x2	-3	D3	When attacking with this weapon, you must subtract 1 from the hit roll.
Frag grenade	6"	Grenade D6	3	0	1	-
Krak grenade	6"	Grenade 1	6	-1	D3	-

WARGEAR OPTIONS	• Any model may take a death mask. • Any model may replace his angelus boltgun with an inferno pistol or a plasma pistol. • Any model may replace his encarmine sword with an encarmine axe or a power fist.

ABILITIES	**And They Shall Know No Fear** (pg 88) **Heirs of Azkaellon:** You can re-roll failed hit rolls for models from this unit if they are within 6" of a **Blood Angels** Warlord. **Death Mask:** Enemy units suffer a -1 modifier to their Leadership while they are within 3" of any models wearing a death mask.	**Jump Pack Assault:** During deployment, you can set up this unit high in the skies instead of placing them on the battlefield. At the end of any of your Movement phases this unit can assault from above – set them up anywhere on the battlefield that is more than 9" away from any enemy models.

FACTION KEYWORDS	**Imperium, Adeptus Astartes, Blood Angels**

KEYWORDS	**Infantry, Jump Pack, Fly, Sanguinary Guard**

Clad in golden armour, the Sanguinary Guard embody the legacy of their Primarch like no other.

DEATH COMPANY DREADNOUGHT

NAME	M	WS	BS	S	T	W	A	Ld	Sv
Death Company Dreadnought	8"	3+	3+	6	7	8	4	7	3+

A Death Company Dreadnought is a single model equipped with two Furioso fists, a storm bolter and a meltagun.

WEAPON	RANGE	TYPE	S	AP	D	ABILITIES
Heavy flamer	8"	Heavy D6	5	-1	1	This weapon automatically hits its target.
Meltagun	12"	Assault 1	8	-4	D6	If the target is within half range of this weapon, roll two dice when inflicting damage with it and discard the lowest result.
Storm bolter	24"	Rapid Fire 2	4	0	1	-
Blood talons	Melee	Melee	x2	-3	D6	-
Furioso fist	Melee	Melee	x2	-3	3	If a model is equipped with two Furioso fists, you can re-roll failed hit rolls when attacking with them.

WARGEAR OPTIONS	• This model may replace its two Furioso fists with blood talons. • This model may replace its storm bolter with a heavy flamer. • This model may replace its meltagun with a heavy flamer. • This model may replace its smoke launchers with a magna-grapple.

ABILITIES	**Black Rage** (pg 88) **Explodes:** If this model is reduced to 0 wounds, roll a D6 before removing the model from the battlefield; on a 6 it explodes, and each unit within 3" suffers D3 mortal wounds. **Insatiable:** This model may move up to 6" when consolidating at the end of the Fight phase.	**Smoke Launchers:** Once per battle, instead of shooting any weapons in the Shooting phase, this model can use smoke launchers if it is equipped with them; until your next Shooting phase your opponent must subtract 1 from all hit rolls for ranged weapons that target this vehicle. **Magna-grapple:** If a model with a magna-grapple targets a **VEHICLE** in the Charge phase, you can add 2 to its charge roll.

FACTION KEYWORDS	**IMPERIUM, ADEPTUS ASTARTES, BLOOD ANGELS, DEATH COMPANY**
KEYWORDS	**VEHICLE, DREADNOUGHT, DEATH COMPANY DREADNOUGHT**

A Blood Angel lost to the Black Rage can cause untold devastation when interred within the towering form of a Dreadnought.

FURIOSO DREADNOUGHT

10 POWER

NAME	M	WS	BS	S	T	W	A	Ld	Sv
Furioso Dreadnought	8"	3+	3+	6	7	8	4	8	3+

A Furioso Dreadnought is a single model equipped with two Furioso fists, a storm bolter and a meltagun.

WEAPON	RANGE	TYPE	S	AP	D	ABILITIES
Frag cannon	8"	Assault 2D6	6	-1	1	This weapon automatically hits its target.
Heavy flamer	8"	Heavy D6	5	-1	1	This weapon automatically hits its target.
Storm bolter	24"	Rapid Fire 2	4	0	1	-
Meltagun	12"	Assault 1	8	-4	D6	If the target is within half range of this weapon, roll two dice when inflicting damage with it and discard the lowest result.
Blood talons	Melee	Melee	x2	-3	D6	-
Furioso fist	Melee	Melee	x2	-3	3	If a model is equipped with two Furioso fists, you can re-roll failed hit rolls when attacking with them.

WARGEAR OPTIONS	• This model may replace one Furioso fist and either its storm bolter or its meltagun with a frag cannon. • This model may replace its two Furioso fists with blood talons. • This model may replace its storm bolter with a heavy flamer. • This model may replace its meltagun with a heavy flamer. • This model may replace its smoke launchers with a magna-grapple.

ABILITIES	**Explodes:** If this model is reduced to 0 wounds, roll a D6 before removing the model from the battlefield; on a 6 it explodes, and each unit within 3" suffers D3 mortal wounds. **Magna-grapple:** If a model with a magna-grapple targets a **VEHICLE** in the Charge phase, you can add 2 to its charge roll.	**Smoke Launchers:** Once per battle, instead of shooting any weapons in the Shooting phase, this model can use smoke launchers if it is equipped with them; until your next Shooting phase your opponent must subtract 1 from all hit rolls for ranged weapons that target this vehicle.

FACTION KEYWORDS	IMPERIUM, ADEPTUS ASTARTES, BLOOD ANGELS
KEYWORDS	VEHICLE, DREADNOUGHT, FURIOSO DREADNOUGHT

BAAL PREDATOR

8 POWER

DAMAGE
Some of this model's characteristics change as it suffers damage, as shown below:

REMAINING W	M	BS	A
6-11+	12"	3+	3
3-5	6"	4+	D3
1-2	3"	5+	1

NAME	M	WS	BS	S	T	W	A	Ld	Sv
Baal Predator	*	6+	*	6	7	11	*	8	3+

A Baal Predator is a single model equipped with a twin assault cannon.

WEAPON	RANGE	TYPE	S	AP	D	ABILITIES
Flamestorm cannon	8"	Assault D6	6	-2	2	This weapon automatically hits its target.
Heavy bolter	36"	Heavy 3	5	-1	1	-
Heavy flamer	8"	Heavy D6	5	-1	1	This weapon automatically hits its target.
Twin assault cannon	24"	Heavy 12	6	-1	1	-

WARGEAR OPTIONS	• This model may replace its twin assault cannon with a flamestorm cannon. • This model may take two heavy bolters or two heavy flamers.

ABILITIES	**Overcharged Engines:** When this model Advances roll 2 dice and pick the highest result. **Explodes:** If this model is reduced to 0 wounds, roll a D6 before removing the model from the battlefield; on a 6 it explodes, and each unit within 6" suffers D3 mortal wounds.	**Smoke Launchers:** Once per battle, instead of shooting any weapons in the Shooting phase, this model can use its smoke launchers; until your next Shooting phase your opponent must subtract 1 from all hit rolls for ranged weapons that target this vehicle.

FACTION KEYWORDS	IMPERIUM, ADEPTUS ASTARTES, BLOOD ANGELS
KEYWORDS	VEHICLE, PREDATOR, BAAL PREDATOR

FLESH TEARERS

Of all the successor Chapters of the Blood Angels, the Flesh Tearers have inherited the most drastic flaws of their genetic heritage. In battle these berserker warriors lose themselves entirely to a frenzied blood-lust, tearing the enemy limb from limb in a horrific orgy of slaughter.

Few Space Marine Chapters have as dark a reputation as the Flesh Tearers. Ever has the eye of the Inquisition and the Ecclesiarchy fallen upon these brutal killers, for such is the carnage and terror they leave in their wake that many believe they must surely be tainted by the touch of Chaos. The tales of the atrocities wrought by the Flesh Tearers grow increasingly grim with each passing decade, and it is only the devastation they have inflicted upon the enemies of the Imperium that has kept them from being further scrutinised.

The Flesh Tearers' home world of Cretacia is a tropical death world that teems with savage life, and contains some of the most ferocious predatory species in the galaxy. It is hard to imagine a more fitting planet for the Chapter to call home. The Flesh Tearers have inherited the fighting skill and courage of their progenitors the Blood Angels, but have also been afflicted with the very worst excesses of the Black Rage, the mindless need to slaughter that threatens to claim each son of Sanguinius. Where many of the Blood Angels' successor Chapters seek to suppress the savagery that boils within their blood, for many years the Flesh Tearers embraced it, exhibiting preference for close assault actions. Indeed, there are few finer melee combatants in all the galaxy than a Flesh Tearer Assault Squad, yet many Imperial Commanders remain reluctant to call upon their skills.

There is good reason for such reticence. Several times in their history, the Flesh Tearers have succumbed entirely to the Black Rage in the midst of combat, and when out of enemies to kill, have turned upon their own allies. There are rumours that entire Astra Militarum regiments and countless civilians have been torn and hacked apart by the chainblades of blood-crazed Flesh Eaters. Some say that during the Chapter's worst excesses, the Red Thirst has combined with the Black Rage, resulting in truly monstrous acts of cannibalism. While the veracity of many of these reports is questionable, it cannot be denied that the Flesh Tearers are prone to losing themselves to their slaughter-lust. Even fellow Adeptus Astartes have fallen victim to this madness – the Space Wolves hold a long-standing grudge against the Flesh Tearers as a result of a particular act of barbarism during the Eclipse Wars that came to be known as Honour's End.

Only through the diplomatic efforts of the Flesh Tearers' current Chapter Master Gabriel Seth has the threat of excommunication been averted. Though he is no less susceptible to the Black Rage

than his battle-brothers, Seth has gone some way towards repairing the strained relations between the Flesh Tearers and their progenitors the Blood Angels. Armed with his colossal two-handed chainsword Blood Reaver, Seth leads his men into the thick of battle, as far away from any civilian zones as possible. There, with only the enemy in sight, can the Flesh Tearers truly embrace their lust for slaughter.

GABRIEL SETH

NAME	M	WS	BS	S	T	W	A	Ld	Sv
Gabriel Seth	6"	2+	2+	4	4	6	4	9	3+

Gabriel Seth is a single model armed with Blood Reaver, a bolt pistol, frag grenades and krak grenades. Only one of this model may be included in your army.

WEAPON	RANGE	TYPE	S	AP	D	ABILITIES
Bolt pistol	12"	Pistol 1	4	0	1	-
Blood Reaver	Melee	Melee	x2	-1	3	Each time you roll a hit roll of 6+ for this weapon, inflict 1 additional hit on the target.
Frag grenade	6"	Grenade D6	3	0	1	-
Krak grenade	6"	Grenade 1	6	-1	D3	-

ABILITIES	And They Shall Know No Fear (pg 88) **Lord of Slaughter:** You can re-roll failed hit rolls for friendly **FLESH TEARERS** units within 6" of Gabriel Seth. **Iron Halo:** Gabriel Seth has a 4+ invulnerable save.	**Whirlwind of Gore:** Roll a D6 each time a friendly **FLESH TEARERS** unit finishes its move within 6" of Gabriel Seth when it consolidates; on a 6 that unit can immediately fight for a second and final time.
FACTION KEYWORDS	**IMPERIUM, ADEPTUS ASTARTES, FLESH TEARERS**	
KEYWORDS	**INFANTRY, CHAPTER MASTER, CHARACTER, GABRIEL SETH**	

Instead of curtailing the bloodlust of his battle-brothers, Chapter Master Gabriel Seth directs it towards the Imperium's enemies.

DARK ANGELS

At the very dawn of the Imperium the Dark Angels were the first founded of all the Adeptus Astartes. Few can match their long history of triumphs in service to mankind. However, behind the façade of their steady disposition lies a sinister obsession, for the Dark Angels are haunted by failings from the distant past.

No matter the foe or the odds, the Dark Angels stubbornly refuse to accept defeat. This tenacity, along with their taciturn character, are traits the Dark Angels inherited from their primogenitor, the Primarch, Lion El'Jonson. Between their grim mien, sombre and often hooded countenance, and the gothic symbolism rife upon their banners and gear of war, it is no surprise that the Dark Angels are feared not only by their enemies but often by their allies as well.

Although proud of the many glories won by the Chapter, the Dark Angels shun platitudes and avoid the vainglorious. The Sons of the Lion, as the Dark Angels are called, seek only to complete each task assigned to them as swiftly and efficiently as possible. This is not purely through a dour monastic outlook and selfless nobility, but something more nefarious. The Inner Circle of the Dark Angels – a secret group composed of the Chapter Master, his hand-chosen officers and veterans of the 1st Company – covertly wage their own secret war.

To outside observers, the Dark Angels are an exemplary Chapter of Adeptus Astartes. They strike swiftly, coordinating assaults with superhuman precision. The battle line advances under cover of fire support, and at the crucial tipping point, rapid deployment of close combat squads breaks all resistance before finishing off the foe. Enemies receive no mercy, yet the Dark Angels do not revel in bloodshed or excess. In the midst of battle they remain stoic, filled not with howling exultations but instead with solemn battle chants and hymns.

Eager not to draw attention, the Dark Angels follow the guidelines of the Codex Astartes, and yet they have petitioned to maintain their two unique fighting companies – the highly mobile 2nd Company (known as the Ravenwing) and the Terminator-armoured squads of the 1st Company (known as the Deathwing). Given the desperate circumstances of the torn and benighted galaxy, as well as the aforementioned companies' service records of excellence, the returned Primarch Roboute Guilliman granted such rights even as the Dark Angels and their successor Chapters began reorganising themselves to fit the dictates of the Ultima Founding.

THE RAVENWING

The 2nd Company is not clad in the dark green of the Chapter, but rather in black. They are a highly specialised formation that fights exclusively from fast-moving vehicles. The majority of the Ravenwing, including the elite Black Knights, fight astride Space Marine bikes. They are supported by brethren piloting varying marks of Land Speeder and swift atmospheric fighters. Fast assaults and reconnaissance are their trademarks. Their speed and daring is unmatched by any other Imperial formation, save perhaps the Great Hunt of the White Scars. There can be no underestimating the hard-hitting shock when the twin wings of the Dark Angels sweep down upon a foe. The fast moving Ravenwing speed into position before using homing devices to allow the Deathwing to teleport to the optimum location for a lethal strike.

THE DEATHWING

The 1st Company of the Dark Angels is one of the most renowned fighting forces in the galaxy. Known as the Deathwing, the entire veteran formation is outfitted in bone white Terminator Armour. The Deathwing is an assault force, able to march through the most intense storms of enemy fire or teleport straight into the fray, ripping the heart from the enemy army with a precision strike.

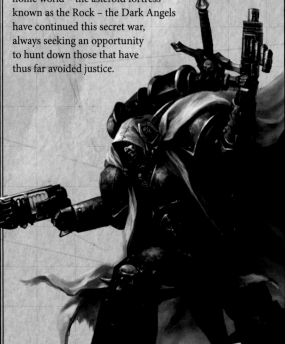

THE HUNT FOR THE FALLEN

As effective as they are at destroying the Emperor's foes, the Inner Circle alone knows that the Ravenwing and Deathwing hone their battle skills with a very specific prey in mind. It is those known as the Fallen that they hunt.

During the Horus Heresy, the Dark Angels protecting the Chapter's home world of Caliban fell under the sway of Chaos. The battle that occurred upon the return of Lion El'Jonson resulted in the destruction of the planet, and in the ensuing cataclysm many of the Fallen Dark Angels were swallowed by the warp and scattered across space and time. All knowledge of their treacherous brethren has been covered up by the leaders of the Chapter, a secret they keep even from those they would call allies. For 10,000 years since, the Dark Angels and their successor Chapters have sought redemption by hunting the Fallen. Using a mountainous shard of their shattered home world – the asteroid fortress known as the Rock – the Dark Angels have continued this secret war, always seeking an opportunity to hunt down those that have thus far avoided justice.

ABILITIES

The following abilities are common to several Dark Angels units:

And They Shall Know No Fear

You can re-roll failed Morale tests for this unit.

Unforgiven

This unit automatically passes Morale tests. In addition, you can re-roll failed hit rolls in the Fight phase for this unit if it is targeting a FALLEN unit.

Jink

If this unit Advances it gains a 5+ invulnerable save against all shooting attacks until the start of your next Movement phase.

WARGEAR

Many of the units you will find on the following pages reference one or more wargear lists. When this is the case, the unit may take any item from the appropriate list on pg 11. The profiles for the weapons in these lists can be found in the appendix (pg 206-209).

DARK ANGELS CHAPTER

The following Space Marines datasheets can be from the Dark Angels Chapter. Those that are replace the <CHAPTER> keyword on their datasheet in all instances with DARK ANGELS. If a Space Marines unit does not appear on the list below, it cannot be from the Dark Angels Chapter, and so cannot have the DARK ANGELS faction keyword. DARK ANGELS PSYKERS generate their psychic powers from the Interromancy discipline (below) instead of the Librarius discipline.

- Apothecary (pg 21)
- Assault Squad (pg 42)
- Chaplain (pg 19)
- Chaplain on Bike (pg 20)
- Company Master [2] – use the Captain (pg 12), Captain in Terminator Armour (pg 12) or Captain in Gravis Armour (pg 13) datasheet
- Company Ancient (pg 23)
- Company Champion [1] (pg 24)
- Company Veterans [3] (pg 26)
- Devastator Squad (pg 51)
- Dreadnought (pg 35)
- Drop Pod (pg 48)
- Hellblaster Squad (pg 52)
- Imperial Space Marine (pg 30)
- Inceptor Squad (pg 43)
- Intercessor Squad (pg 30)
- Land Raider (pg 58)
- Land Raider Crusader (pg 59)
- Land Raider Excelsior (pg 61)
- Land Raider Redeemer (pg 60)
- Librarian [2] (pg 14)
- Librarian in Terminator Armour [2] (pg 15)
- Librarian on Bike (pg 15) [2]
- Predator (pg 54)
- Primaris Ancient (pg 24)

- Primaris Lieutenants (pg 22)
- Razorback (pg 48)
- Rhino (pg 46)
- Rhino Primaris (pg 47)
- Scout Squad (pg 29)
- Servitors (pg 16)
- Tactical Squad (pg 28)
- Techmarine (pg 16)
- Techmarine on Bike (pg 17)
- Venerable Dreadnought [2] (pg 36)
- Vindicator (pg 55)
- Whirlwind (pg 54)

[1] This model replaces his master-crafted power sword with a blade of Caliban (pg 215). He cannot take any other options.

[2] These units gain the DEATHWING keyword and the Unforgiven ability.

[3] Any model in this unit may take a combat shield (pg 209).

INTERROMANCY DISCIPLINE

Before the battle, generate the psychic powers for PSYKERS that can use powers from the Interromancy discipline using the table below. You can either roll a D3 to generate their powers randomly (re-roll any duplicate results), or you can select the psychic powers you wish the psyker to have.

INTERROMANCY DISCIPLINE

D3	PSYCHIC POWER
1	**Mind Worm** *Mind Worm* has a warp charge value of 6. If manifested, select an enemy unit within 12" of the psyker. That unit suffers a mortal wound and may only be chosen to attack in the Fight phase after all other eligible units have made their attacks. This effect lasts until the end of your turn.
2	**Aversion** *Aversion* has a warp charge value of 6. If manifested, select an enemy unit within 24" of the psyker. Until your next Psychic phase, your opponent must subtract 1 from all hit rolls made for that unit.
3	**Engulfing Fear** *Engulfing Fear* has a warp charge value of 6. If manifested, your opponent must roll 2 dice and discard the lowest result when taking Morale tests for any unit that is within 6" of the psyker in the Morale phase.

DARK ANGELS SUCCESSOR CHAPTERS

There are many esteemed Space Marine Chapters that trace their origins to the gene-seed of the Dark Angels. From the mysterious Consecrators to the ferocious Disciples of Caliban, all uphold the grim legacy of Lion El'Jonson. If you wish to theme your army as a Dark Angels successor Chapter, use the rules presented in this section but substitute the DARK ANGELS keyword in all instances on the datasheets with the name of your Dark Angels successor Chapter. Note, however, that named characters that can only be included in your army once cannot be from any other Chapter – Azrael is the Supreme Grand Master of the Dark Angels Chapter, and not any successor Chapter.

AZRAEL

NAME	M	WS	BS	S	T	W	A	Ld	Sv
Azrael	6"	2+	2+	4	4	6	5	9	2+

Azrael is a single model armed with the Sword of Secrets, the Lion's Wrath, a bolt pistol, frag grenades and krak grenades. Only one of this model may be included in your army.

WEAPON	RANGE	TYPE	S	AP	D	ABILITIES
Bolt pistol	12"	Pistol 1	4	0	1	-
Lion's Wrath		When attacking with this weapon, choose one or both of the profiles below. If you choose both, subtract 1 from all hit rolls for this weapon.				
- Master-crafted boltgun	24"	Rapid Fire 1	4	-1	2	-
- Plasma gun	24"	Rapid Fire 1	7	-3	1	This weapon can be supercharged by the bearer before firing. If they do so, increase the Strength and Damage of the weapon by 1 this turn. On any hit rolls of 1 when firing supercharge, the bearer is slain after all of the weapon's shots have been resolved.
Sword of Secrets	Melee	Melee	+2	-3	D3	Each time you make a wound roll of 6+ for this weapon, the target suffers a mortal wound in addition to any other damage.
Frag grenade	6"	Grenade D6	3	0	1	-
Krak grenade	6"	Grenade 1	6	-1	D3	-

ABILITIES		
	Unforgiven (pg 107)	**Lion Helm:** Azrael is accompanied by a relic bearer who carries the Lion Helm, an artefact that generates a powerful force field. As a result, all friendly **Dark Angels** models within 6" of Azrael have a 4+ invulnerable save. The relic bearer model must always remain as close to Azrael as possible, but is otherwise ignored for all gaming purposes. Remove the relic bearer if Azrael is slain.
	Chapter Master: You can re-roll failed hit rolls for friendly **Dark Angels** units that are within 6" of Azrael.	
	Supreme Tactician: If your army is Battle-forged, you receive 1 additional Command Point if Azrael is your Warlord.	

FACTION KEYWORDS	IMPERIUM, ADEPTUS ASTARTES, DARK ANGELS, DEATHWING

KEYWORDS	CHARACTER, INFANTRY, CHAPTER MASTER, AZRAEL

BELIAL

8 POWER

NAME	M	WS	BS	S	T	W	A	Ld	Sv
Belial	5"	2+	2+	4	4	6	4	9	2+

Belial is a single model armed with the Sword of Silence and a storm bolter. Only one of this model may be included in your army.

WEAPON	RANGE	TYPE	S	AP	D	ABILITIES
Storm bolter	24"	Rapid Fire 2	4	0	1	-
Lightning claw	Melee	Melee	User	-2	1	You can re-roll failed wound rolls for this weapon. If a model is armed with two lightning claws, each time it fights it can make 1 additional attack with them.
Sword of Silence	Melee	Melee	+1	-3	2	This weapon always wounds on a 2+, unless the target is a **VEHICLE**.
Thunder hammer	Melee	Melee	x2	-3	3	When attacking with this weapon, you must subtract 1 from the hit roll.

WARGEAR OPTIONS	• Belial may replace his storm bolter and the Sword of Silence with two lightning claws or a thunder hammer and storm shield.

| ABILITIES | **Unforgiven** (pg 107)

Rites of Battle: You can re-roll hit rolls of 1 for friendly **DARK ANGELS** units within 6" of this model.

Grand Master of the Deathwing: You can re-roll failed hit rolls for friendly **DEATHWING** units within 6" of Belial.

Storm Shield: A model equipped with a storm shield has a 3+ invulnerable save. | **Parrying Blade:** If Belial is armed with the Sword of Silence, your opponent must subtract 1 from hit rolls for attacks that target him in the Fight phase.

Iron Halo: Belial has a 4+ invulnerable save.

Teleport Strike: During deployment, you can set up Belial in a teleportarium chamber instead of placing him on the battlefield. At the end of any of your Movement phases Belial can teleport into battle – set him up anywhere on the battlefield that is more than 9" from any enemy models. |

FACTION KEYWORDS	IMPERIUM, ADEPTUS ASTARTES, DARK ANGELS, DEATHWING
KEYWORDS	CHARACTER, INFANTRY, GRAND MASTER, TERMINATOR, BELIAL

Belial is the Lord of the Deathwing, a warrior whose mastery of the blade is matched by few in all the galaxy.

SAMMAEL
ON CORVEX

NAME	M	WS	BS	S	T	W	A	Ld	Sv
Sammael on Corvex	14"	2+	2+	4	6	6	5	9	3+

Sammael on Corvex is a single model armed with the Raven Sword, a bolt pistol, frag grenades and krak grenades. His jetbike *Corvex* is equipped with a plasma cannon and a twin storm bolter. Only one SAMMAEL may be included in your army.

WEAPON	RANGE	TYPE	S	AP	D	ABILITIES
Bolt pistol	12"	Pistol 1	4	0	1	-
Plasma cannon		When attacking with this weapon, choose one of the profiles below.				
- Standard	36"	Heavy D3	7	-3	1	-
- Supercharge	36"	Heavy D3	8	-3	2	On a hit roll of 1, the bearer is slain after all of this weapon's shots have been resolved.
Twin storm bolter	24"	Rapid Fire 4	4	0	1	-
Raven Sword	Melee	Melee	+1	-3	2	This weapon has Strength x2 if Sammael charged in the preceding Charge phase.

ABILITIES		
	And They Shall Know No Fear, Jink (pg 107) **Rites of Battle:** You can re-roll hit rolls of 1 for friendly DARK ANGELS units within 6" of this model. **Iron Halo:** This model has a 4+ invulnerable save.	**Grand Master of the Ravenwing:** You can re-roll failed hit rolls for friendly RAVENWING units within 6" of this model. **Swift Judgement:** When this model Advances, add 2D6" to its Move characteristic for that Movement phase instead of rolling a dice.

FACTION KEYWORDS	IMPERIUM, ADEPTUS ASTARTES, DARK ANGELS, RAVENWING
KEYWORDS	BIKER, CHARACTER, GRAND MASTER, FLY, SAMMAEL

SAMMAEL
IN SABLECLAW

NAME	M	WS	BS	S	T	W	A	Ld	Sv
Sammael in Sableclaw	16"	2+	2+	4	6	7	5	9	3+

Sammael in Sableclaw is a single model armed with the Raven Sword. His Land Speeder *Sableclaw* is equipped with a twin assault cannon and a twin heavy bolter. Only one SAMMAEL may be included in your army.

WEAPON	RANGE	TYPE	S	AP	D	ABILITIES
Twin assault cannon	24"	Heavy 12	6	-1	1	-
Twin heavy bolter	36"	Heavy 6	5	-1	1	-
Raven Sword	Melee	Melee	+1	-3	2	This weapon has Strength x2 if Sammael charged in the preceding Charge phase.

ABILITIES		
	And They Shall Know No Fear, Jink (pg 107) **Rites of Battle:** You can re-roll hit rolls of 1 for friendly DARK ANGELS units within 6" of this model. **Grand Master of the Ravenwing:** You can re-roll failed hit rolls for friendly RAVENWING units within 6" of this model.	**Sableclaw:** Enemy units can target this model in the Shooting phase even if it is not the closest model, despite it being a CHARACTER. **Iron Halo:** This model has a 4+ invulnerable save. **Explodes:** If this model is reduced to 0 Wounds, roll a D6 before removing it from the battlefield; on a 6 it explodes, and each unit within 3" suffers a mortal wound.

FACTION KEYWORDS	IMPERIUM, ADEPTUS ASTARTES, DARK ANGELS, RAVENWING
KEYWORDS	CHARACTER, VEHICLE, GRAND MASTER, LAND SPEEDER, FLY, SAMMAEL

INTERROGATOR-CHAPLAIN

6 POWER

NAME	M	WS	BS	S	T	W	A	Ld	Sv
Interrogator-Chaplain	6"	2+	3+	4	4	5	3	9	3+

An Interrogator-Chaplain is a single model armed with a crozius arcanum, a bolt pistol, frag grenades and krak grenades.

WEAPON	RANGE	TYPE	S	AP	D	ABILITIES
Bolt pistol	12"	Pistol 1	4	0	1	-
Boltgun	24"	Rapid Fire 1	4	0	1	-
Crozius arcanum	Melee	Melee	+1	-1	2	-
Power fist	Melee	Melee	x2	-3	D3	When attacking with this weapon, you must subtract 1 from the hit roll.
Frag grenade	6"	Grenade D6	3	0	1	-
Krak grenade	6"	Grenade 1	6	-1	D3	-

WARGEAR OPTIONS	• This model may replace his bolt pistol with a boltgun, or an item from either the *Pistols*, *Combi-weapons* or *Melee Weapons* list. • This model may take a power fist. • This model may take a jump pack (**Power Rating +1**). If it does, its Move characteristic is increased to 12" and it gains the **JUMP PACK** and **FLY** keywords.

ABILITIES	**Unforgiven** (pg 107) **Rosarius:** This model has a 4+ invulnerable save. **Litanies of Hate:** You can re-roll failed hit rolls in the Fight phase for friendly **DARK ANGELS** units within 6" of this model. **Aura of Dread:** Enemy units within 6" of this model subtract 1 from their Leadership characteristic.	**Spiritual Leaders:** All friendly **DARK ANGELS** units within 6" of this model can use his Leadership instead of their own. **Jump Pack Assault:** During deployment, if this model has a jump pack, you can set it up high in the skies instead of placing it on the battlefield. At the end of any of your Movement phases this model can assault from above – set it up anywhere on the battlefield that is more than 9" away from any enemy models.

FACTION KEYWORDS	**IMPERIUM, ADEPTUS ASTARTES, DARK ANGELS, DEATHWING**
KEYWORDS	**CHARACTER, INFANTRY, CHAPLAIN, INTERROGATOR-CHAPLAIN**

An Interrogator-Chaplain's every strike is directed to agonise the foe, to break their resolve and thus uncover their darkest secrets.

INTERROGATOR-CHAPLAIN
IN TERMINATOR ARMOUR

7 POWER

NAME	M	WS	BS	S	T	W	A	Ld	Sv
Interrogator-Chaplain in Terminator Armour	5"	2+	3+	4	4	6	3	9	2+

An Interrogator-Chaplain in Terminator Armour is a single model armed with a crozius arcanum and storm bolter.

WEAPON	RANGE	TYPE	S	AP	D	ABILITIES
Storm bolter	24"	Rapid Fire 2	4	0	1	-
Crozius arcanum	Melee	Melee	+1	-1	2	-
Lightning claw	Melee	Melee	User	-2	1	You can re-roll failed wound rolls for this weapon. If a model is armed with two lightning claws, each time it fights it can make 1 additional attack with them.
Power fist	Melee	Melee	x2	-3	D3	When attacking with this weapon, you must subtract 1 from the hit roll.

WARGEAR OPTIONS	• This model may replace his storm bolter with a lightning claw, a power fist, or an item from either the *Terminator Combi-weapons* or *Terminator Melee Weapons* wargear list.

ABILITIES	**Unforgiven** (pg 107)	**Spiritual Leaders:** All friendly **DARK ANGELS** units within 6" of this model can use his Leadership instead of their own.
	Rosarius: This model has a 4+ invulnerable save.	
	Litanies of Hate: You can re-roll failed hit rolls in the Fight phase for friendly **DARK ANGELS** units within 6" of this model.	**Teleport Strike:** During deployment, you can set up this unit in a teleportarium chamber instead of placing it on the battlefield. At the end of any of your Movement phases this unit can teleport into battle – set it up anywhere on the battlefield that is more than 9" from any enemy models.
	Aura of Dread: Enemy units within 6" of this model subtract 1 from their Leadership characteristic.	

FACTION KEYWORDS	**IMPERIUM, ADEPTUS ASTARTES, DARK ANGELS, DEATHWING**
KEYWORDS	**CHARACTER, INFANTRY, CHAPLAIN, TERMINATOR, INTERROGATOR-CHAPLAIN**

INTERROGATOR-CHAPLAIN
on Bike

NAME	M	WS	BS	S	T	W	A	Ld	Sv
Interrogator-Chaplain on Bike	14"	2+	3+	4	5	6	3	9	3+

An Interrogator-Chaplain on Bike is a single model armed with a crozius arcanum, a bolt pistol, frag grenades and krak grenades. His Space Marine bike is equipped with a twin boltgun.

WEAPON	RANGE	TYPE	S	AP	D	ABILITIES
Bolt pistol	12"	Pistol 1	4	0	1	-
Boltgun	24"	Rapid Fire 1	4	0	1	-
Twin boltgun	24"	Rapid fire 2	4	0	1	-
Crozius arcanum	Melee	Melee	+1	-1	2	-
Power fist	Melee	Melee	x2	-3	D3	When attacking with this weapon, you must subtract 1 from the hit roll.
Frag grenade	6"	Grenade D6	3	0	1	-
Krak grenade	6"	Grenade 1	6	-1	D3	-

WARGEAR OPTIONS	• This model may replace his bolt pistol with a boltgun, or an item from either the *Pistols*, *Combi-weapons* or *Melee Weapons* list. • This model may take a power fist.

ABILITIES	**Unforgiven** (pg 107) **Rosarius:** This model has a 4+ invulnerable save. **Litanies of Hate:** You can re-roll failed hit rolls in the Fight phase for friendly **Dark Angels** units within 6" of this model.	**Aura of Dread:** Enemy units within 6" of this model subtract 1 from their Leadership characteristic. **Spiritual Leaders:** All friendly **Dark Angels** units within 6" of this model can use his Leadership instead of their own.

FACTION KEYWORDS	IMPERIUM, ADEPTUS ASTARTES, DARK ANGELS, DEATHWING

KEYWORDS	BIKER, CHARACTER, CHAPLAIN, INTERROGATOR-CHAPLAIN

ASMODAI

NAME	M	WS	BS	S	T	W	A	Ld	Sv
Asmodai	6"	2+	3+	4	4	5	3	9	3+

Asmodai is a single model armed with the Blades of Reason, a crozius arcanum, a bolt pistol, frag grenades and krak grenades. Only one of this model may be included in your army.

WEAPON	RANGE	TYPE	S	AP	D	ABILITIES
Bolt pistol	12"	Pistol 1	4	0	1	-
Blades of Reason	Melee	Melee	User	0	D6	-
Crozius arcanum	Melee	Melee	+1	-1	2	-
Frag grenade	6"	Grenade D6	3	0	1	-
Krak grenade	6"	Grenade 1	6	-1	D3	-

ABILITIES	**Unforgiven** (pg 107) **Rosarius:** This model has a 4+ invulnerable save. **Spiritual Leaders:** All friendly **Dark Angels** units within 6" of Asmodai can use his Leadership instead of their own.	**Exemplar of Hate:** You can re-roll failed hit rolls in the Fight phase for friendly **Dark Angels** units that are within 6" of Asmodai. In addition, increase the Attacks characteristic of friendly **Dark Angels Infantry** and **Biker** units by 1 whilst they are within 6" of Asmodai. **Aura of Dread:** Enemy units within 6" of Asmodai subtract 1 from their Leadership characteristic.

FACTION KEYWORDS	IMPERIUM, ADEPTUS ASTARTES, DARK ANGELS, DEATHWING

KEYWORDS	CHARACTER, INFANTRY, CHAPLAIN, ASMODAI

EZEKIEL

NAME	M	WS	BS	S	T	W	A	Ld	Sv
Ezekiel	6"	2+	2+	4	4	5	3	9	2+

Ezekiel is a single model armed with Traitor's Bane, the Deliverer, frag grenades and krak grenades. Only one of this model may be included in your army.

WEAPON	RANGE	TYPE	S	AP	D	ABILITIES
The Deliverer	12"	Pistol 1	4	-1	2	-
Traitor's Bane	Melee	Melee	+1	-3	D3	Add 1 to this weapon's damage if the target is a **Psyker**.
Frag grenade	6"	Grenade D6	3	0	1	-
Krak grenade	6"	Grenade 1	6	-1	D3	-

ABILITIES	Unforgiven (pg 107)	**Psychic Hood:** You can add 1 to Deny the Witch tests you take for Ezekiel against enemy **Psykers** within 12".
	Book of Salvation: Any friendly **Dark Angels Infantry** or **Biker** models within 6" of Ezekiel that are slain in the Fight phase may pile in and make a single close combat attack before being removed.	**Keeper of the Keys:** Ezekiel has a 4+ invulnerable save.

PSYKER	Ezekiel can attempt to manifest two psychic powers in each friendly Psychic phase, and attempt to deny two psychic powers in each enemy Psychic phase. He knows the *Smite* power and three psychic powers from the Interromancy discipline (pg 107).

FACTION KEYWORDS	**Imperium, Adeptus Astartes, Dark Angels, Deathwing**
KEYWORDS	**Character, Infantry, Librarian, Psyker, Ezekiel**

DEATHWING APOTHECARY

NAME	M	WS	BS	S	T	W	A	Ld	Sv
Deathwing Apothecary	5"	3+	3+	4	4	5	2	8	2+

A Deathwing Apothecary is a single model armed with a storm bolter.

WEAPON	RANGE	TYPE	S	AP	D	ABILITIES
Storm bolter	24"	Rapid Fire 2	4	0	1	-

ABILITIES	Unforgiven (pg 107)	**Narthecium:** At the end of any of your Movement phases, the Deathwing Apothecary can attempt to heal or revive a single model. Select a friendly **Dark Angels Infantry** or **Biker** unit within 3" of the Apothecary. If that unit contains a wounded model, it immediately regains D3 lost wounds. If the chosen unit contains no wounded models but one or more of its models have been slain during the battle, roll a D6. On a 4+ a single slain model is returned to the unit with 1 wound remaining. If a Deathwing Apothecary fails to revive a model in this manner he can do nothing else for the remainder of the turn (shoot, charge, fight etc.) as he recovers the gene-seed of the fallen warrior. A unit can only be the target of the Narthecium ability once in each turn.
	Crux Terminatus: This model has a 5+ invulnerable save.	
	Teleport Strike: During deployment, you can set up this model in a teleportarium chamber instead of placing it on the battlefield. At the end of any of your Movement phases this model can teleport into battle – set it up anywhere on the battlefield that is more than 9" from any enemy models.	

FACTION KEYWORDS	**Imperium, Adeptus Astartes, Dark Angels, Deathwing**
KEYWORDS	**Character, Infantry, Apothecary, Terminator**

DEATHWING ANCIENT

POWER 7

NAME	M	WS	BS	S	T	W	A	Ld	Sv
Deathwing Ancient	5"	3+	3+	4	4	5	3	8	2+

The Deathwing Ancient is a single model armed with a power fist and storm bolter. Only one of this model may be included in your army.

WEAPON	RANGE	TYPE	S	AP	D	ABILITIES
Storm bolter	24"	Rapid Fire 2	4	0	1	-
Chainfist	Melee	Melee	x2	-4	2	When attacking with this weapon, you must subtract 1 from the hit roll.
Lightning claw	Melee	Melee	User	-2	1	You can re-roll failed wound rolls for this weapon. If a model is armed with two lightning claws, each time it fights it can make 1 additional attack with them.
Power fist	Melee	Melee	x2	-3	D3	When attacking with this weapon, you must subtract 1 from the hit roll.
Thunder hammer	Melee	Melee	x2	-3	3	When attacking with this weapon, you must subtract 1 from the hit roll.

WARGEAR OPTIONS	• This model may replace his power fist and storm bolter with two lightning claws or a thunder hammer and storm shield. • This model may replace his power fist with a chainfist.

ABILITIES	**Unforgiven** (pg 107) **Deathwing Company Banner:** Friendly **DEATHWING** units have +1 Attack while they are within 6" of any Deathwing company banners. **Crux Terminatus:** This model has a 5+ invulnerable save.	**Storm Shield:** A model equipped with a storm shield has a 3+ invulnerable save. **Teleport Strike:** During deployment, you can set up this model in a teleportarium chamber instead of placing it on the battlefield. At the end of any of your Movement phases this model can teleport into battle – set it up anywhere on the battlefield that is more than 9" from any enemy models.

FACTION KEYWORDS	IMPERIUM, ADEPTUS ASTARTES, DARK ANGELS, DEATHWING
KEYWORDS	CHARACTER, INFANTRY, ANCIENT, TERMINATOR

DEATHWING CHAMPION

POWER 6

NAME	M	WS	BS	S	T	W	A	Ld	Sv
Deathwing Champion	5"	2+	3+	4	4	5	3	8	2+

The Deathwing Champion is a single model armed with a halberd of Caliban. Only one of this model may be included in your army.

WEAPON	RANGE	TYPE	S	AP	D	ABILITIES
Halberd of Caliban	Melee	Melee	+3	-4	D3	Each time the bearer fights, it can make D3 additional attacks with this weapon if the target unit contains 5 or more models.

ABILITIES	**Unforgiven** (pg 107) **Honour or Death:** You can re-roll failed hit rolls for this model in the Fight phase if it targets a **CHARACTER**. In addition, this model must always perform a Heroic Intervention when possible.	**Terminator Armour:** This model has a 5+ invulnerable save. **Teleport Strike:** During deployment, you can set up this model in a teleportarium chamber instead of placing it on the battlefield. At the end of any of your Movement phases this model can teleport into battle – set it up anywhere on the battlefield that is more than 9" from any enemy models.

FACTION KEYWORDS	IMPERIUM, ADEPTUS ASTARTES, DARK ANGELS, DEATHWING
KEYWORDS	CHARACTER, INFANTRY, TERMINATOR, DEATHWING CHAMPION

DEATHWING TERMINATOR SQUAD

12 POWER

NAME	M	WS	BS	S	T	W	A	Ld	Sv
Deathwing Terminator	5"	3+	3+	4	4	2	2	8	2+
Deathwing Sergeant	5"	3+	3+	4	4	2	3	9	2+

This unit contains 1 Deathwing Sergeant and 4 Deathwing Terminators. It can include up to 5 additional Deathwing Terminators (**Power Rating +12**).
• Each Deathwing Terminator is armed with a power fist and a storm bolter.
• The Deathwing Sergeant is armed with a power sword and storm bolter.

WEAPON	RANGE	TYPE	S	AP	D	ABILITIES
Plasma cannon	When attacking with this weapon, choose one of the profiles below.					
- Standard	36"	Heavy D3	7	-3	1	-
- Supercharge	36"	Heavy D3	8	-3	2	On a hit roll of 1, the bearer is slain after all of this weapon's shots have been resolved.
Storm bolter	24"	Rapid Fire 2	4	0	1	-
Chainfist	Melee	Melee	x2	-4	2	When attacking with this weapon, you must subtract 1 from the hit roll.
Lightning claw	Melee	Melee	User	-2	1	You can re-roll failed wound rolls for this weapon. If a model is armed with two lightning claws, each time it fights it can make 1 additional attack with them.
Power fist	Melee	Melee	x2	-3	D3	When attacking with this weapon, you must subtract 1 from the hit roll.
Power sword	Melee	Melee	User	-3	1	-
Thunder hammer	Melee	Melee	x2	-3	3	When attacking with this weapon, you must subtract 1 from the hit roll.

WARGEAR OPTIONS	
	• Any model may replace all of its weapons with two lightning claws or a thunder hammer and storm shield.
	• Any model may replace its power fist with a chainfist.
	• For every five models in the squad, one Deathwing Terminator may take a plasma cannon or an item from the *Terminator Heavy Weapons* list.
	• This unit may be accompanied by a Watcher in the Dark.

ABILITIES	
	Unforgiven (pg 107) **Terminator Armour:** Models in this unit have a 5+ invulnerable save. **Watcher in the Dark:** Once per game, if an enemy psychic power affects a unit of Deathwing Terminators that is accompanied by a Watcher in the Dark, roll a dice. On a 3+ the power has no effect on this unit (all other targets are affected normally). Remove the Watcher in the Dark model from play after this roll has been made, whether successful or not. The Watcher in the Dark model must always remain as close to this unit as possible, but is otherwise ignored for all other gaming purposes. Remove the Watcher in the Dark if this unit is slain. **Storm Shield:** A model equipped with a storm shield has a 3+ invulnerable save. **Teleport Strike:** During deployment, you can set up this unit in a teleportarium chamber instead of placing it on the battlefield. At the end of any of your Movement phases this unit can teleport into battle – set it up anywhere on the battlefield that is more than 9" from any enemy models.

FACTION KEYWORDS	IMPERIUM, ADEPTUS ASTARTES, DARK ANGELS, DEATHWING
KEYWORDS	INFANTRY, TERMINATOR, DEATHWING TERMINATOR SQUAD

DEATHWING KNIGHTS

NAME	M	WS	BS	S	T	W	A	Ld	Sv
Deathwing Knights	5"	3+	3+	4	4	2	2	8	2+
Knight Master	5"	3+	3+	4	4	2	3	9	2+

This unit contains 4 Deathwing Knights and 1 Knight Master. It can include up to 5 additional Deathwing Knights (**Power Rating +12**).
• Each Deathwing Knight is armed with a mace of absolution and a storm shield.
• The Knight Master is armed with a flail of the Unforgiven and a storm shield.

WEAPON	RANGE	TYPE	S	AP	D	ABILITIES
Flail of the Unforgiven	Melee	Melee	+2	-3	2	Excess damage from this weapon is not lost; instead, keep allocating damage to another model in the target unit until either all the damage has been allocated or the target unit is destroyed.
Mace of absolution	Melee	Melee	x2	-2	3	-

WARGEAR OPTIONS	• This unit may be accompanied by a Watcher in the Dark.

ABILITIES	**Unforgiven** (pg 107)	**Watcher in the Dark:** Once per game, if an enemy psychic power affects a unit of Deathwing Knights that is accompanied by a Watcher in the Dark, roll a dice. On a 3+ the power has no effect on this unit (all other targets are affected normally). Remove the Watcher in the Dark model from play after this roll has been made, whether successful or not. The Watcher in the Dark model must always remain as close to this unit as possible, but is otherwise ignored for all other gaming purposes. Remove the Watcher in the Dark if this unit is slain.
	Storm Shield: Models in this unit have a 3+ invulnerable save.	
	Teleport Strike: During deployment, you can set up this unit in a teleportarium chamber instead of placing it on the battlefield. At the end of any of your Movement phases this unit can teleport into battle – set it up anywhere on the battlefield that is more than 9" from any enemy models.	

FACTION KEYWORDS	**IMPERIUM, ADEPTUS ASTARTES, DARK ANGELS, DEATHWING**
KEYWORDS	**INFANTRY, TERMINATOR, DEATHWING KNIGHTS**

Driven on by the rage of an ancient betrayal, Deathwing Knights fight with a cold, vengeful fury.

RAVENWING APOTHECARY

NAME	M	WS	BS	S	T	W	A	Ld	Sv
Ravenwing Apothecary	14"	3+	3+	4	5	5	3	8	3+

A Ravenwing Apothecary is a single model armed with a Corvus hammer, a bolt pistol, frag grenades and krak grenades. His Space Marine bike is equipped with a plasma talon.

WEAPON	RANGE	TYPE	S	AP	D	ABILITIES
Bolt pistol	12"	Pistol 1	4	0	1	-
Plasma talon	When attacking with this weapon, choose one of the profiles below.					
- Standard	18"	Assault 2	7	-3	1	-
- Supercharge	18"	Assault 2	8	-3	2	On a hit roll of 1, the bearer is slain after all of this weapon's shots have been resolved.
Ravenwing grenade launcher	When attacking with this weapon, choose one of the profiles below.					
- Frag shell	24"	Assault D6	3	0	1	-
- Krak shell	24"	Assault 2	6	-1	D3	-
Corvus hammer	Melee	Melee	+1	-1	1	Each wound roll of 6+ made for this weapon causes D3 damage instead of 1.
Frag grenade	6"	Grenade D6	3	0	1	-
Krak grenade	6"	Grenade 1	6	-1	D3	-

WARGEAR OPTIONS	• This model may replace his plasma talon with a Ravenwing grenade launcher.
ABILITIES	**And They Shall Know No Fear, Jink** (pg 107) **Turbo-boost:** When this model Advances, add 6" to its Move characteristic for that Movement phase instead of rolling a dice. **Narthecium:** At the end of any of your Movement phases, the Ravenwing Apothecary can attempt to heal or revive a single model. Select a friendly **Dark Angels Infantry** or **Biker** unit within 3" of the Apothecary. If that unit contains a wounded model, it immediately regains D3 lost wounds. If the chosen unit contains no wounded models but one or more of its models have been slain during the battle, roll a D6. On a 4+ a single slain model is returned to the unit with 1 wound remaining. If a Ravenwing Apothecary fails to revive a model in this manner he can do nothing else for the remainder of the turn (shoot, charge, fight etc.) as he recovers the gene-seed of the fallen warrior. A unit can only be the target of the Narthecium ability once in each turn.
FACTION KEYWORDS	**Imperium, Adeptus Astartes, Dark Angels, Ravenwing**
KEYWORDS	**Biker, Character, Apothecary**

RAVENWING ANCIENT

6 POWER

NAME	M	WS	BS	S	T	W	A	Ld	Sv
Ravenwing Ancient	14"	3+	3+	4	5	5	3	8	3+

The Ravenwing Ancient is a single model armed with a Corvus hammer, a bolt pistol, frag grenades and krak grenades. His Space Marine bike is equipped with a plasma talon. Only one of this model may be included in your army.

WEAPON	RANGE	TYPE	S	AP	D	ABILITIES
Bolt pistol	12"	Pistol 1	4	0	1	-
Plasma talon	When attacking with this weapon, choose one of the profiles below.					
- Standard	18"	Assault 2	7	-3	1	-
- Supercharge	18"	Assault 2	8	-3	2	On a hit roll of 1, the bearer is slain after all of this weapon's shots have been resolved.
Ravenwing grenade launcher	When attacking with this weapon, choose one of the profiles below.					
- Frag shell	24"	Assault D6	3	0	1	-
- Krak shell	24"	Assault 2	6	-1	D3	-
Corvus hammer	Melee	Melee	+1	-1	1	Each wound roll of 6+ made for this weapon causes D3 damage instead of 1.
Frag grenade	6"	Grenade D6	3	0	1	-
Krak grenade	6"	Grenade 1	6	-1	D3	-

WARGEAR OPTIONS
- This model may replace his plasma talon with a Ravenwing grenade launcher.

ABILITIES

And They Shall Know No Fear, Jink (pg 107)

Sacred Standard: Friendly **RAVENWING** units have +1 Attack while they are within 6" of any sacred standards.

Turbo-boost: When this model Advances, add 6" to its Move characteristic for that Movement phase instead of rolling a dice.

FACTION KEYWORDS   IMPERIUM, ADEPTUS ASTARTES, DARK ANGELS, RAVENWING

KEYWORDS   BIKER, CHARACTER, ANCIENT

RAVENWING CHAMPION

6 POWER

NAME	M	WS	BS	S	T	W	A	Ld	Sv
Ravenwing Champion	14"	2+	3+	4	5	5	3	8	3+

The Ravenwing Champion is a single model armed with a blade of Caliban, a bolt pistol, frag grenades and krak grenades. His Space Marine bike is equipped with a plasma talon. Only one of this model may be included in your army.

WEAPON	RANGE	TYPE	S	AP	D	ABILITIES
Bolt pistol	12"	Pistol 1	4	0	1	-
Plasma talon	When attacking with this weapon, choose one of the profiles below.					
- Standard	18"	Assault 2	7	-3	1	-
- Supercharge	18"	Assault 2	8	-3	2	On a hit roll of 1, the bearer is slain after all of this weapon's shots have been resolved.
Blade of Caliban	Melee	Melee	+3	-3	D3	-
Frag grenade	6"	Grenade D6	3	0	1	-
Krak grenade	6"	Grenade 1	6	-1	D3	-

ABILITIES

And They Shall Know No Fear, Jink (pg 107)

Turbo-boost: When this model Advances, add 6" to its Move characteristic for that Movement phase instead of rolling a dice.

Honour or Death: You can re-roll failed hit rolls for this model in the Fight phase if it targets a **CHARACTER**.
In addition, this model must always perform a Heroic Intervention when possible.

FACTION KEYWORDS   IMPERIUM, ADEPTUS ASTARTES, DARK ANGELS, RAVENWING

KEYWORDS   BIKER, CHARACTER, RAVENWING CHAMPION

RAVENWING BIKE SQUAD

NAME	M	WS	BS	S	T	W	A	Ld	Sv
Ravenwing Biker	14"	3+	3+	4	5	2	1	7	3+
Ravenwing Sergeant	14"	3+	3+	4	5	2	2	8	3+
Ravenwing Attack Bike	14"	3+	3+	4	5	4	1	7	3+

This unit contains 1 Ravenwing Sergeant and 2 Ravenwing Bikers. It can include up to 3 additional Ravenwing Bikers (**Power Rating +5**) or up to 5 additional Ravenwing Bikers (**Power Rating +9**). It can also include a single Ravenwing Attack Bike (**Power Rating +3**).
- Ravenwing Bikers and Sergeants are each armed with a bolt pistol, frag grenades and krak grenades. Each of their Space Marine bikes is equipped with a twin boltgun.
- A Ravenwing Attack Bike is equipped with a twin boltgun and a heavy bolter, and is crewed by two Dark Angels armed with a bolt pistol, frag grenades and krak grenades.

WEAPON	RANGE	TYPE	S	AP	D	ABILITIES
Bolt pistol	12"	Pistol 1	4	0	1	-
Heavy bolter	36"	Heavy 3	5	-1	1	-
Multi-melta	24"	Heavy 1	8	-4	D6	If the target is within half range of this weapon, roll two dice when inflicting damage with it and discard the lowest result.
Twin boltgun	24"	Rapid fire 2	4	0	1	-
Chainsword	Melee	Melee	User	0	1	Each time the bearer fights, it can make 1 additional attack with this weapon.
Frag grenade	6"	Grenade D6	3	0	1	-
Krak grenade	6"	Grenade 1	6	-1	D3	-

WARGEAR OPTIONS	• Any Ravenwing Biker may replace his bolt pistol with a chainsword. • The Ravenwing Sergeant may replace his bolt pistol with an item from the *Sergeant Equipment* list. • Up to two Ravenwing Bikers may take an item from the *Special Weapons* list. • The Ravenwing Attack Bike may replace its heavy bolter with a multi-melta.

ABILITIES	**And They Shall Know No Fear, Jink** (pg 107) **Turbo-boost:** When this unit Advances, add 6" to its Move characteristic for that Movement phase instead of rolling a dice.	**Combat Squads:** Before any models are deployed at the start of the game a Ravenwing Bike Squad containing 9 models may be split into two units, one of which has 4 models including the Ravenwing Attack Bike.

FACTION KEYWORDS	IMPERIUM, ADEPTUS ASTARTES, DARK ANGELS, RAVENWING

KEYWORDS	BIKER, RAVENWING BIKE SQUAD

Mounted upon their lightning-fast bikes, the Ravenwing roar into battle on the trail of the Fallen.

RAVENWING ATTACK BIKE SQUAD

3 POWER

NAME	M	WS	BS	S	T	W	A	Ld	Sv
Ravenwing Attack Bike	14"	3+	3+	4	5	4	1	7	3+

This unit contains 1 Ravenwing Attack Bike. It can include 1 additional Ravenwing Attack Bike (**Power Rating +3**) or 2 additional Ravenwing Attack Bikes (**Power Rating +6**). Each model is equipped with a twin boltgun and a heavy bolter, and is crewed by two Dark Angels armed with a bolt pistol, frag grenades and krak grenades.

WEAPON	RANGE	TYPE	S	AP	D	ABILITIES
Bolt pistol	12"	Pistol 1	4	0	1	-
Heavy bolter	36"	Heavy 3	5	-1	1	-
Multi-melta	24"	Heavy 1	8	-4	D6	If the target is within half range of this weapon, roll two dice when inflicting damage with it and discard the lowest result.
Twin boltgun	24"	Rapid fire 2	4	0	1	-
Frag grenade	6"	Grenade D6	3	0	1	-
Krak grenade	6"	Grenade 1	6	-1	D3	-

WARGEAR OPTIONS	• Any model may replace its heavy bolter with a multi-melta.	
ABILITIES	And They Shall Know No Fear, Jink (pg 107)	**Turbo-boost:** When this unit Advances, add 6" to its Move characteristic for that Movement phase instead of rolling a dice.
FACTION KEYWORDS	IMPERIUM, ADEPTUS ASTARTES, DARK ANGELS, RAVENWING	
KEYWORDS	BIKER, RAVENWING ATTACK BIKE SQUAD	

RAVENWING LAND SPEEDERS

6 POWER

NAME	M	WS	BS	S	T	W	A	Ld	Sv
Ravenwing Land Speeder	16"	3+	3+	4	5	6	2	7	3+

This unit contains 1 Ravenwing Land Speeder. It can include up to 4 additional Ravenwing Land Speeders (**Power Rating +6 per model**). Each model is equipped with a heavy bolter.

WEAPON	RANGE	TYPE	S	AP	D	ABILITIES
Assault cannon	24"	Heavy 6	6	-1	1	-
Heavy bolter	36"	Heavy 3	5	-1	1	-
Heavy flamer	8"	Heavy D6	5	-1	1	This weapon automatically hits its target.
Multi-melta	24"	Heavy 1	8	-4	D6	If the target is within half range of this weapon, roll two dice when inflicting damage with it and discard the lowest result.
Typhoon missile launcher	When attacking with this weapon, choose one of the profiles below.					
- Frag missiles	48"	Heavy 2D6	4	0	1	-
- Krak missiles	48"	Heavy 2	8	-2	D6	-

WARGEAR OPTIONS	• Any model may replace its heavy bolter with a multi-melta or a heavy flamer. • Any model may take an assault cannon, a heavy flamer, a typhoon missile launcher, a heavy bolter or a multi-melta.	
ABILITIES	And They Shall Know No Fear, Jink (pg 107) **Anti-grav Upwash:** Models in this unit have a Move characteristic of 20", instead of 16", whilst their unit contains 3 or more models.	**Explodes:** If a model in this unit is reduced to 0 wounds, roll a D6 before removing it from the battlefield. On a 6 it explodes, and each unit within 3" suffers a mortal wound.
FACTION KEYWORDS	IMPERIUM, ADEPTUS ASTARTES, DARK ANGELS, RAVENWING	
KEYWORDS	VEHICLE, LAND SPEEDER, FLY, RAVENWING LAND SPEEDER	

RAVENWING DARKSHROUD

7 POWER

NAME	M	WS	BS	S	T	W	A	Ld	Sv
Ravenwing Darkshroud	12"	3+	3+	4	6	9	3	8	3+

A Ravenwing Darkshroud is a single model equipped with a heavy bolter.

WEAPON	RANGE	TYPE	S	AP	D	ABILITIES
Assault cannon	24"	Heavy 6	6	-1	1	-
Heavy bolter	36"	Heavy 3	5	-1	1	-

WARGEAR OPTIONS	• This model may replace its heavy bolter with an assault cannon.

ABILITIES	Jink (pg 107)	Explodes: If a model in this unit is reduced to 0 wounds, roll a D6 before removing it from the battlefield. On a 6 it explodes, and each unit within D6" suffers D3 mortal wounds.
	Icon of Old Caliban: Your opponent must subtract 1 from any hit rolls they make for shooting attacks that target friendly **DARK ANGELS** units within 6" of this model.	

FACTION KEYWORDS	IMPERIUM, ADEPTUS ASTARTES, DARK ANGELS, RAVENWING
KEYWORDS	VEHICLE, LAND SPEEDER, FLY, RAVENWING DARKSHROUD

NEPHILIM JETFIGHTER

9 POWER

NAME	M	WS	BS	S	T	W	A	Ld	Sv
Nephilim Jetfighter	*	6+	*	6	6	10	3	8	3+

DAMAGE
Some of this model's characteristics change as it suffers damage, as shown below:

REMAINING W	M	BS
6-10+	20-50"	3+
3-5	20-35"	4+
1-2	20"	5+

A Nephilim Jetfighter is a single model equipped with an avenger mega bolter, a twin heavy bolter, and two blacksword missile launchers.

WEAPON	RANGE	TYPE	S	AP	D	ABILITIES
Avenger mega bolter	36"	Heavy 10	6	-1	1	-
Blacksword missile launcher	36"	Heavy 1	7	-3	2	-
Twin heavy bolter	36"	Heavy 6	5	-1	1	-
Twin lascannon	48"	Heavy 2	9	-3	D6	-

WARGEAR OPTIONS	• This model may replace its avenger mega bolter with a twin lascannon.

ABILITIES	Jink (pg 107)	Strafing Run: You can add 1 to hit rolls for this model when targeting an enemy in the Shooting phase that cannot **FLY**.
	Supersonic: Each time this model moves, first pivot it on the spot up to 90° (this does not contribute to how far the model moves), and then move the model straight forwards. Note that it cannot pivot again after the initial pivot. When this model Advances, increase its Move characteristic by 20" until the end of the phase – do not roll a dice.	Crash and Burn: If this model is reduced to 0 wounds, roll a D6 before removing the model from the battlefield; on a 6 it crashes and explodes, and each unit within 6" suffers D3 mortal wounds.
		Airborne: This model cannot charge, can only be charged by units that can **FLY**, and can only attack or be attacked in the Fight phase by units that can **FLY**.
	Hard to Hit: Your opponent must subtract 1 from hit rolls for attacks that target this model in the Shooting phase.	

FACTION KEYWORDS	IMPERIUM, ADEPTUS ASTARTES, DARK ANGELS, RAVENWING
KEYWORDS	VEHICLE, FLY, NEPHILIM JETFIGHTER

RAVENWING DARK TALON

9 POWER

NAME	M	WS	BS	S	T	W	A	Ld	Sv
Ravenwing Dark Talon	*	6+	*	6	6	10	3	8	3+

DAMAGE
Some of this model's characteristics change as it suffers damage, as shown below:

REMAINING W	M	BS	RIFT VORTEX
6-10+	20-40"	3+	3+
3-5	20-30"	4+	4+
1-2	20"	5+	5+

A Ravenwing Dark Talon is a single model equipped with two hurricane bolters and a rift cannon.

WEAPON	RANGE	TYPE	S	AP	D	ABILITIES
Hurricane bolter	24"	Rapid Fire 6	4	0	1	-
Rift cannon	18"	Heavy D3	10	-3	3	If a unit suffers any damage from this weapon, roll a dice and consult the damage table above. If the result equals or beats the relevant number in the Rift Vortex column, the target unit suffers a further D3 mortal wounds.

ABILITIES	
	Jink (pg 107)

Stasis Bomb: Once per game, this model can drop a stasis bomb as it flies over an enemy unit in its Movement phase. After the Ravenwing Dark Talon has moved, pick one enemy unit that it flew over. Then, roll a D6 for each model in the enemy unit (up to a maximum of 10 dice). For each roll of a 4+, the target unit suffers a mortal wound.

Hover Jet: Before this model moves in your Movement phase, you can declare it will hover. Its Move characteristic becomes 20" until the end of the phase, and it loses the Airborne, Hard to Hit and Supersonic abilities until the beginning of your next Movement phase.

Hard to Hit: Your opponent must subtract 1 from hit rolls for attacks that target this model in the Shooting phase.

Supersonic: Each time this model moves, first pivot it on the spot up to 90° (this does not contribute to how far the model moves), and then move the model straight forwards. Note that it cannot pivot again after the initial pivot. When this model Advances, increase its Move characteristic by 20" until the end of the phase – do not roll a dice.

Crash and Burn: If this model is reduced to 0 wounds, roll a D6 before removing the model from the battlefield; on a 6 it crashes and explodes, and each unit within 6" suffers D3 mortal wounds.

Airborne: This model cannot charge, can only be charged by units that can **FLY**, and can only attack or be attacked in the Fight phase by units that can **FLY**.

Strafing Run: You can add 1 to hit rolls for this model when targeting an enemy in the Shooting phase that cannot **FLY**.

FACTION KEYWORDS	IMPERIUM, ADEPTUS ASTARTES, DARK ANGELS, RAVENWING
KEYWORDS	VEHICLE, FLY, RAVENWING DARK TALON

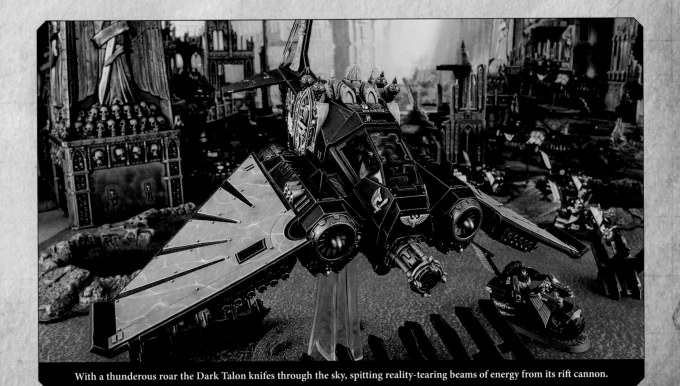

With a thunderous roar the Dark Talon knifes through the sky, spitting reality-tearing beams of energy from its rift cannon.

RAVENWING BLACK KNIGHTS

NAME	M	WS	BS	S	T	W	A	Ld	Sv
Ravenwing Black Knight	14"	3+	3+	4	5	2	2	8	3+
Ravenwing Huntmaster	14"	3+	3+	4	5	2	3	8	3+

This unit contains 1 Ravenwing Huntmaster and 2 Ravenwing Black Knights. It can include up to 2 additional Ravenwing Black Knights (**Power Rating +5**) or up to 7 additional Ravenwing Black Knights (**Power Rating +17**). Each model is armed with a Corvus hammer, a bolt pistol, frag grenades and krak grenades. Each of their Space Marine bikes is equipped with a plasma talon.

WEAPON	RANGE	TYPE	S	AP	D	ABILITIES
Bolt pistol	12"	Pistol 1	4	0	1	-
Plasma talon	When attacking with this weapon, choose one of the profiles below.					
- Standard	18"	Assault 2	7	-3	1	-
- Supercharge	18"	Assault 2	8	-3	2	On a hit roll of 1, the bearer is slain after all of this weapon's shots have been resolved.
Ravenwing grenade launcher	When attacking with this weapon, choose one of the profiles below.					
- Frag shell	24"	Assault D6	3	0	1	-
- Krak shell	24"	Assault 2	6	-1	D3	-
Corvus hammer	Melee	Melee	+1	-1	1	Each wound roll of 6+ made for this weapon causes D3 damage instead of 1.
Power axe	Melee	Melee	+1	-2	1	-
Power lance	Melee	Melee	+2	-1	1	-
Power maul	Melee	Melee	+2	-1	1	-
Power sword	Melee	Melee	User	-3	1	-
Frag grenade	6"	Grenade D6	3	0	1	-
Krak grenade	6"	Grenade 1	6	-1	D3	-
Melta bomb	4"	Grenade 1	8	-4	D6	-

WARGEAR OPTIONS	• For every 3 models in the unit, one Ravenwing Black Knight may replace his plasma talon with a Ravenwing grenade launcher. • The Ravenwing Huntmaster may replace his Corvus hammer with a power sword, power axe, power maul or power lance. • The Ravenwing Huntmaster may take melta bombs.
ABILITIES	And They Shall Know No Fear, Jink (pg 107) **Turbo-boost:** When this unit Advances, add 6" to its Move characteristic for that Movement phase instead of rolling a dice.
FACTION KEYWORDS	IMPERIUM, ADEPTUS ASTARTES, DARK ANGELS, RAVENWING
KEYWORDS	BIKER, RAVENWING BLACK KNIGHTS

RAVENWING LAND SPEEDER VENGEANCE

NAME	M	WS	BS	S	T	W	A	Ld	Sv
Ravenwing Land Speeder Vengeance	12"	3+	3+	4	6	9	3	8	3+

A Ravenwing Land Speeder Vengeance is a single model equipped with a heavy bolter and a plasma storm battery.

WEAPON	RANGE	TYPE	S	AP	D	ABILITIES
Assault cannon	24"	Heavy 6	6	-1	1	-
Heavy bolter	36"	Heavy 3	5	-1	1	-
Plasma storm battery	When attacking with this weapon, choose one of the profiles below.					
- Standard	36"	Heavy D6	7	-3	2	-
- Supercharge	36"	Heavy D6	8	-3	3	If you make one or more hit rolls of 1, the bearer suffers 3 mortal wounds after all of this weapon's shots have been resolved, and the plasma storm battery cannot be used for the rest of the battle.

WARGEAR OPTIONS	• This model may replace its heavy bolter with an assault cannon.
ABILITIES	And They Shall Know No Fear, Jink (pg 107) Explodes: If this model is reduced to 0 wounds, roll a D6 before removing it from the battlefield. On a 6 it explodes, and each unit within D6" suffers D3 mortal wounds.
FACTION KEYWORDS	IMPERIUM, ADEPTUS ASTARTES, DARK ANGELS, RAVENWING
KEYWORDS	VEHICLE, LAND SPEEDER, FLY, RAVENWING LAND SPEEDER VENGEANCE

The plasma storm battery mounted upon a Land Speeder Vengeance unleashes an incinerating storm of super-heated matter.

FORTRESS OF REDEMPTION

20 POWER

NAME	M	WS	BS	S	T	W	A	Ld	Sv
Fortress of Redemption	0	-	✳	0	10	30	0	9	3+

DAMAGE
Some of this model's characteristics change as it suffers damage, as shown below:

REMAINING W	BS
21-30+	5+
11-20	6+
1-10	7+

A Fortress of Redemption is a single model equipped with a twin Icarus lascannon and a redemption missile silo.

WEAPON	RANGE	TYPE	S	AP	D	ABILITIES
Heavy bolter	36"	Heavy 3	5	-1	1	-
Redemption missile silo	When attacking with this weapon, choose one of the profiles below.					
- Fragstorm missile	18-96"	Heavy 2D6	4	0	1	-
- Krakstorm missile	18-96"	Heavy D6	8	-3	D3	-
Twin Icarus lascannon	96"	Heavy 2D6	9	-3	D6	Add 1 to all hit rolls made for this weapon against targets that can **FLY**. Subtract 1 from the hit rolls made for this weapon against all other targets.

WARGEAR OPTIONS	• This model may take up to four heavy bolters.

ABILITIES	**Immobile:** This model cannot move for any reason, nor can it fight in the Fight phase. Enemy models automatically hit this model in the Fight phase – do not make hit rolls. However, this model can still shoot if there are enemy models within 1" of it, and friendly units can still target enemy units that are within 1" of this model. **Automated Weapons:** Unless a friendly unit is embarked inside this model, each of its weapons can only target the nearest visible enemy. If two units are equally close, you may choose which is targeted. **Fire Points:** 15 models embarked in this model can shoot in their Shooting phase, measuring and drawing line of sight from any point on this model. They can do this even if enemy models are within 1" of this model.	**Magazine Explosion:** If this model is reduced to 0 wounds, roll a D6 before removing it from the battlefield and before any embarked models disembark. On a 6 its magazine explodes, and each unit within 2D6" suffers D6 mortal wounds. **Designer's Note:** *If you cannot physically remove this model from your battlefield when it is destroyed (because, for example, it is glued to the surface) then regardless of whether its magazine explodes or not, it is wrecked – from that point on, models can no longer embark inside it, it can no longer shoot etc.*

TRANSPORT	This model can transport any number of **INFANTRY CHARACTERS** and one other **INFANTRY** unit, up to a maximum of 30 models. **Designer's Note:** *When you embark models onto a Fortress of Redemption, you may find it useful to place some of them on the battlements to remind you which unit(s) are inside the fortification.*

FACTION KEYWORDS	**UNALIGNED**
KEYWORDS	**BUILDING, VEHICLE, TRANSPORT, FORTRESS OF REDEMPTION**

Grim of aspect, bearing aloft the heraldry of their secretive past, the Dark Angels charge the traitors of the Black Legion.

SPACE WOLVES

With blood-chilling howls the warriors of the Space Wolves hurl themselves into battle, hacking and tearing with a primal, predatory ferocity. Mighty warriors whose deeds and sagas stretch back to the dawn of the Imperium, the Sons of Russ are amongst Humanity's most redoubtable defenders.

Savage warriors hailing from the icy death world of Fenris, the Space Wolves are a stubbornly individualistic Chapter who have little patience for the petty bureaucracies of the Imperium. They fight to honour the memory of their lost Primarch, Leman Russ, and to deliver the wrath of the Emperor of Mankind – known to them as the Allfather. The legends told of the Space Wolves are beyond count, for they have battled across the galaxy since the earliest days of the Imperium, falling upon those who would threaten Humanity with unbridled aggression.

Space Wolves certainly appear little more than barbarous savages at first glance, with their untamed manes bound up with runestones, and their storm-grey armour bedecked with totems and kill-trophies. Any such belief quickly evaporates in the face of a Space Wolf assault, however, for the Sons of Russ fight with a vicious, predatory cunning. Individualistic by nature, the Wolves eschew much of the Codex Astartes, preferring to organise their armies according to their own ancient ways.

The youngest and most inexperienced of the Wolves are known as Blood Claws, and learn to master their berserker rage in the gore-strewn arena of melee combat. Older, more seasoned warriors

join the ranks of the Grey Hunters, wily and adaptable killers who have fought upon countless battlefields. Only the wisest and most capable live long enough to earn their place amongst the Long Fangs, those venerable grey-hairs who punish the enemy from afar with pinpoint barrages from their heavy weapons, or the Wolf Guard, loyal veterans that serve under each Great Company's Wolf Lord. Unlike most other Space Marines Chapters, the Space Wolves source their scouts from within the ranks of their veteran fighters, rather than assigning the role to neophytes. These Wolf Scouts drift like wraiths behind the enemy line, wreaking bloody havoc upon their supply chain with acts of sabotage and well-timed assassinations.

The Space Wolves favour aggressive, rapid assaults. They utilise a number of unique and devastatingly powerful war assets to tear the throat from the enemy before they can bring their guns to bear. Thunderwolf Cavalry bound across the battlefield, the slavering jaws of these monstrous wolf-steeds as deadly a weapon as the swords and guns of the Space Marines who sit astride them. Stormwolf assault craft swoop down upon the foe, helfrost cannons firing even as Blood Claws leap from their landing ramps with joyful roars bursting from their lungs. Rune Priests summon the

howling gales and lightning storms of Fenris to send vortexes of primal destruction tearing through the enemy's ranks. Wolf Lords whose acts are told and retold by the Chapter's skalds in epic verse forge new sagas upon the corpses of their enemies, carving a red path through all who dare challenge them.

CURSE OF THE WULFEN

All Space Wolves are marked by a flaw in their gene-seed, a strain of mutation known as the Canis Helix. This abnormality is what grants the warriors of this Chapter their feral, lupine appearance, and invests them with the predatory rage that makes them so fearsome in battle. In some unfortunate Space Wolves, it bestows a far darker change. The body mutates and twists agonisingly, bones reforming, canines elongating and thick fur piercing its way through flesh. Wracked by unimaginable pain, the unfortunate victim is overwhelmed by the curse of his tainted blood, and becomes one of the feral monsters known as the Wulfen. Most of these blood-maddened creatures roam the wilds of Fenris, ever searching for fresh prey to rip apart with their razor-sharp jaws, but a number have been captured by the Space Wolves and confined to the lower levels of the Chapter's fortress monastery, the Fang. There they are armed and armoured, and kept under watchful guard until such a time that they can be unleashed on the Space Wolves' foes. Only the venerable and wise Wolf Priests can maintain a modicum of control over these monsters in battle, where their feral savagery can be unleashed upon enemy formations with gory results.

UNTAMED WOLVES

The Space Wolves' most famous act of devastation occurred upon Prospero, home world of the traitorous Thousand Sons Legion. This gleaming paradise was burned to ashes by the vengeful Wolves after the Primarch Magnus the Red was found guilty of using sorcerous powers forbidden by the Emperor. In truth it was the Warmaster Horus who tricked Leman Russ and his Legion into sacking Prospero against their father's wishes, but nevertheless it ignited a bitter hatred between the Space Wolves and the Thousand Sons that exists to this day.

Ever short-tempered and stubborn, the Wolves of Fenris have made enemies within the Imperium as well as without. Long has the Inquisition desired to bring them to heel, frustrated by their wilful and rebellious nature, and suspicious of their strange rituals and unnatural appearance. An ancient animosity also exists between the Spaces Wolves and the Dark Angels Chapter, and has brought the two Imperial forces to the brink of open hostility on more than one occasion.

SPACE WOLVES ARMY LIST

This section contains all of the datasheets that you will need in order to fight battles with your Space Wolves miniatures. Each datasheet includes the characteristics profiles of the unit it describes, as well as any wargear and special abilities it may have. Some rules are common to several Space Wolves units, and are described below and referenced on the datasheets.

> 'They have us outnumbered a hundred to one. Their aircraft darken the skies, their tanks churn the ground to mud, and all we have is our axes and our ill temper. Hardly a fair fight, is it my Wolves? Let them pray their weakling gods have pity on them, for we shall not.'
>
> *- Logan Grimnar*

ABILITIES

The following ability is common to several Space Wolves units:

And They Shall Know No Fear

You can re-roll failed Morale tests for this unit.

SPACE WOLVES CHAPTER

The following Space Marines datasheets can be from the Space Wolves Chapter. Those that do replace the <CHAPTER> keyword on their datasheet in all instances with **SPACE WOLVES**. If a Space Marines unit does not appear on the list below, it cannot be from the Space Wolves Chapter, and so cannot have the **SPACE WOLVES** Faction keyword.

- Dreadnought (pg 35)
- Drop Pod (pg 48)
- Hellblaster Squad (pg 52)
- Imperial Space Marine (pg 30)
- Inceptor Squad (pg 43)
- Intercessor Squad (pg 30)
- Land Raider [1] (pg 58)
- Land Raider Crusader [1] (pg 59)
- Land Raider Excelsior [1] (pg 61)
- Land Raider Redeemer [1] (pg 60)
- Land Speeders (pg 46)
- Predator (pg 54)
- Primaris Ancient (pg 24)
- Primaris Lieutenants (pg 22)
- Razorback (pg 48)
- Rhino (pg 46)
- Rhino Primaris (pg 47)
- Servitors (pg 16)
- Venerable Dreadnought (pg 36)
- Vindicator (pg 55)
- Whirlwind (pg 54)
- Wolf Lord – use the Captain (pg 12) or Captain in Gravis Armour (pg 13) datasheet
- Wolf Lord in Terminator Armour – use the Captain in Terminator Armour datasheet (pg 12)
- Wolf Lord on Bike – use the Captain on Bike datasheet (pg 14)

[1] These vehicles can also transport Wulfen. Each Wulfen model takes the space of two other models.

SPACE WOLVES DREADNOUGHT WARGEAR

SPACE WOLVES Dreadnoughts and Venerable Dreadnoughts wield a number of weapons that are unique to their Chapter.

Replace the wargear options on these datasheets with the following:

- Instead of an assault cannon, this model can be equipped with a helfrost cannon or a weapon from the *Dreadnought Heavy Weapons* list (pg 11).
- Instead of a Dreadnought combat weapon and a storm bolter, this model can be equipped with a missile launcher or a twin autocannon.
- Instead of a storm bolter, this model can be equipped with a heavy flamer.
- Instead of a Dreadnought combat weapon, this model can be equipped with a great wolf claw.

Add the following wargear option and ability to the datasheet for **SPACE WOLVES** Venerable Dreadnoughts:

- Instead of an assault cannon, Dreadnought combat weapon and storm bolter, this model can be equipped with a Fenrisian great axe and blizzard shield.

Blizzard Shield: A model equipped with a blizzard shield has a 3+ invulnerable save.

TEMPESTAS DISCIPLINE

Before the battle, generate the psychic powers for **PSYKERS** that can use the Tempestas discipline using the table below. You can either roll a D3 to generate their powers randomly (re-roll any duplicate results), or you can select the powers you wish the psyker to have.

TEMPESTAS DISCIPLINE

D3	PSYCHIC POWER
1	**Storm Caller** *Storm Caller* has a warp charge value of 6. If manifested, then until the start of your next Psychic phase, the psyker and any friendly **SPACE WOLVES** units within 6" of him gain the benefit of being in cover.
2	**Tempest's Wrath** *Tempest's Wrath* has a warp charge value of 6. If manifested, pick an enemy unit within 18" of the psyker. Your opponent must subtract 1 from any hit rolls they make for that unit until the start of your next Psychic phase.
3	**Jaws of the World Wolf** *Jaws of the World Wolf* has a warp charge value of 7. If manifested, pick an enemy unit within 18" of the psyker, other than a **VEHICLE**. Roll 2D6 and subtract the target's Move characteristic – the target unit suffers a number of mortal wounds equal to the result.

WARGEAR

Many of the units you will find on the following pages reference one or more of the following wargear lists. When this is the case, the unit may take any item from the appropriate list below. The profiles for the items in these lists can be found in the appendix (pg 206-209 and 218-219).

SPACE WOLVES COMBI-WEAPONS
- Storm bolter
- Combi-plasma
- Combi-flamer
- Combi-melta

SPACE WOLVES MELEE WEAPONS
- Chainsword
- Frost axe
- Frost sword
- Lightning claw
- Power axe
- Power fist
- Power maul
- Power sword
- Thunder hammer
- Wolf claw

SPACE WOLVES SPECIAL WEAPONS
- Flamer
- Plasma gun
- Meltagun

SPACE WOLVES HEAVY WEAPONS
- Heavy bolter
- Lascannon
- Missile launcher
- Multi-melta
- Plasma cannon

SPACE WOLVES TERMINATOR MELEE WEAPONS
- Chainfist
- Frost axe
- Frost sword
- Lightning claw
- Power axe
- Power fist
- Power maul
- Power sword
- Thunder hammer
- Wolf claw

LOGAN GRIMNAR

NAME	M	WS	BS	S	T	W	A	Ld	Sv
Logan Grimnar	5"	2+	2+	4	4	7	5	9	2+

Logan Grimnar is a single model armed with the Axe Morkai and a storm bolter. Your army can only include one **LOGAN GRIMNAR**.

WEAPON	RANGE	TYPE	S	AP	D	ABILITIES
Storm bolter	24"	Rapid Fire 2	4	0	1	-
The Axe Morkai	When attacking with this weapon, choose one of the profiles below.					
- One-handed	Melee	Melee	+2	-3	D3	-
- Two-handed	Melee	Melee	x2	-3	3	When attacking with this weapon, you must subtract 1 from the hit roll.

ABILITIES	
And They Shall Know No Fear (pg 130)	**Belt of Russ:** Logan Grimnar has a 4+ invulnerable save.
Chapter Master: You can re-roll failed hit rolls for friendly **SPACE WOLVES** units that are within 6" of Logan Grimnar.	**Teleport Strike:** During deployment, you can set up Logan Grimnar in a teleportarium chamber instead of placing him on the battlefield. At the end of any of your Movement phases he can use a teleport strike to arrive on the battlefield – set him up anywhere on the battlefield that is more than 9" away from any enemy models.
High King of Fenris: You do not need to take Morale tests for friendly **WOLF GUARD** units within 6" of Logan Grimnar.	

FACTION KEYWORDS	IMPERIUM, ADEPTUS ASTARTES, SPACE WOLVES
KEYWORDS	CHARACTER, INFANTRY, CHAPTER MASTER, TERMINATOR, WOLF LORD, LOGAN GRIMNAR

LOGAN GRIMNAR
ON STORMRIDER

NAME	M	WS	BS	S	T	W	A	Ld	Sv
Logan Grimnar on Stormrider	*	2+	2+	4	6	12	5	9	3+

DAMAGE

Some of this model's characteristics change as it suffers damage, as shown below:

REMAINING W	M	ADDITIONAL ATTACKS
7-12+	10"	6
4-6	7"	5
1-3	4"	4

Logan Grimnar on *Stormrider* is a single model. Logan Grimnar rides atop *Stormrider* and is armed with the Axe Morkai and a storm bolter. *Stormrider* is drawn into battle by the High King's trusty Thunderwolves, Tyrnak and Fenrir, who attack with a flurry of teeth and claws. Your army can only include one **LOGAN GRIMNAR**.

WEAPON	RANGE	TYPE	S	AP	D	ABILITIES
Logan Grimnar						
Storm bolter	24"	Rapid Fire 2	4	0	1	-
The Axe Morkai	When attacking with this weapon, choose one of the profiles below.					
- One-handed	Melee	Melee	+2	-3	D3	-
- Two-handed	Melee	Melee	x2	-3	3	When attacking with this weapon, you must subtract 1 from the hit roll.
Tyrnak and Fenrir						
Flurry of teeth and claws	Melee	Melee	5	-1	1	After Logan Grimnar makes his close combat attacks, you can attack with Tyrnak and Fenrir. Make a number of additional attacks as shown in the damage chart above, using this weapon profile.

ABILITIES	
And They Shall Know No Fear (pg 130)	**Belt of Russ:** Logan Grimnar has a 4+ invulnerable save.
Chapter Master: You can re-roll failed hit rolls for friendly **SPACE WOLVES** units that are within 6" of Logan Grimnar.	**High King of Fenris:** You do not need to take Morale tests for friendly **WOLF GUARD** units within 6" of Logan Grimnar.
Alpha Predators: You can re-roll failed charge rolls for this model.	

FACTION KEYWORDS	IMPERIUM, ADEPTUS ASTARTES, SPACE WOLVES
KEYWORDS	CHARACTER, VEHICLE, CHAPTER MASTER, STORMRIDER, WOLF LORD, LOGAN GRIMNAR

WOLF LORD
ON THUNDERWOLF

NAME	M	WS	BS	S	T	W	A	Ld	Sv
Wolf Lord on Thunderwolf	10"	2+	2+	4	5	7	4	9	3+

A Wolf Lord on Thunderwolf is a single model armed with a chainsword, bolt pistol, frag grenades and krak grenades. He rides to battle atop a Thunderwolf, who attacks with crushing teeth and claws.

WEAPON	RANGE	TYPE	S	AP	D	ABILITIES
Wolf Lord						
Bolt pistol	12"	Pistol 1	4	0	1	-
Boltgun	24"	Rapid Fire 1	4	0	1	-
Plasma pistol	When attacking with this weapon, choose one of the profiles below.					
- Standard	12"	Pistol 1	7	-3	1	-
- Supercharge	12"	Pistol 1	8	-3	2	On a hit roll of 1, the bearer is slain.
Chainsword	Melee	Melee	User	0	1	Each time the bearer fights, it can make 1 additional attack with this weapon.
Frag grenade	6"	Grenade D6	3	0	1	-
Krak grenade	6"	Grenade 1	6	-1	D3	-
Thunderwolf						
Crushing teeth and claws	Melee	Melee	5	-1	1	After a model on this mount makes its close combat attacks, you can attack with its mount. Make 3 additional attacks, using this weapon profile.

WARGEAR OPTIONS	• This model may replace its chainsword with an item from the *Space Wolves Melee Weapons* list. • This model may replace its bolt pistol with a boltgun, plasma pistol, storm shield or an item from the *Space Wolves Combi-weapons* or *Space Wolves Melee Weapons* lists.
ABILITIES	**And They Shall Know No Fear** (pg 130) **Belt of Russ:** This model has a 4+ invulnerable save. **Jarl of Fenris:** You can re-roll hit rolls of 1 for friendly **SPACE WOLVES** units within 6" of this model. **Storm Shield:** A model equipped with a storm shield has a 3+ invulnerable save.
FACTION KEYWORDS	**IMPERIUM, ADEPTUS ASTARTES, SPACE WOLVES**
KEYWORDS	**CAVALRY, CHARACTER, THUNDERWOLF, WOLF LORD**

Mounted upon his chariot, *Stormrider*, Logan Grimnar leads his Champions of Fenris into battle.

RAGNAR BLACKMANE

7 POWER

NAME	M	WS	BS	S	T	W	A	Ld	Sv
Ragnar Blackmane	6"	2+	2+	4	4	5	5	9	3+
Svangir	12"	3+	7+	4	4	1	3	4	6+
Ulfgir	12"	3+	7+	4	4	1	3	4	6+

Ragnar Blackmane is a single model armed with Frostfang, a bolt pistol, frag grenades and krak grenades. Only one of this model may be included in your army.
- Ragnar's unit may include his two loyal Fenrisian Wolves, Svangir and Ulfgir (**Power Rating +1**). Svangir and Ulfgir attack with their teeth and claws.

WEAPON	RANGE	TYPE	S	AP	D	ABILITIES
Bolt pistol	12"	Pistol 1	4	-0	1	-
Frostfang	Melee	Melee	+1	-4	2	-
Teeth and claws	Melee	Melee	User	-1	1	-
Frag grenade	6"	Grenade D6	3	0	1	-
Krak grenade	6"	Grenade 1	6	-1	D3	-

ABILITIES		
	And They Shall Know No Fear (pg 130) **Belt of Russ:** Ragnar Blackmane has a 4+ invulnerable save. **War Howl:** You can re-roll failed charge rolls for friendly **Space Wolves** units within 6" of Ragnar Blackmane.	**Jarl of Fenris:** You can re-roll hit rolls of 1 for friendly **Space Wolves** units within 6" of Ragnar Blackmane. **Insane Bravado:** Ragnar Blackmane can perform a Heroic Intervention if he is within 6" of an enemy unit instead of only 3", and if he does so he can move 6" rather than 3".

FACTION KEYWORDS	IMPERIUM, ADEPTUS ASTARTES, SPACE WOLVES
KEYWORDS	CHARACTER, INFANTRY, WOLF LORD, RAGNAR BLACKMANE

KROM DRAGONGAZE

6 POWER

NAME	M	WS	BS	S	T	W	A	Ld	Sv
Krom Dragongaze	6"	2+	2+	4	4	5	5	9	3+

Krom Dragongaze is a single model armed with Wyrmclaw, a bolt pistol, frag grenades and krak grenades. Only one of this model may be included in your army.

WEAPON	RANGE	TYPE	S	AP	D	ABILITIES
Bolt pistol	12"	Pistol 1	4	0	1	-
Wyrmclaw	Melee	Melee	+2	-2	D3	-
Frag grenade	6"	Grenade D6	3	0	1	-
Krak grenade	6"	Grenade 1	6	-1	D3	-

ABILITIES		
	And They Shall Know No Fear (pg 130) **Jarl of Fenris:** You can re-roll hit rolls of 1 for friendly **Space Wolves** units within 6" of Krom Dragongaze.	**The Fierce-eye:** Enemy units that are within 3" of Krom Dragongaze at the start of the Morale phase must reduce their Leadership by 1 for the duration of the phase. **Belt of Russ:** Krom Dragongaze has a 4+ invulnerable save.

FACTION KEYWORDS	IMPERIUM, ADEPTUS ASTARTES, SPACE WOLVES
KEYWORDS	CHARACTER, INFANTRY, WOLF LORD, KROM DRAGONGAZE

HARALD DEATHWOLF

NAME	M	WS	BS	S	T	W	A	Ld	Sv
Harald Deathwolf	10"	2+	2+	4	5	7	4	9	3+

Harald Deathwolf is a single model armed with Glacius, a bolt pistol, frag grenades and krak grenades. He rides to battle atop his Thunderwolf, Icetooth, who attacks with crushing teeth and claws. Only one of this model may be included in your army.

WEAPON	RANGE	TYPE	S	AP	D	ABILITIES
Harald Deathwolf						
Bolt pistol	12"	Pistol 1	4	0	1	-
Glacius	Melee	Melee	+2	-2	2	If a model suffers any unsaved wounds from this weapon but is not slain, roll a D6; on a 6, the target suffers a mortal wound.
Frag grenade	6"	Grenade D6	3	0	1	-
Krak grenade	6"	Grenade 1	6	-1	D3	-
Icetooth						
Crushing teeth and claws	Melee	Melee	5	-1	1	After a model on this mount makes its close combat attacks, you can attack with its mount. Make 3 additional attacks, using this weapon profile.

ABILITIES	**And They Shall Know No Fear** (pg 130)	**Jarl of Fenris:** You can re-roll hit rolls of 1 for friendly **Space Wolves** units within 6" of Harald Deathwolf.
	Expert Hunter: During deployment, you can set up Harald Deathwolf ready to outflank his prey instead of placing him on the battlefield. At the end of any of your Movement phases he can join the battle – set him up so that he is within 12" of any battlefield edge of your choice and more than 9" away from any enemy models.	**Lord of the Wolfkin:** All friendly **Thunderwolf** units and friendly units of Fenrisian Wolves or Cyberwolves within 6" in the Morale phase can use Harald Deathwolf's Leadership instead of their own.
	Storm Shield: Harald Deathwolf has a 3+ invulnerable save.	**Mantle of the Troll King:** Add 1 to any saving throws you make for Harald Deathwolf against shooting attacks.

FACTION KEYWORDS	IMPERIUM, ADEPTUS ASTARTES, SPACE WOLVES
KEYWORDS	CAVALRY, CHARACTER, THUNDERWOLF, WOLF LORD, HARALD DEATHWOLF

Hot-blooded and deadly, Wolf Lord Krom Dragongaze advances at the head of his warriors.

CANIS WOLFBORN

NAME	M	WS	BS	S	T	W	A	Ld	Sv
Canis Wolfborn	10"	2+	5+	4	5	6	4	8	3+

Canis Wolfborn is a single model armed with two wolf claws, a bolt pistol, frag grenades, and krak grenades. He rides to battle atop his Thunderwolf, Fangir, who attacks with crushing teeth and claws. Only one of this model may be included in your army.

WEAPON	RANGE	TYPE	S	AP	D	ABILITIES
Canis Wolfborn						
Bolt pistol	12"	Pistol 1	4	0	1	-
Wolf claw	Melee	Melee	+1	-2	1	You can re-roll failed wound rolls for this weapon. A model armed with two wolf claws can make 1 additional attack with this weapon.
Frag grenade	6"	Grenade D6	3	0	1	-
Krak grenade	6"	Grenade 1	6	-1	D3	-
Fangir						
Crushing teeth and claws	Melee	Melee	5	-1	1	After a model on this mount makes its close combat attacks, you can attack with its mount. Make 3 additional attacks, using this weapon profile.

ABILITIES	And They Shall Know No Fear (pg 130)	**Alpha Predator:** You can re-roll failed charge rolls for Canis Wolfborn.
	Born of Wolves: You can make 1 additional teeth and claws or crushing teeth and claws attack in the Fight phase for all friendly models in **Thunderwolf**, Fenrisian Wolves or Cyberwolves units that are within 6" of Canis Wolfborn at the start of the phase.	**Champion of the Deathwolves:** You can re-roll wound rolls of 1 for friendly **Space Wolves** units that are within 6" of Canis Wolfborn.

FACTION KEYWORDS	**Imperium, Adeptus Astartes, Space Wolves**
KEYWORDS	**Cavalry, Character, Thunderwolf, Wolf Guard, Canis Wolfborn**

Canis Wolfborn has a unique affinity with the wolves of Fenris, and puts this to deadly effect upon the field of battle.

RUNE PRIEST

NAME	M	WS	BS	S	T	W	A	Ld	Sv
Rune Priest	6"	2+	3+	4	4	4	3	9	3+

A Rune Priest is a single model armed with a runic axe, bolt pistol, frag grenades and krak grenades.

WEAPON	RANGE	TYPE	S	AP	D	ABILITIES
Bolt pistol	12"	Pistol 1	4	0	1	-
Plasma pistol	When attacking with this weapon, choose one of the profiles below.					
- Standard	12"	Pistol 1	7	-3	1	-
- Supercharge	12"	Pistol 1	8	-3	2	On a hit roll of 1, the bearer is slain.
Runic axe	Melee	Melee	+1	-2	D3	-
Runic stave	Melee	Melee	+2	-1	D3	-
Runic sword	Melee	Melee	User	-3	D3	-
Frag grenade	6"	Grenade D6	3	0	1	-
Krak grenade	6"	Grenade 1	6	-1	D3	-

WARGEAR OPTIONS	
	• This model may take a psychic hood. • This model may take runic armour. • This model may replace its runic axe with a runic stave or a runic sword. • This model may replace its bolt pistol with a plasma pistol or an item from the *Space Wolves Combi-weapons* list. • This model may take a jump pack (**Power Rating +1**). If it does, its Move characteristic becomes 12" and it gains the **Jump Pack** and **Fly** keywords.

ABILITIES	
	And They Shall Know No Fear (pg 130) **Runic Armour:** A model equipped with runic armour has a 5+ invulnerable save. **Psychic Hood:** You can add 1 to any Deny the Witch tests you make for a model equipped with a psychic hood against an enemy **Psyker** within 12".	**Jump Pack Assault:** If this model has a jump pack, when you set it up during deployment, it can be set up high in the skies, ready to strike, instead of being placed on the battlefield. If it is, it can make a sudden assault to arrive on the battlefield at the end of any of your Movement phases; when it does so set it up anywhere that is more than 9" from any enemy models.

PSYKER	This model can attempt to manifest two psychic powers in each friendly Psychic phase, and attempt to deny one psychic power in each enemy Psychic phase. It knows the *Smite* power and one psychic power from the Tempestas discipline (pg 131).

FACTION KEYWORDS	**Imperium, Adeptus Astartes, Space Wolves**
KEYWORDS	**Character, Infantry, Psyker, Rune Priest**

Rune Priests howl invocations to harness and unleash the powers of the storm upon their foes.

RUNE PRIEST
IN TERMINATOR ARMOUR

NAME	M	WS	BS	S	T	W	A	Ld	Sv
Rune Priest in Terminator Armour	5"	2+	3+	4	4	5	3	9	2+

A Rune Priest in Terminator Armour is a single model armed with a runic axe and storm bolter.

WEAPON	RANGE	TYPE	S	AP	D	ABILITIES
Storm bolter	24"	Rapid Fire 2	4	0	1	-
Runic axe	Melee	Melee	+1	-2	D3	-
Runic stave	Melee	Melee	+2	-1	D3	-
Runic sword	Melee	Melee	User	-3	D3	-

WARGEAR OPTIONS	
	• This model may take a psychic hood.
	• This model may take Runic Terminator armour.
	• This model may replace its runic axe with a runic stave or a runic sword.
	• This model may replace its storm bolter with an item from the *Space Wolves Combi-weapons* list.

ABILITIES

And They Shall Know No Fear (pg 130)

Psychic Hood: You can add 1 to any Deny the Witch tests you make for a model equipped with a psychic hood against an enemy PSYKER within 12".

Crux Terminatus: This model has a 5+ invulnerable save.

Runic Terminator Armour: A model equipped with Runic Terminator armour has a 4+ invulnerable save.

Teleport Strike: During deployment, you can set up this model in a teleportarium chamber instead of placing it on the battlefield. At the end of any of your Movement phases this model can use a teleport strike to arrive on the battlefield – set it up anywhere on the battlefield that is more than 9" away from any enemy models.

PSYKER

This model can attempt to manifest two psychic powers in each friendly Psychic phase, and attempt to deny one psychic power in each enemy Psychic phase. It knows the *Smite* power and one psychic power from the Tempestas discipline (pg 131).

FACTION KEYWORDS

IMPERIUM, ADEPTUS ASTARTES, SPACE WOLVES

KEYWORDS

CHARACTER, INFANTRY, TERMINATOR, PSYKER, RUNE PRIEST

RUNE PRIEST
ON BIKE

NAME	M	WS	BS	S	T	W	A	Ld	Sv
Rune Priest on Bike	14"	2+	3+	4	5	5	3	9	3+

A Rune Priest on Bike is a single model armed with a runic axe, bolt pistol, frag grenades and krak grenades. He rides into battle on a Space Marine bike equipped with a twin boltgun.

WEAPON	RANGE	TYPE	S	AP	D	ABILITIES
Bolt pistol	12"	Pistol 1	4	0	1	-
Plasma pistol	When attacking with this weapon, choose one of the profiles below.					
- Standard	12"	Pistol 1	7	-3	1	-
- Supercharge	12"	Pistol 1	8	-3	2	On a hit roll of 1, the bearer is slain.
Twin boltgun	24"	Rapid Fire 2	4	0	1	-
Runic axe	Melee	Melee	+1	-2	D3	-
Runic stave	Melee	Melee	+2	-1	D3	-
Runic sword	Melee	Melee	User	-3	D3	-
Frag grenade	6"	Grenade D6	3	0	1	-
Krak grenade	6"	Grenade 1	6	-1	D3	-

WARGEAR OPTIONS	• This model may take a psychic hood. • This model may take runic armour. • This model may replace its runic axe with a runic stave or a runic sword. • This model may replace its bolt pistol with a plasma pistol or an item from the *Space Wolves Combi-weapons* list.

ABILITIES	**And They Shall Know No Fear** (pg 130) **Psychic Hood:** You can add 1 to any Deny the Witch tests you make for a model equipped with a psychic hood against an enemy **PSYKER** within 12".	**Runic Armour:** A model equipped with runic armour has a 5+ invulnerable save. **Turbo-boost:** When this model Advances, add 6" to its Move characteristic for that Movement phase instead of rolling a dice.

PSYKER	This model can attempt to manifest two psychic powers in each friendly Psychic phase, and attempt to deny one psychic power in each enemy Psychic phase. It knows the *Smite* power and one psychic power from the Tempestas discipline (pg 131).

FACTION KEYWORDS	**IMPERIUM, ADEPTUS ASTARTES, SPACE WOLVES**

KEYWORDS	**BIKER, CHARACTER, PSYKER, RUNE PRIEST**

NJAL STORMCALLER

7 POWER

NAME	M	WS	BS	S	T	W	A	Ld	Sv
Njal Stormcaller	6"	2+	2+	4	4	5	3	9	2+

Njal Stormcaller is a single model armed with the Staff of the Stormcaller, a bolt pistol, frag grenades and krak grenades. Njal is accompanied by his psyber-raven, Nightwing. Your army can only include one **NJAL STORMCALLER**.

WEAPON	RANGE	TYPE	S	AP	D	ABILITIES
Bolt pistol	12"	Pistol 1	4	0	1	-
Nightwing	12"	Assault D6	3	0	1	-
Staff of the Stormcaller	Melee	Melee	+2	-1	D3	-
Frag grenade	6"	Grenade D6	3	0	1	-
Krak grenade	6"	Grenade 1	6	-1	D3	-

ABILITIES	**And They Shall Know No Fear** (pg 130) **Lord of Tempests:** You can add 1 to any Psychic tests you make for Njal Stormcaller. **Psychic Hood:** You can add 1 to any Deny the Witch tests you make for Njal Stormcaller against an enemy **PSYKER** within 12".	**Runic Armour:** Njal Stormcaller has a 5+ invulnerable save. **Staff of the Stormcaller:** You can re-roll one failed Deny the Witch test for Njal Stormcaller in each of your opponent's Psychic phases.
PSYKER	Njal Stormcaller can attempt to manifest two psychic powers in each friendly Psychic phase, and attempt to deny two psychic powers in each enemy Psychic phase. He knows the *Smite* power and three psychic powers from the Tempestas discipline (pg 131).	
FACTION KEYWORDS	**IMPERIUM, ADEPTUS ASTARTES, SPACE WOLVES**	
KEYWORDS	**CHARACTER, INFANTRY, RUNE PRIEST, PSYKER, NJAL STORMCALLER**	

NJAL STORMCALLER
IN RUNIC TERMINATOR ARMOUR

9 POWER

NAME	M	WS	BS	S	T	W	A	Ld	Sv
Njal Stormcaller in Runic Terminator Armour	5"	2+	2+	4	4	6	3	9	2+

Njal Stormcaller in Runic Terminator Armour is a single model armed with the Staff of the Stormcaller and a bolt pistol. Njal is accompanied by his psyber-raven, Nightwing. Your army can only include one **NJAL STORMCALLER**.

WEAPON	RANGE	TYPE	S	AP	D	ABILITIES
Bolt pistol	12"	Pistol 1	4	0	1	-
Nightwing	12"	Assault D6	3	0	1	-
Staff of the Stormcaller	Melee	Melee	+2	-1	D3	-

ABILITIES	**And They Shall Know No Fear** (pg 130) **Lord of Tempests:** You can add 1 to any Psychic tests you make for Njal Stormcaller. **Psychic Hood:** You can add 1 to any Deny the Witch tests you make for Njal Stormcaller against an enemy **PSYKER** within 12". **Runic Terminator Armour:** Njal Stormcaller has a 4+ invulnerable save.	**Staff of the Stormcaller:** You can re-roll one failed Deny the Witch test for Njal Stormcaller in each of your opponent's Psychic phases. **Teleport Strike:** During deployment, you can set up Njal Stormcaller in a teleportarium chamber instead of placing him on the battlefield. At the end of any of your Movement phases he can use a teleport strike to arrive on the battlefield – set him up anywhere on the battlefield that is more than 9" away from any enemy models.
PSYKER	Njal Stormcaller can attempt to manifest two psychic powers in each friendly Psychic phase, and attempt to deny two psychic powers in each enemy Psychic phase. He knows the *Smite* power and three psychic powers from the Tempestas discipline (pg 131).	
FACTION KEYWORDS	**IMPERIUM, ADEPTUS ASTARTES, SPACE WOLVES**	
KEYWORDS	**CHARACTER, INFANTRY, RUNE PRIEST, TERMINATOR, PSYKER, NJAL STORMCALLER**	

WOLF PRIEST

NAME	M	WS	BS	S	T	W	A	Ld	Sv
Wolf Priest	6"	2+	3+	4	4	4	3	9	3+

A Wolf Priest is a single model armed with a crozius arcanum, bolt pistol, frag grenades and krak grenades.

WEAPON	RANGE	TYPE	S	AP	D	ABILITIES
Bolt pistol	12"	Pistol 1	4	0	1	-
Plasma pistol	When attacking with this weapon, choose one of the profiles below.					
- Standard	12"	Pistol 1	7	-3	1	-
- Supercharge	12"	Pistol 1	8	-3	2	On a hit roll of 1, the bearer is slain.
Crozius arcanum	Melee	Melee	+1	-1	2	-
Frag grenade	6"	Grenade D6	3	0	1	-
Krak grenade	6"	Grenade 1	6	-1	D3	-

WARGEAR OPTIONS	• This model may replace its bolt pistol with a plasma pistol or an item from the *Space Wolves Combi-weapons* list. • This model may take a jump pack (**Power Rating +1**). If it does, its Move characteristic becomes 12" and it gains the **JUMP PACK** and **FLY** keywords.

ABILITIES	**And They Shall Know No Fear** (pg 130) **Jump Pack Assault:** If this model has a jump pack, when you set it up during deployment, it can be set up high in the skies, ready to strike, instead of being placed on the battlefield. If it is, it can make a sudden assault to arrive on the battlefield at the end of any of your Movement phases; when it does so set it up anywhere that is more than 9" from any enemy models. **Oath of War:** You can re-roll failed hit rolls in the Fight phase for friendly **SPACE WOLVES** units within 6" of this model.	**Spiritual Leader:** All friendly **SPACE WOLVES** units within 6" of this model in the Morale phase can use its Leadership instead of their own. **Wolf Amulet:** This model has a 4+ invulnerable save. **Healing Balms:** At the end of your Movement phase a Wolf Priest can attempt to heal a single model. To do so, select a **SPACE WOLVES INFANTRY**, **BIKER** or **CAVALRY** unit within 3" of him. If that unit contains a wounded model, it is healed and immediately regains up to D3 lost wounds. A unit can only be the target of Healing Balms once in each turn.

FACTION KEYWORDS	IMPERIUM, ADEPTUS ASTARTES, SPACE WOLVES
KEYWORDS	CHARACTER, INFANTRY, WOLF PRIEST

5 POWER

WOLF PRIEST
in Terminator Armour

NAME	M	WS	BS	S	T	W	A	Ld	Sv
Wolf Priest in Terminator Armour	5"	2+	3+	4	4	5	3	9	2+

A Wolf Priest in Terminator Armour is a single model armed with a crozius arcanum and storm bolter.

WEAPON	RANGE	TYPE	S	AP	D	ABILITIES
Storm bolter	24"	Rapid Fire 2	4	0	1	-
Crozius arcanum	Melee	Melee	+1	-1	2	-

WARGEAR OPTIONS	• This model may replace its storm bolter with an item from the *Space Wolves Combi-weapons* list.

ABILITIES

And They Shall Know No Fear (pg 130)

Teleport Strike: During deployment, you can set up this model in a teleportarium chamber instead of placing it on the battlefield. At the end of any of your Movement phases this model can use a teleport strike to arrive on the battlefield – set it up anywhere on the battlefield that is more than 9" away from any enemy models.

Oath of War: You can re-roll failed hit rolls in the Fight phase for friendly **SPACE WOLVES** units within 6" of this model.

Spiritual Leader: All friendly **SPACE WOLVES** units within 6" of this model in the Morale phase can use its Leadership instead of their own.

Healing Balms: At the end of your Movement phase a Wolf Priest in Terminator Armour can attempt to heal a single model. To do so, select a **SPACE WOLVES INFANTRY, BIKER** or **CAVALRY** unit within 3" of him. If that unit contains a wounded model, it is healed and immediately regains up to D3 lost wounds. A unit can only be the target of Healing Balms once in each turn.

Wolf Amulet: This model has a 4+ invulnerable save.

FACTION KEYWORDS	IMPERIUM, ADEPTUS ASTARTES, SPACE WOLVES
KEYWORDS	CHARACTER, INFANTRY, TERMINATOR, WOLF PRIEST

WOLF PRIEST
on Bike

NAME	M	WS	BS	S	T	W	A	Ld	Sv
Wolf Priest on Bike	14"	2+	3+	4	5	5	3	9	3+

A Wolf Priest on Bike is a single model armed with a crozius arcanum, bolt pistol, frag grenades and krak grenades. He rides into battle on a Space Marine bike equipped with a twin boltgun.

WEAPON	RANGE	TYPE	S	AP	D	ABILITIES
Bolt pistol	12"	Pistol 1	4	0	1	-
Plasma pistol	When attacking with this weapon, choose one of the profiles below.					
- Standard	12"	Pistol 1	7	-3	1	-
- Supercharge	12"	Pistol 1	8	-3	2	On a hit roll of 1, the bearer is slain.
Twin boltgun	24"	Rapid Fire 2	4	0	1	-
Crozius arcanum	Melee	Melee	+1	-1	2	-
Frag grenade	6"	Grenade D6	3	0	1	-
Krak grenade	6"	Grenade 1	6	-1	D3	-

WARGEAR OPTIONS	• This model may replace its bolt pistol with a plasma pistol or an item from the *Space Wolves Combi-weapons* list.

ABILITIES

And They Shall Know No Fear (pg 130)

Oath of War: You can re-roll failed hit rolls in the Fight phase for friendly **SPACE WOLVES** units within 6" of this model.

Spiritual Leader: All friendly **SPACE WOLVES** units within 6" of this model in the Morale phase can use its Leadership instead of their own.

Wolf Amulet: This model has a 4+ invulnerable save.

Healing Balms: At the end of your Movement phase a Wolf Priest on Bike can attempt to heal a single model. To do so, select a **SPACE WOLVES INFANTRY, BIKER** or **CAVALRY** unit within 3" of him. If that unit contains a wounded model, it is healed and immediately regains up to D3 lost wounds. A unit can only be the target of Healing Balms once in each turn.

Turbo-boost: When this model Advances, add 6" to its Move characteristic for that Movement phase instead of rolling a dice.

FACTION KEYWORDS	IMPERIUM, ADEPTUS ASTARTES, SPACE WOLVES
KEYWORDS	BIKER, CHARACTER, WOLF PRIEST

ULRIK THE SLAYER

NAME	M	WS	BS	S	T	W	A	Ld	Sv
Ulrik the Slayer	6"	2+	2+	4	4	5	4	9	3+

Ulrik the Slayer is a single model armed with a crozius arcanum, plasma pistol, frag grenades and krak grenades. Only one of this model may be included in your army.

WEAPON	RANGE	TYPE	S	AP	D	ABILITIES
Plasma pistol	When attacking with this weapon, choose one of the profiles below.					
- Standard	12"	Pistol 1	7	-3	1	-
- Supercharge	12"	Pistol 1	8	-3	2	On a hit roll of 1, the bearer is slain.
Crozius arcanum	Melee	Melee	+1	-1	2	-
Frag grenade	6"	Grenade D6	3	0	1	-
Krak grenade	6"	Grenade 1	6	-1	D3	-

ABILITIES	And They Shall Know No Fear (pg 130) **Healing Balms:** At the end of your Movement phase, Ulrik the Slayer can attempt to heal a single model. To do so, select a **Space Wolves Infantry**, **Biker** or **Cavalry** unit within 3" of him. If that unit contains a wounded model, it is healed and immediately regains up to D3 lost wounds. A unit can only be the target of Healing Balms once in each turn. **Wolf Amulet:** Ulrik the Slayer has a 4+ invulnerable save.	**Slayer's Oath:** You can re-roll failed hit rolls in the Fight phase for friendly **Space Wolves** units within 6" of this model. If Ulrik the Slayer kills an enemy **Character** or **Monster**, then for the rest of the battle, you can add 1 to any wound rolls you make in the Fight phase for any friendly **Space Wolves** units within 6" of him. **Wolf Helm of Russ:** All friendly **Space Wolves** units within 9" of Ulrik the Slayer in the Morale phase can use his Leadership instead of their own.
FACTION KEYWORDS	**Imperium, Adeptus Astartes, Space Wolves**	
KEYWORDS	**Character, Infantry, Wolf Priest, Ulrik the Slayer**	

Ulrik the Slayer is ancient and wise, but no less deadly a warrior for all his centuries of life.

WOLF GUARD BATTLE LEADER

NAME	M	WS	BS	S	T	W	A	Ld	Sv
Wolf Guard Battle Leader	6"	2+	3+	4	4	4	4	8	3+

A Wolf Guard Battle Leader is a single model armed with a chainsword, bolt pistol, frag grenades and krak grenades.

WEAPON	RANGE	TYPE	S	AP	D	ABILITIES
Bolt pistol	12"	Pistol 1	4	0	1	-
Boltgun	24"	Rapid Fire 1	4	0	1	-
Plasma pistol	When attacking with this weapon, choose one of the profiles below.					
- Standard	12"	Pistol 1	7	-3	1	-
- Supercharge	12"	Pistol 1	8	-3	2	On a hit roll of 1, the bearer is slain.
Chainsword	Melee	Melee	User	0	1	Each time the bearer fights, it can make 1 additional attack with this weapon.
Frag grenade	6"	Grenade D6	3	0	1	-
Krak grenade	6"	Grenade 1	6	-1	D3	-

WARGEAR OPTIONS	
	• This model may replace its chainsword with an item from the *Space Wolves Melee Weapons* list.
	• This model may replace its bolt pistol with a boltgun, plasma pistol, storm shield, or an item from the *Space Wolves Combi-weapons* or *Space Wolves Melee Weapons* lists.
	• This model may take a jump pack (**Power Rating +1**). If it does, its Move characteristic becomes 12" and it gains the **Jump Pack** and **Fly** keywords.

ABILITIES		
	And They Shall Know No Fear (pg 130)	**Jump Pack Assault:** If this model has a jump pack, when you set it up during deployment, it can be set up high in the skies, ready to strike, instead of being placed on the battlefield. If it is, it can make a sudden assault to arrive on the battlefield at the end of any of your Movement phases; when it does so set it up anywhere that is more than 9" from any enemy models.
	Storm Shield: A model equipped with a storm shield has a 3+ invulnerable save.	
	Huskarl to the Jarl: You can re-roll wound rolls of 1 for friendly **Space Wolves** units that are within 6" of this model.	

FACTION KEYWORDS	**Imperium, Adeptus Astartes, Space Wolves**
KEYWORDS	**Character, Infantry, Wolf Guard, Battle Leader**

Heavily equipped packs of Wolf Guard storm into battle through the bitter snows of a frozen world.

WOLF GUARD BATTLE LEADER
ON BIKE

6 POWER

NAME	M	WS	BS	S	T	W	A	Ld	Sv
Wolf Guard Battle Leader on Bike	14"	2+	3+	4	5	5	4	8	3+

A Wolf Guard Battle Leader on Bike is a single model armed with a chainsword, bolt pistol, frag grenades and krak grenades. He rides into battle on a Space Marine bike equipped with a twin boltgun.

WEAPON	RANGE	TYPE	S	AP	D	ABILITIES
Bolt pistol	12"	Pistol 1	4	0	1	-
Boltgun	24"	Rapid Fire 1	4	0	1	-
Plasma pistol	When attacking with this weapon, choose one of the profiles below.					
- Standard	12"	Pistol 1	7	-3	1	-
- Supercharge	12"	Pistol 1	8	-3	2	On a hit roll of 1, the bearer is slain.
Twin boltgun	24"	Rapid Fire 2	4	0	1	-
Chainsword	Melee	Melee	User	0	1	Each time the bearer fights, it can make 1 additional attack with this weapon.
Frag grenade	6"	Grenade D6	3	0	1	-
Krak grenade	6"	Grenade 1	6	-1	D3	-

WARGEAR OPTIONS	• This model may replace its chainsword with an item from the *Space Wolves Melee Weapons* list. • This model may replace its bolt pistol with a boltgun, plasma pistol, storm shield, or an item from the *Space Wolves Combi-weapons* or *Space Wolves Melee Weapons* lists.

ABILITIES	**And They Shall Know No Fear** (pg 130) **Huskarl to the Jarl:** You can re-roll wound rolls of 1 for friendly **SPACE WOLVES** units that are within 6" of this model.	**Storm Shield:** A model equipped with a storm shield has a 3+ invulnerable save. **Turbo-boost:** When this model Advances, add 6" to its Move characteristic for that Movement phase instead of rolling a dice.

FACTION KEYWORDS	IMPERIUM, ADEPTUS ASTARTES, SPACE WOLVES
KEYWORDS	BIKER, CHARACTER, WOLF GUARD, BATTLE LEADER

WOLF GUARD BATTLE LEADER
IN TERMINATOR ARMOUR

6 POWER

NAME	M	WS	BS	S	T	W	A	Ld	Sv
Wolf Guard Battle Leader in Terminator Armour	5"	2+	3+	4	4	5	4	8	2+

A Wolf Guard Battle Leader in Terminator Armour is a single model armed with a power sword and storm bolter.

WEAPON	RANGE	TYPE	S	AP	D	ABILITIES
Storm bolter	24"	Rapid Fire 2	4	0	1	-
Power sword	Melee	Melee	User	-3	1	-

WARGEAR OPTIONS	• This model may replace its power sword with an item from the *Space Wolves Melee Weapons* list. • This model may replace its storm bolter with a storm shield or an item from the *Space Wolves Combi-weapons* or *Space Wolves Melee Weapons* lists.

ABILITIES	**And They Shall Know No Fear** (pg 130) **Crux Terminatus:** This model has a 5+ invulnerable save. **Huskarl to the Jarl:** You can re-roll wound rolls of 1 for friendly **SPACE WOLVES** units that are within 6" of this model.	**Storm Shield:** A model equipped with a storm shield has a 3+ invulnerable save. **Teleport Strike:** During deployment, you can set up this model in a teleportarium chamber instead of placing it on the battlefield. At the end of any of your Movement phases this model can use a teleport strike to arrive on the battlefield – set it up anywhere on the battlefield that is more than 9" away from any enemy models.

FACTION KEYWORDS	IMPERIUM, ADEPTUS ASTARTES, SPACE WOLVES
KEYWORDS	CHARACTER, INFANTRY, TERMINATOR, WOLF GUARD, BATTLE LEADER

WOLF GUARD BATTLE LEADER
ON THUNDERWOLF

NAME	M	WS	BS	S	T	W	A	Ld	Sv
Wolf Guard Battle Leader on Thunderwolf	10"	2+	3+	4	5	6	4	8	3+

A Wolf Guard Battle Leader on Thunderwolf is a single model armed with a chainsword, bolt pistol, frag grenades and krak grenades. He rides to battle atop a Thunderwolf, who attacks with crushing teeth and claws.

WEAPON	RANGE	TYPE	S	AP	D	ABILITIES
Wolf Guard Battle Leader						
Bolt pistol	12"	Pistol 1	4	0	1	-
Boltgun	24"	Rapid Fire 1	4	0	1	-
Plasma pistol	When attacking with this weapon, choose one of the profiles below.					
- Standard	12"	Pistol 1	7	-3	1	-
- Supercharge	12"	Pistol 1	8	-3	2	On a hit roll of 1, the bearer is slain.
Chainsword	Melee	Melee	User	0	1	Each time the bearer fights, it can make 1 additional attack with this weapon.
Frag grenade	6"	Grenade D6	3	0	1	-
Krak grenade	6"	Grenade 1	6	-1	D3	-
Thunderwolf						
Crushing teeth and claws	Melee	Melee	5	-1	1	After a model on this mount makes its close combat attacks, you can attack with its mount. Make 3 additional attacks, using this weapon profile.

WARGEAR OPTIONS	• This model may replace its chainsword, with an item from the *Space Wolves Melee Weapons* list. • This model may replace its bolt pistol with a boltgun, plasma pistol, storm shield, or an item from the *Space Wolves Combi-weapons* or *Space Wolves Melee Weapons* lists.
ABILITIES	**And They Shall Know No Fear** (pg 130) **Storm Shield:** A model equipped with a storm shield has a 3+ invulnerable save.	**Huskarl to the Jarl:** You can re-roll wound rolls of 1 for friendly **SPACE WOLVES** units that are within 6" of this model.
FACTION KEYWORDS	**IMPERIUM, ADEPTUS ASTARTES, SPACE WOLVES**
KEYWORDS	**CAVALRY, CHARACTER, THUNDERWOLF, WOLF GUARD, BATTLE LEADER**

BJORN THE FELL-HANDED

NAME	M	WS	BS	S	T	W	A	Ld	Sv
Bjorn the Fell-handed	8"	2+	2+	7	8	8	5	9	3+

Bjorn the Fell-Handed is a single model armed with Trueclaw, an assault cannon and a heavy flamer. Only one of this model may be included in your army.

WEAPON	RANGE	TYPE	S	AP	D	ABILITIES
Assault cannon	24"	Heavy 6	6	-1	1	-
Heavy flamer	8"	Heavy D6	5	-1	1	This weapon automatically hits its target.
Heavy plasma cannon	When attacking with this weapon, choose one of the profiles below.					
- Standard	36"	Heavy D3	7	-3	1	-
- Supercharge	36"	Heavy D3	8	-3	2	For each hit roll of 1, the bearer suffers 1 mortal wound after all of this weapon's shots have been resolved.
Helfrost cannon	When attacking with this weapon, choose one of the profiles below. If a model suffers any unsaved wounds from this weapon but is not slain, roll a D6; on a 6, the target suffers a mortal wound.					
- Dispersed beam	24"	Heavy D3	6	-2	1	-
- Focused beam	24"	Heavy 1	8	-4	D6	-
Twin lascannon	48"	Heavy 2	9	-3	D6	-
Trueclaw	Melee	Melee	+5	-4	D6	You can re-roll failed wound rolls for this weapon.

WARGEAR OPTIONS	• Bjorn the Fell-Handed may replace his assault cannon with a helfrost cannon, heavy plasma cannon or twin lascannon.

ABILITIES	**And They Shall Know No Fear** (pg 130) **Ancient Tactician:** If your army is Battle-forged, you receive 1 additional Command Point if it includes Bjorn the Fell-Handed. **Last of the Company of Russ:** You can re-roll hit rolls of 1 for friendly **SPACE WOLVES** units that are within 6" of Bjorn the Fell-Handed.	**Legendary Tenacity:** Roll a D6 each time Bjorn the Fell-Handed loses a wound; on a roll of 5+ that wound is not lost. **Smoke Launchers:** Once per game, instead of shooting any weapons in the Shooting phase, Bjorn the Fell-Handed can use his Smoke Launchers; until your next Shooting phase your opponent must subtract 1 from all hit rolls for ranged weapons that target him.

FACTION KEYWORDS	**IMPERIUM, ADEPTUS ASTARTES, SPACE WOLVES**
KEYWORDS	**CHARACTER, VEHICLE, DREADNOUGHT, BJORN THE FELL-HANDED**

Bjorn the Fell-Handed leads his ancient brothers into battle against the Daemons of Tzeentch.

BLOOD CLAWS

NAME	M	WS	BS	S	T	W	A	Ld	Sv
Blood Claw	6"	3+	4+	4	4	1	1	7	3+
Blood Claw Pack Leader	6"	3+	4+	4	4	1	2	7	3+
Wolf Guard Pack Leader	6"	3+	3+	4	4	1	2	8	3+
Wolf Guard Pack Leader in Terminator Armour	5"	3+	3+	4	4	2	2	8	2+

This unit contains 1 Blood Claw Pack Leader and 4 Blood Claws. It can include up to 5 additional Blood Claws (**Power Rating +4**) or up to 10 additional Blood Claws (**Power Rating +8**). It can also include either a Wolf Guard Pack Leader (**Power Rating +2**) or a Wolf Guard Pack Leader in Terminator Armour (**Power Rating +3**).

- The Blood Claws, Blood Claw Pack Leader and Wolf Guard Pack Leader are each armed with a chainsword, bolt pistol, frag grenades and krak grenades.
- A Wolf Guard Pack Leader in Terminator Armour is armed with a power sword and storm bolter.

WEAPON	RANGE	TYPE	S	AP	D	ABILITIES
Bolt pistol	12"	Pistol 1	4	0	1	-
Plasma pistol	When attacking with this weapon, choose one of the profiles below.					
- Standard	12"	Pistol 1	7	-3	1	-
- Supercharge	12"	Pistol 1	8	-3	2	On a hit roll of 1, the bearer is slain.
Storm bolter	24"	Rapid Fire 2	4	0	1	-
Chainsword	Melee	Melee	User	0	1	Each time the bearer fights, it can make 1 additional attack with this weapon.
Power axe	Melee	Melee	+1	-2	1	-
Power fist	Melee	Melee	x2	-3	D3	When attacking with this weapon, you must subtract 1 from the hit roll.
Power sword	Melee	Melee	User	-3	1	-
Frag grenade	6"	Grenade D6	3	0	1	-
Krak grenade	6"	Grenade 1	6	-1	D3	-

WARGEAR OPTIONS	
	- One Blood Claw may replace his chainsword with an item from the *Space Wolves Special Weapons* list. If the unit includes 15 models, one additional Blood Claw may also do this.
	- One Blood Claw may replace his bolt pistol with a plasma pistol.
	- The Blood Claw Pack Leader may replace his chainsword with a power sword, power axe or power fist.
	- The Wolf Guard Pack Leader may replace his chainsword with an item from the *Space Wolves Melee Weapons* list; he may also replace his bolt pistol with a plasma pistol or an item from the *Space Wolves Combi-weapons* list.
	- The Wolf Guard Pack Leader in Terminator Armour may replace his power sword with an item from the *Space Wolves Terminator Melee Weapons* list; he may also replace his storm bolter with a storm shield or an item from the *Space Wolves Combi-weapons* list.

ABILITIES	
And They Shall Know No Fear (pg 130)	**Headstrong:** Unless this unit contains a Wolf Guard Pack Leader or Wolf Guard Pack Leader in Terminator Armour, or is within 6" of a friendly **WOLF GUARD**, it must declare a charge in its Charge phase if it is possible to do so.
Berserk Charge: On a turn in which they make a successful charge, you can make 1 additional attack in the Fight phase with all models in this unit.	
Storm shield: A model equipped with a storm shield has a 3+ invulnerable save.	**Crux Terminatus:** A Wolf Guard Pack Leader in Terminator Armour has a 5+ invulnerable save.

FACTION KEYWORDS	IMPERIUM, ADEPTUS ASTARTES, SPACE WOLVES
KEYWORDS	INFANTRY, BLOOD CLAWS

LUKAS THE TRICKSTER

6 POWER

NAME	M	WS	BS	S	T	W	A	Ld	Sv
Lukas the Trickster	6"	2+	3+	4	4	4	4	8	3+

Lukas the Trickster is a single model armed with the Claw of the Jackalwolf, a plasma pistol, frag grenades and krak grenades. Only one of this model may be included in your army.

WEAPON	RANGE	TYPE	S	AP	D	ABILITIES
Plasma pistol	When attacking with this weapon, choose one of the profiles below.					
- Standard	12"	Pistol 1	7	-3	1	-
- Supercharge	12"	Pistol 1	8	-3	2	On a hit roll of 1, the bearer is slain.
Claw of the Jackalwolf	Melee	Melee	+1	-2	2	You can re-roll failed wound rolls for this weapon.
Frag grenade	6"	Grenade D6	3	0	1	-
Krak grenade	6"	Grenade 1	6	-1	D3	-

ABILITIES

And They Shall Know No Fear (pg 130)

Blood Claws Hero: You can add 1 to hit rolls you make for friendly **BLOOD CLAW** units within 6" of Lukas the Trickster.

Master of Mischief: Subtract 1 from the Leadership of all units (friend or foe) within 3" of Lukas the Trickster at the start of the Morale phase for the duration of the phase.

The Last Laugh: If Lukas the Trickster is slain in the Fight phase, both players roll a dice, re-rolling ties: if you roll lowest, nothing happens; if you roll highest, the unit that landed the blow immediately suffers D6 mortal wounds.

Pelt of the Doppegangrel: Your opponent must subtract 1 from any hit rolls for attacks that target Lukas the Trickster in the Fight phase.

FACTION KEYWORDS	IMPERIUM, ADEPTUS ASTARTES, SPACE WOLVES
KEYWORDS	CHARACTER, INFANTRY, BLOOD CLAW, LUKAS THE TRICKSTER

Lukas the Trickster lunges into the fight with a mocking grin upon his feral features.

GREY HUNTERS

NAME	M	WS	BS	S	T	W	A	Ld	Sv
Grey Hunter	6"	3+	3+	4	4	1	1	7	3+
Grey Hunter Pack Leader	6"	3+	3+	4	4	1	2	7	3+
Wolf Guard Pack Leader	6"	3+	3+	4	4	1	2	8	3+
Wolf Guard Pack Leader in Terminator Armour	5"	3+	3+	4	4	2	2	8	2+

This unit contains 1 Grey Hunter Pack Leader and 4 Grey Hunters. It can include up to 5 additional Grey Hunters (**Power Rating +5**). It can also include either a Wolf Guard Pack Leader (**Power Rating +2**) or a Wolf Guard Pack Leader in Terminator Armour (**Power Rating +3**).
• The Grey Hunters and Grey Hunter Pack Leader are each armed with a boltgun, bolt pistol, frag grenades and krak grenades.
• A Wolf Guard Pack Leader is armed with a chainsword, bolt pistol, frag grenades and krak grenades.
• A Wolf Guard Pack Leader in Terminator Armour is armed with a power sword and storm bolter.

WEAPON	RANGE	TYPE	S	AP	D	ABILITIES
Bolt pistol	12"	Pistol 1	4	0	1	-
Boltgun	24"	Rapid Fire 1	4	0	1	-
Plasma pistol	When attacking with this weapon, choose one of the profiles below.					
- Standard	12"	Pistol 1	7	-3	1	-
- Supercharge	12"	Pistol 1	8	-3	2	On a hit roll of 1, the bearer is slain.
Storm bolter	24"	Rapid Fire 2	4	0	1	-
Chainsword	Melee	Melee	User	0	1	Each time the bearer fights, it can make 1 additional attack with this weapon.
Power axe	Melee	Melee	1	-2	1	-
Power fist	Melee	Melee	x2	-3	D3	When attacking with this weapon, you must subtract 1 from the hit roll.
Power sword	Melee	Melee	User	-3	1	-
Frag grenade	6"	Grenade D6	3	0	1	-
Krak grenade	6"	Grenade 1	6	-1	D3	-

WARGEAR OPTIONS	
	• Any Grey Hunter may take a chainsword.
	• One Grey Hunter may take a wolf standard.
	• For each five models in the unit, one Grey Hunter may replace his boltgun with an item from the *Space Wolves Special Weapons* list.
	• One Grey Hunter may replace his bolt pistol with a plasma pistol.
	• The Grey Hunter Pack Leader may take a chainsword, power axe, power fist or power sword.
	• The Wolf Guard Pack Leader may replace his chainsword with an item from the *Space Wolves Melee Weapons* list; he may also replace his bolt pistol with a plasma pistol or an item from the *Space Wolves Combi-weapons* list.
	• The Wolf Guard Pack Leader in Terminator Armour may replace his power sword with an item from the *Space Wolves Terminator Melee Weapons* list; he may also replace his storm bolter with a storm shield or an item from the *Space Wolves Combi-weapons* list.

ABILITIES	
	And They Shall Know No Fear (pg 130)
	Wolf Standard: You can re-roll any dice rolls of 1 when making an Advance or charge move for a unit that has a wolf standard.
	Crux Terminatus: A Wolf Guard Pack Leader in Terminator Armour has a 5+ invulnerable save.
	Storm Shield: A model equipped with a storm shield has a 3+ invulnerable save.

FACTION KEYWORDS	**IMPERIUM, ADEPTUS ASTARTES, SPACE WOLVES**
KEYWORDS	**INFANTRY, GREY HUNTERS**

IRON PRIEST

An Iron Priest is a single model armed with a thunder hammer, boltgun, servo-arm, frag grenades and krak grenades.

NAME	M	WS	BS	S	T	W	A	Ld	Sv
Iron Priest	6"	2+	3+	4	4	4	3	8	2+

WEAPON	RANGE	TYPE	S	AP	D	ABILITIES
Bolt pistol	12"	Pistol 1	4	0	1	-
Boltgun	24"	Rapid Fire 1	4	0	1	-
Helfrost pistol	12"	Pistol 1	8	-4	D3	If a model suffers any unsaved wounds from this weapon but is not slain, roll a D6; on a 6, the target suffers a mortal wound.
Servo-arm	Melee	Melee	x2	-2	3	Each servo-arm can only be used to make one attack each time this model fights. When a model attacks with this weapon, you must subtract 1 from the hit roll.
Tempest hammer	Melee	Melee	x2	-3	3	If a model suffers any unsaved wounds from this weapon but is not slain, roll a D6; on a 6, the target suffers a mortal wound.
Thunder hammer	Melee	Melee	x2	-3	3	When attacking with this weapon, you must subtract 1 from the hit roll.
Frag grenade	6"	Grenade D6	3	0	1	-
Krak grenade	6"	Grenade 1	6	-1	D3	-

WARGEAR OPTIONS	• This model may replace its thunder hammer with a tempest hammer. • This model may replace its boltgun with a bolt pistol or a helfrost pistol.
ABILITIES	**And They Shall Know No Fear** (pg 130) **Battlesmith:** At the end of your Movement phase, this model can repair a single **SPACE WOLVES VEHICLE** within 1" of him. That model immediately regains D3 wounds lost earlier in the battle. A model can only be repaired once per turn.
FACTION KEYWORDS	**IMPERIUM, ADEPTUS ASTARTES, SPACE WOLVES**
KEYWORDS	**CHARACTER, INFANTRY, IRON PRIEST**

From tempest hammers to helfrost pistols, Iron Priests wield many ancient and terrifying weapons of war.

IRON PRIEST
ON BIKE

6 POWER

NAME	M	WS	BS	S	T	W	A	Ld	Sv
Iron Priest on Bike	14"	2+	3+	4	5	5	3	8	2+

An Iron Priest on Bike is a single model armed with a thunder hammer, boltgun, servo-arm, frag grenades and krak grenades. He rides into battle on a Space Marine bike equipped with a twin boltgun.

WEAPON	RANGE	TYPE	S	AP	D	ABILITIES
Bolt pistol	12"	Pistol 1	4	0	1	-
Boltgun	24"	Rapid Fire 1	4	0	1	-
Helfrost pistol	12"	Pistol 1	8	-4	D3	If a model suffers any unsaved wounds from this weapon but is not slain, roll a D6; on a 6, the target suffers a mortal wound.
Plasma pistol	When attacking with this weapon, choose one of the profiles below.					
- Standard	12"	Pistol 1	7	-3	1	-
- Supercharge	12"	Pistol 1	8	-3	2	On a hit roll of 1, the bearer is slain.
Twin boltgun	24"	Rapid fire 2	4	0	1	-
Servo-arm	Melee	Melee	x2	-2	3	Each servo-arm can only be used to make one attack each time this model fights. When a model attacks with this weapon, you must subtract 1 from the hit roll.
Tempest hammer	Melee	Melee	x2	-3	3	If a model suffers any unsaved wounds from this weapon but is not slain, roll a D6; on a 6, the target suffers a mortal wound.
Thunder hammer	Melee	Melee	x2	-3	3	When attacking with this weapon, you must subtract 1 from the hit roll.
Frag grenade	6"	Grenade D6	3	0	1	-
Krak grenade	6"	Grenade 1	6	-1	D3	-

WARGEAR OPTIONS	• This model may replace its thunder hammer with a tempest hammer. • This model may replace its boltgun with a bolt pistol or a helfrost pistol.
ABILITIES	**And They Shall Know No Fear** (pg 130) **Turbo-boost:** When this model Advances, add 6" to its Move characteristic for that Movement phase instead of rolling a dice.	**Battlesmith:** At the end of your Movement phase, if he didn't move more than 6", this model can repair a single SPACE WOLVES VEHICLE within 1" of him. That model immediately regains D3 wounds lost earlier in the battle. A model can only be repaired once per turn.
FACTION KEYWORDS	**IMPERIUM, ADEPTUS ASTARTES, SPACE WOLVES**
KEYWORDS	**BIKER, CHARACTER, IRON PRIEST**

IRON PRIEST
on Thunderwolf

7 POWER

NAME	M	WS	BS	S	T	W	A	Ld	Sv
Iron Priest on Thunderwolf	10"	2+	3+	4	5	6	3	8	2+

An Iron Priest on Thunderwolf is a single model armed with a thunder hammer, boltgun, servo-arm, frag grenades and krak grenades. His Thunderwolf attacks with its crushing teeth and claws.

WEAPON	RANGE	TYPE	S	AP	D	ABILITIES
Iron Priest						
Bolt pistol	12"	Pistol 1	4	0	1	-
Boltgun	24"	Rapid Fire 1	4	0	1	-
Helfrost pistol	12"	Pistol 1	8	-4	D3	If a model suffers any unsaved wounds from this weapon but is not slain, roll a D6; on a 6, the target suffers a mortal wound.
Plasma pistol	When attacking with this weapon, choose one of the profiles below.					
- Standard	12"	Pistol 1	7	-3	1	-
- Supercharge	12"	Pistol 1	8	-3	2	On a hit roll of 1, the bearer is slain.
Servo-arm	Melee	Melee	x2	-2	3	Each servo-arm can only be used to make one attack each time this model fights. When a model attacks with this weapon, you must subtract 1 from the hit roll.
Tempest hammer	Melee	Melee	x2	-3	3	If a model suffers any unsaved wounds from this weapon but is not slain, roll a D6; on a 6, the target suffers a mortal wound.
Thunder hammer	Melee	Melee	x2	-3	3	When attacking with this weapon, you must subtract 1 from the hit roll.
Frag grenade	6"	Grenade D6	3	0	1	-
Krak grenade	6"	Grenade 1	6	-1	D3	-
Thunderwolf						
Crushing teeth and claws	Melee	Melee	5	-1	1	After a model on this mount makes its close combat attacks, you can attack with its mount. Make 3 additional attacks, using this weapon profile.

WARGEAR OPTIONS	• This model may replace its thunder hammer with a tempest hammer. • This model may replace its boltgun with a bolt pistol or a helfrost pistol.
ABILITIES	**And They Shall Know No Fear** (pg 130) **Battlesmith:** At the end of your Movement phase, if he didn't move more than 6", this model can repair a single SPACE WOLVES VEHICLE within 1" of him. That model immediately regains D3 wounds lost earlier in the battle. A model can only be repaired once per turn.
FACTION KEYWORDS	IMPERIUM, ADEPTUS ASTARTES, SPACE WOLVES
KEYWORDS	CAVALRY, CHARACTER, THUNDERWOLF, IRON PRIEST

CYBERWOLVES

1 POWER

NAME	M	WS	BS	S	T	W	A	Ld	Sv
Cyberwolf	10"	3+	-	4	4	2	3	4	4+

This unit contains 1 Cyberwolf. It can include up to 4 additional Cyberwolves (**Power Rating +1 per model**). Each model attacks with its teeth and claws.

WEAPON	RANGE	TYPE	S	AP	D	ABILITIES
Teeth and claws	Melee	Melee	User	-1	1	-

ABILITIES	**Swift Hunters:** You can re-roll failed charge rolls for this unit.
FACTION KEYWORDS	IMPERIUM, ADEPTUS ASTARTES, SPACE WOLVES
KEYWORDS	BEAST, CYBERWOLVES

WOLF SCOUTS

4 POWER

NAME	M	WS	BS	S	T	W	A	Ld	Sv
Wolf Scout	6"	3+	3+	4	4	1	1	7	4+
Wolf Scout Pack Leader	6"	3+	3+	4	4	1	2	7	4+
Wolf Guard Pack Leader	6"	3+	3+	4	4	1	2	8	3+

This unit contains 1 Wolf Scout Pack Leader and 4 Wolf Scouts. It can include up to 5 additional Wolf Scouts (**Power Rating +4**). It can also include a Wolf Guard Pack Leader (**Power Rating +2**).
• The Wolf Scouts and Wolf Scout Pack Leader are each armed with a boltgun, bolt pistol, frag grenades and krak grenades.
• A Wolf Guard Pack Leader is armed with a boltgun, bolt pistol, frag grenades and krak grenades.

WEAPON	RANGE	TYPE	S	AP	D	ABILITIES
Astartes shotgun	12"	Assault 2	4	0	1	If the target is within half range, add 1 to this weapon's Strength.
Bolt pistol	12"	Pistol 1	4	0	1	-
Boltgun	24"	Rapid Fire 1	4	0	1	-
Heavy bolter	36"	Heavy 3	5	-1	1	-
Missile launcher	When attacking with this weapon, choose one of the profiles below.					
- Frag missile	48"	Heavy D6	4	0	1	-
- Krak missile	48"	Heavy 1	8	-2	D6	-
Plasma pistol	When attacking with this weapon, choose one of the profiles below.					
- Standard	12"	Pistol 1	7	-3	1	-
- Supercharge	12"	Pistol 1	8	-3	2	On a hit roll of 1, the bearer is slain.
Sniper rifle	36"	Heavy 1	4	0	1	This weapon may target a **CHARACTER** even if it is not the closest enemy unit. If you roll a wound roll of 6+ for this weapon, it inflicts a mortal wound in addition to its normal damage.
Chainsword	Melee	Melee	User	0	1	Each time the bearer fights, it can make 1 additional attack with this weapon.
Combat knife	Melee	Melee	User	0	1	Each time the bearer fights, it can make 1 additional attack with this weapon.
Frag grenade	6"	Grenade D6	3	0	1	-
Krak grenade	6"	Grenade 1	6	-1	D3	-

WARGEAR OPTIONS	
	• Any Wolf Scout or Wolf Scout Pack Leader may take a camo cloak. • Any Wolf Scout or Wolf Scout Pack Leader replace its boltgun with a chainsword, combat knife, sniper rifle or Astartes shotgun. • One Wolf Scout may replace his boltgun with a heavy bolter, missile launcher or an item from the *Space Wolves Special Weapons* list. • One Wolf Scout may replace his boltgun with an item from the *Space Wolves Melee Weapons* list, or replace his bolt pistol with a plasma pistol. • The Wolf Scout Pack Leader may replace his boltgun with an item from the *Space Wolves Melee Weapons* list, or replace his bolt pistol with a plasma pistol. • The Wolf Guard Pack Leader may replace his boltgun with an item from the *Space Wolves Melee Weapons* list; he may also replace his bolt pistol with a plasma pistol or an item from the *Space Wolves Combi-weapons* list.

ABILITIES	
	And They Shall Know No Fear (pg 130) **Camo Cloaks:** If every model in a unit has a camo cloak you can add 2 to saving throws made for models in the unit when they receive the benefits of cover, instead of 1.	**Behind Enemy Lines:** During deployment, you can set up this unit behind enemy lines instead of placing it on the battlefield. At the end of any of your Movement phases the unit can join the battle – set it up so that he is within 6" of any battlefield edge of your choice and more than 9" away from any enemy models.

FACTION KEYWORDS	**IMPERIUM, ADEPTUS ASTARTES, SPACE WOLVES**
KEYWORDS	**INFANTRY, SCOUT, WOLF SCOUTS**

WULFEN

NAME	M	WS	BS	S	T	W	A	Ld	Sv
Wulfen	7"	3+	5+	5	4	2	3	7	4+
Wulfen Pack Leader	7"	3+	5+	5	4	2	4	7	4+

This unit contains 1 Wulfen Pack Leader and 4 Wulfen. It can include up to 5 additional Wulfen (**Power Rating +13**).
• Each Wulfen fights with its Wulfen claws.
• The Wulfen Pack Leader is armed with frost claws.

WEAPON	RANGE	TYPE	S	AP	D	ABILITIES
Stormfrag auto-launcher	12"	Assault D3	4	0	1	-
Frost claws	Melee	Melee	+1	-2	1	Each time the bearer fights, it can make 1 additional attack with this weapon. You can re-roll failed wound rolls for this weapon.
Great frost axe	Melee	Melee	+3	-3	D3	The bearer can make 1 additional attack with this weapon on a turn in which it has charged.
Thunder hammer	Melee	Melee	x2	-3	3	When attacking with this weapon, you must subtract 1 from the hit roll.
Wulfen claws	Melee	Melee	User	-1	1	-

WARGEAR OPTIONS	• Any model may take a stormfrag auto-launcher. • Any Wulfen may replace their Wulfen claws with frost claws, a great frost axe or a thunder hammer and storm shield.

ABILITIES	**And They Shall Know No Fear** (pg 130) **Bounding Lope:** Models in this unit can Advance and charge in the same turn, and can re-roll failed charge rolls. **Death Frenzy:** Roll a D6 each time a model in this unit loses a wound; on a roll of 5+ that wound is not lost. If a model in this unit is slain in the Fight phase, once the unit that slew them has made its attacks, you can attack with them before removing their model as casualty, even if they have already attacked that phase. **Storm Shield:** A model equipped with a storm shield has a 3+ invulnerable save.	**Curse of the Wulfen (Hunt):** You can re-roll failed charge rolls for friendly **SPACE WOLVES INFANTRY**, **BIKER** and **CAVALRY** units that are within 6" of this unit at the start of the Charge phase. This range of this ability is doubled to 12" for friendly **BLOOD CLAW** units. Units of Wulfen are never affected by this ability. **Curse of the Wulfen (Kill):** You can make 1 additional attack for models in friendly **SPACE WOLVES INFANTRY**, **BIKER** and **CAVALRY** units that are within 6" of this unit when they make their attacks. This range of this ability is doubled to 12" for friendly **BLOOD CLAW** units. Units of Wulfen are never affected by this ability, nor are units that have already been affected by the Curse of the Wulfen (Hunt) earlier in the turn.

FACTION KEYWORDS	IMPERIUM, ADEPTUS ASTARTES, SPACE WOLVES

KEYWORDS	INFANTRY, WULFEN

The Wulfen lope into battle with ferocious howls, swinging their outsized weapons with feral fury.

LONE WOLF

5 POWER

NAME	M	WS	BS	S	T	W	A	Ld	Sv
Lone Wolf	6"	2+	3+	4	4	3	3	8	3+

A Lone Wolf is a single model armed with a chainsword, bolt pistol, frag grenades and krak grenades.

WEAPON	RANGE	TYPE	S	AP	D	ABILITIES
Bolt pistol	12"	Pistol 1	4	0	1	-
Plasma pistol	When attacking with this weapon, choose one of the profiles below.					
- Standard	12"	Pistol 1	7	-3	1	-
- Supercharge	12"	Pistol 1	8	-3	2	On a hit roll of 1, the bearer is slain.
Chainsword	Melee	Melee	User	0	1	Each time the bearer fights, it can make 1 additional attack with this weapon.
Frag grenade	6"	Grenade D6	3	0	1	-
Krak grenade	6"	Grenade 1	6	-1	D3	-

WARGEAR OPTIONS

- This model may replace its chainsword with an item from the *Space Wolves Melee Weapons* list.
- This model may replace its bolt pistol with a storm shield, plasma pistol or an item from the *Space Wolves Combi-weapons* list.

ABILITIES

And They Shall Know No Fear (pg 130)

A Glorious Death…: Roll a D6 each time this model loses his final wound; on a roll of 4+ that wound is not lost. In addition, if this model is slain in the Fight phase, once the unit that slew him has made its attacks, you can attack with him before removing his model as casualty, even if he has already attacked that phase.

…Worthy of a Saga: You can re-roll failed wound rolls of 1 for this model when attacking a **CHARACTER** or **MONSTER** in the Fight phase.

An Army of One: This model can never have a Warlord Trait.

Storm Shield: A model equipped with a storm shield has a 3+ invulnerable save.

FACTION KEYWORDS

IMPERIUM, ADEPTUS ASTARTES, SPACE WOLVES

KEYWORDS

CHARACTER, INFANTRY, LONE WOLF

Every Lone Wolf goes to battle determined to avenge his fallen pack-mates.

LONE WOLF
IN TERMINATOR ARMOUR

7 POWER

NAME	M	WS	BS	S	T	W	A	Ld	Sv
Lone Wolf in Terminator Armour	5"	2+	3+	4	4	4	3	9	2+

A Lone Wolf in Terminator Armour is a single model armed with a power sword and storm bolter.

WEAPON	RANGE	TYPE	S	AP	D	ABILITIES
Storm bolter	24"	Rapid Fire 2	4	0	1	-
Power sword	Melee	Melee	User	-3	1	-

WARGEAR OPTIONS	
	• This model may replace its power sword with an item from the *Space Wolves Terminator Melee Weapons* list. • This model may replace its storm bolter with a storm shield or an item from the *Space Wolves Combi-weapons* list.

ABILITIES	
	And They Shall Know No Fear (pg 130) **Teleport Strike:** During deployment, you can set up this model in a teleportarium chamber instead of placing it on the battlefield. At the end of any of your Movement phases this model can use a teleport strike to arrive on the battlefield – set it up anywhere on the battlefield that is more than 9" away from any enemy models. **Crux Terminatus:** This model has a 5+ invulnerable save. **Storm Shield:** A model equipped with a storm shield has a 3+ invulnerable save.	**A Glorious Death…:** Roll a D6 each time this model loses his final wound; on a roll of 4+ that wound is not lost. In addition, if this model is slain in the Fight phase, once the unit that slew him has made its attacks, you can attack with him before removing his model as casualty, even if he has already attacked that phase. **…Worthy of a Saga:** You can re-roll failed wound rolls of 1 for this model when attacking a **CHARACTER** or **MONSTER** in the Fight phase. **An Army of One:** This model can never have a Warlord Trait.

FACTION KEYWORDS	IMPERIUM, ADEPTUS ASTARTES, SPACE WOLVES
KEYWORDS	CHARACTER, INFANTRY, TERMINATOR, LONE WOLF

MURDERFANG

10 POWER

NAME	M	WS	BS	S	T	W	A	Ld	Sv
Murderfang	8"	2+	3+	6	7	8	5	8	3+

Murderfang is a single model armed with the Murderclaws, a storm bolter and a heavy flamer. Only one of this model may be included in your army.

WEAPON	RANGE	TYPE	S	AP	D	ABILITIES
Heavy flamer	8"	Heavy D6	5	-1	1	This weapon automatically hits its target.
Storm bolter	24"	Rapid Fire 2	4	0	1	-
The Murderclaws	Melee	Melee	x2	-3	3	You can re-roll failed wound rolls for this weapon.

ABILITIES	
	And They Shall Know No Fear (pg 130) **Murderlust:** You can re-roll any failed charge rolls for Murderfang.

FACTION KEYWORDS	IMPERIUM, ADEPTUS ASTARTES, SPACE WOLVES
KEYWORDS	CHARACTER, VEHICLE, DREADNOUGHT, MURDERFANG

WOLF GUARD

NAME	M	WS	BS	S	T	W	A	Ld	Sv
Wolf Guard	6"	3+	3+	4	4	1	2	8	3+
Wolf Guard Pack Leader	6"	3+	3+	4	4	1	3	8	3+

This unit contains 1 Wolf Guard Pack Leader and 4 Wolf Guard. It can include up to 5 additional Wolf Guard (**Power Rating +9**). Each model is armed with a boltgun, bolt pistol, frag grenades and krak grenades.

WEAPON	RANGE	TYPE	S	AP	D	ABILITIES
Bolt pistol	12"	Pistol 1	4	0	1	-
Boltgun	24"	Rapid Fire 1	4	0	1	-
Plasma pistol	When attacking with this weapon, choose one of the profiles below.					
- Standard	12"	Pistol 1	7	-3	1	-
- Supercharge	12"	Pistol 1	8	-3	2	On a hit roll of 1, the bearer is slain.
Chainsword	Melee	Melee	User	0	1	Each time the bearer fights, it can make 1 additional attack with this weapon.
Frag grenade	6"	Grenade D6	3	0	1	-
Krak grenade	6"	Grenade 1	6	-1	D3	-

WARGEAR OPTIONS	• Any model may replace its boltgun with an item from the *Space Wolves Combi-weapons* list.
	• Any model may take an item from the *Space Wolves Melee Weapons* list.
	• Any model may replace its bolt pistol with a storm shield, plasma pistol or an item from the *Space Wolves Melee Weapons* list.
	• The entire unit may take jump packs (**Power Rating +1 per 5 models**). If it does, its Move characteristic becomes 12" and it gains the **JUMP PACK** and **FLY** keywords.

ABILITIES	**And They Shall Know No Fear** (pg 130)	**Jump Pack Assault:** If this unit has jump packs, when you set it up during deployment, it can be set up high in the skies, ready to strike, instead of being placed on the battlefield. If it is, it can make a sudden assault to arrive on the battlefield at the end of any of your Movement phases; when it does so set it up anywhere that is more than 9" from any enemy models.
	Storm Shield: A model equipped with a storm shield has a 3+ invulnerable save.	

FACTION KEYWORDS	**IMPERIUM, ADEPTUS ASTARTES, SPACE WOLVES**
KEYWORDS	**INFANTRY, WOLF GUARD**

Each member of a Wolf Guard pack is a hero with a mighty wyrd, saga-sung warriors who fight with their favoured weapons.

WOLF GUARD
on Bikes

NAME	M	WS	BS	S	T	W	A	Ld	Sv
Wolf Guard on Bike	14"	3+	3+	4	5	2	2	8	3+
Wolf Guard Pack Leader on Bike	14"	3+	3+	4	5	2	3	8	3+

This unit contains 1 Wolf Guard Pack Leader on Bike and 4 Wolf Guard on Bikes. It can include up to 5 additional Wolf Guard on Bikes (**Power Rating +14**). Each model is armed with a chainsword, bolt pistol, frag grenades and krak grenades and rides into battle on a Space Marine bike equipped with a twin boltgun.

WEAPON	RANGE	TYPE	S	AP	D	ABILITIES
Bolt pistol	12"	Pistol 1	4	0	1	-
Boltgun	24"	Rapid Fire 1	4	0	1	-
Plasma pistol	When attacking with this weapon, choose one of the profiles below.					
- Standard	12"	Pistol 1	7	-3	1	-
- Supercharge	12"	Pistol 1	8	-3	2	On a hit roll of 1, the bearer is slain.
Twin boltgun	24"	Rapid fire 2	4	0	1	-
Chainsword	Melee	Melee	User	0	1	Each time the bearer fights, it can make 1 additional attack with this weapon.
Frag grenade	6"	Grenade D6	3	0	1	-
Krak grenade	6"	Grenade 1	6	-1	D3	-

WARGEAR OPTIONS	
	• Any model may take a boltgun or an item from the *Space Wolves Combi-weapons* list.
	• Any model may replace its chainsword with an item from the *Space Wolves Melee Weapons* list.
	• Any model may replace its bolt pistol with a storm shield, plasma pistol or an item from the *Space Wolves Melee Weapons* list.

ABILITIES	
And They Shall Know No Fear (pg 130)	**Turbo-boost:** When this unit Advances, add 6" to its Move characteristic for that Movement phase instead of rolling a dice.
Storm Shield: A model equipped with a storm shield has a 3+ invulnerable save.	

FACTION KEYWORDS	IMPERIUM, ADEPTUS ASTARTES, SPACE WOLVES
KEYWORDS	BIKER, WOLF GUARD

ARJAC ROCKFIST

NAME	M	WS	BS	S	T	W	A	Ld	Sv
Arjac Rockfist	5"	2+	3+	5	4	5	4	8	2+

Arjac Rockfist is a single model armed with Foehammer. Only one of this model may be included in your army.

WEAPON	RANGE	TYPE	S	AP	D	ABILITIES
Foehammer (shooting)	12"	Assault 1	x2	-3	D3	When attacking **CHARACTERS** or **MONSTERS**, this weapon has a Damage of 3.
Foehammer (melee)	Melee	Melee	x2	-3	D3	

ABILITIES	
And They Shall Know No Fear (pg 130)	**Teleport Strike:** During deployment, you can set up Arjac Rockfist in his Strike Cruiser's teleportarium instead of placing him on the battlefield. At the end of any of your Movement phases he can use a teleport strike to arrive on the battlefield – set him up anywhere on the battlefield that is more than 9" away from any enemy models.
The Anvil Shield: Arjac Rockfist has a 3+ invulnerable save. In addition, reduce all damage suffered by Arjac Rockfist by 1 (to a minimum of 1).	
Champion of the Kingsguard: You can re-roll failed hit rolls for Arjac Rockfist in the Fight phase when targeting a **CHARACTER**. In addition, you can make 1 additional attack in the Fight phase for all models in friendly **WOLF GUARD** units within 6" of Arjac Rockfist at the start of the phase.	**Thane to the High King:** You can re-roll wound rolls of 1 for friendly **SPACE WOLVES** units that are within 6" of this model.

FACTION KEYWORDS	IMPERIUM, ADEPTUS ASTARTES, SPACE WOLVES
KEYWORDS	CHARACTER, INFANTRY, TERMINATOR, WOLF GUARD, ARJAC ROCKFIST

WOLF GUARD
IN TERMINATOR ARMOUR

15 POWER

NAME	M	WS	BS	S	T	W	A	Ld	Sv
Wolf Guard in Terminator Armour	5"	3+	3+	4	4	2	2	8	2+
Wolf Guard Pack Leader in Terminator Armour	5"	3+	3+	4	4	2	3	8	2+

This unit contains 1 Wolf Guard Pack Leader in Terminator Armour and 4 Wolf Guard in Terminator Armour. It can include up to 5 additional Wolf Guard in Terminator Armour (**Power Rating +15**).
- Each Wolf Guard in Terminator Armour is armed with a power fist and storm bolter.
- The Wolf Guard Pack Leader in Terminator Armour is armed with a power sword and storm bolter.

WEAPON	RANGE	TYPE	S	AP	D	ABILITIES
Cyclone missile launcher	When attacking with this weapon, choose one of the profiles below.					
- Frag missile	36"	Heavy 2D3	4	0	1	-
- Krak missile	36"	Heavy 2	8	-2	D6	-
Storm bolter	24"	Rapid Fire 2	4	0	1	-
Power fist	Melee	Melee	x2	-3	D3	When attacking with this weapon, you must subtract 1 from the hit roll.
Power sword	Melee	Melee	User	-3	1	-

WARGEAR OPTIONS	
	• Any model may replace its power fist or power sword with an item from the *Space Wolves Terminator Melee Weapons* list.
	• Any model may replace its storm bolter with a storm shield or an item from the *Space Wolves Combi-weapons* or *Space Wolves Terminator Melee Weapons* lists.
	• For each five models, one Wolf Guard in Terminator Armour may take a cyclone missile launcher or replace their storm bolter with an item from the *Terminator Heavy Weapons* list.

ABILITIES		
	And They Shall Know No Fear (pg 130)	**Teleport Strike:** During deployment, you can set up this unit in a teleportarium chamber instead of placing it on the battlefield. At the end of any of your Movement phases this unit can use a teleport strike to arrive on the battlefield – set it up anywhere on the battlefield that is more than 9" away from any enemy models.
	Crux Terminatus: All models in this unit have a 5+ invulnerable save.	
	Storm Shield: A model equipped with a storm shield has a 3+ invulnerable save.	

FACTION KEYWORDS	IMPERIUM, ADEPTUS ASTARTES, SPACE WOLVES
KEYWORDS	INFANTRY, TERMINATOR, WOLF GUARD

SWIFTCLAWS

6 POWER

NAME	M	WS	BS	S	T	W	A	Ld	Sv
Swiftclaw	14"	3+	4+	4	5	2	1	7	3+
Swiftclaw Pack Leader	14"	3+	4+	4	5	2	2	7	3+
Swiftclaw Attack Bike	14"	3+	4+	4	5	4	2	7	3+
Wolf Guard Bike Leader	14"	3+	3+	4	5	2	2	8	3+

This unit contains 1 Swiftclaw Pack Leader and 2 Swiftclaws. It can include up to 3 additional Swiftclaws (**Power Rating +5**) or up to 7 additional Swiftclaws (**Power Rating +11**). It can also include a single Swiftclaw Attack Bike (**Power Rating +3**) and a Wolf Guard Bike Leader (**Power Rating +3**).

- The Swiftclaws and the Swiftclaw Pack Leader are each armed with a bolt pistol, frag grenades and krak grenades, and rides into battle on a Space Marine bike equipped with a twin boltgun.
- The Swiftclaw Attack Bike is crewed by two Swiftclaws armed with bolt pistols, frag grenades and krak grenades, and is itself equipped with a twin boltgun and a heavy bolter.
- A Wolf Guard Bike Leader is armed with a bolt pistol, frag grenades and krak grenades, and rides into battle on a Space Marine bike equipped with a twin boltgun.

WEAPON	RANGE	TYPE	S	AP	D	ABILITIES
Bolt pistol	12"	Pistol 1	4	0	1	-
Heavy bolter	36"	Heavy 3	5	-1	1	-
Multi-melta	24"	Heavy 1	8	-4	D6	If the target is within half range of this weapon, roll two dice when inflicting damage with it and discard the lowest result.
Plasma pistol	When attacking with this weapon, choose one of the profiles below.					
- Standard	12"	Pistol 1	7	-3	1	-
- Supercharge	12"	Pistol 1	8	-3	2	On a hit roll of 1, the bearer is slain.
Twin boltgun	24"	Rapid fire 2	4	0	1	-
Chainsword	Melee	Melee	User	0	1	Each time the bearer fights, it can make 1 additional attack with this weapon.
Frag grenade	6"	Grenade D6	3	0	1	-
Krak grenade	6"	Grenade 1	6	-1	D3	-

WARGEAR OPTIONS	
	- Any model may replace its bolt pistol with a chainsword.
	- One Swiftclaw or Swiftclaw Pack Leader may replace their bolt pistol with a plasma pistol or an item from the *Space Wolves Special Weapons* list.
	- The Swiftclaw Pack Leader may replace his bolt pistol with an item from the *Space Wolves Melee Weapons* list.
	- The Wolf Guard Bike Leader may replace his bolt pistol with an item from the *Space Wolves Melee Weapons* or *Space Wolves Combi-weapons* list.
	- The Swiftclaw Attack Bike may replace its heavy bolter with a multi-melta.

ABILITIES	
	And They Shall Know No Fear (pg 130) **Berserk Charge:** On a turn in which they make a successful charge, you can make 1 additional attack in the Fight phase with all models in the unit.
	Headstrong: Unless this unit contains a Wolf Guard Bike Leader, or is within 6" of a friendly **WOLF GUARD**, it must declare a charge in its Charge phase if it is possible to do so. **Turbo-boost:** When this unit Advances, add 6" to its Move characteristic for that Movement phase instead of rolling a dice.

FACTION KEYWORDS	IMPERIUM, ADEPTUS ASTARTES, SPACE WOLVES
KEYWORDS	BIKER, BLOOD CLAW, SWIFTCLAWS

SWIFTCLAW ATTACK BIKES

NAME	M	WS	BS	S	T	W	A	Ld	Sv
Swiftclaw Attack Bike	14"	3+	4+	4	5	4	2	7	3+

This unit contains 1 Swiftclaw Attack Bike. It can include 1 additional Swiftclaw Attack Bike (**Power Rating +3**) or 2 additional Swiftclaw Attack Bikes (**Power Rating +6**). Each model is crewed by two Swiftclaws armed with bolt pistols, frag grenades and krak grenades, and is itself equipped with a twin boltgun and a heavy bolter.

WEAPON	RANGE	TYPE	S	AP	D	ABILITIES
Bolt pistol	12"	Pistol 1	4	0	1	-
Heavy bolter	36"	Heavy 3	5	-1	1	-
Multi-melta	24"	Heavy 1	8	-4	D6	If the target is within half range of this weapon, roll two dice when inflicting damage with it and discard the lowest result.
Twin boltgun	24"	Rapid fire 2	4	0	1	-
Frag grenade	6"	Grenade D6	3	0	1	-
Krak grenade	6"	Grenade 1	6	-1	D3	-

WARGEAR OPTIONS	• Any model may replace its heavy bolter with a multi-melta.

ABILITIES	**And They Shall Know No Fear** (pg 130)	**Headstrong:** Unless this unit is within 6" of a friendly **Wolf Guard**, it must declare a charge in its Charge phase if it possible to do so.
	Berserk Charge: On a turn in which they make a successful charge, you can make 1 additional attack in the Fight phase with all models in the unit.	**Turbo-boost:** When this unit Advances, add 6" to its Move characteristic for that Movement phase instead of rolling a dice.

FACTION KEYWORDS	**Imperium, Adeptus Astartes, Space Wolves**
KEYWORDS	**Biker, Blood Claw, Swiftclaw Attack Bikes**

Powerful engines howl like feral beasts as the Swiftclaw Bikers speed into battle.

STORMWOLF

DAMAGE
Some of this model's characteristics change as it suffers damage, as shown below:

REMAINING W	M	BS
8-14+	20-50"	3+
4-7	20-35"	4+
1-3	20"	5+

NAME	M	WS	BS	S	T	W	A	Ld	Sv
Stormwolf	*	6+	*	8	7	14	3	8	3+

A Stormwolf is a single model armed with two lascannons, two twin heavy bolters and a twin helfrost cannon.

WEAPON	RANGE	TYPE	S	AP	D	ABILITIES
Lascannon	48"	Heavy 1	9	-3	D6	-
Skyhammer missile launcher	60"	Heavy 3	7	-1	D3	Add 1 to all hit rolls made for this weapon against targets that can FLY. Subtract 1 from the hit rolls made for this weapon against all other targets.
Twin heavy bolter	36"	Heavy 6	5	-1	1	-
Twin helfrost cannon						When attacking with this weapon, choose one of the profiles below. If a model suffers any unsaved wounds from this weapon but is not slain, roll a D6; on a 6, the target suffers a mortal wound.
- Dispersed beam	24"	Heavy 2D3	6	-2	1	-
- Focused beam	24"	Heavy 2	8	-4	D6	-
Twin multi-melta	24"	Heavy 2	8	-4	D6	If the target is within half range of this weapon, roll two dice when inflicting damage with it and discard the lowest result.

WARGEAR OPTIONS	• This model may replace its twin heavy bolters with two twin multi-meltas or a skyhammer missile launcher.
ABILITIES	**Crash and Burn:** If this model is reduced to 0 wounds, roll a D6 before removing it from the battlefield and before any embarked models disembark. On a 6 it crashes in a fiery explosion and each unit within 6" suffers D6 mortal wounds. **Hover Jet:** Before this model moves in your Movement phase, you can declare it will hover. Its Move characteristic becomes 20" until the end of the phase, and it loses the Airborne, Hard to Hit and Supersonic abilities until the beginning of your next Movement phase. **Power of the Machine Spirit:** This model can move and fire Heavy weapons without suffering the penalty to its hit rolls.	**Airborne:** This model cannot charge, can only be charged by units that can Fly, and can only attack or be attacked in the Fight phase by units that can Fly. **Hard to Hit:** Your opponent must subtract 1 from hit rolls for attacks that target this model in the Shooting phase. **Supersonic:** Each time this model moves, first pivot it on the spot up to 90° (this does not contribute to how far the model moves), and then move the model straight forwards. Note that it cannot pivot again after the initial pivot. When this model Advances, increase its Move characteristic by 20" until the end of the phase – do not roll a dice.
TRANSPORT	A Stormwolf can transport 16 SPACE WOLVES INFANTRY models. Each TERMINATOR, JUMP PACK or Wulfen model takes the space of two other models. It may not transport PRIMARIS models.
FACTION KEYWORDS	IMPERIUM, ADEPTUS ASTARTES, SPACE WOLVES
KEYWORDS	VEHICLE, TRANSPORT, FLY, STORMWOLF

THUNDERWOLF CAVALRY

8 POWER

NAME	M	WS	BS	S	T	W	A	Ld	Sv
Thunderwolf Cavalry	10"	3+	3+	4	5	3	2	8	3+
Thunderwolf Cavalry Pack Leader	10"	3+	3+	4	5	3	3	8	3+

This unit contains 1 Thunderwolf Cavalry Pack Leader and 2 Thunderwolf Cavalry. It can include up to 3 additional Thunderwolf Cavalry (**Power Rating +8**). Each model is armed with a chainsword, bolt pistol, frag grenades and krak grenades, and rides to battle atop a fearsome Thunderwolf, who attacks with crushing teeth and claws.

WEAPON	RANGE	TYPE	S	AP	D	ABILITIES
Thunderwolf Cavalry & Thunderwolf Cavalry Pack Leader						
Bolt pistol	12"	Pistol 1	4	0	1	-
Boltgun	24"	Rapid Fire 1	4	0	1	-
Plasma pistol	When attacking with this weapon, choose one of the profiles below.					
- Standard	12"	Pistol 1	7	-3	1	-
- Supercharge	12"	Pistol 1	8	-3	2	On a hit roll of 1, the bearer is slain.
Chainsword	Melee	Melee	User	0	1	Each time the bearer fights, it can make 1 additional attack with this weapon.
Frag grenade	6"	Grenade D6	3	0	1	-
Krak grenade	6"	Grenade 1	6	-1	D3	-
Thunderwolf						
Crushing teeth and claws	Melee	Melee	5	-1	1	After a model on this mount makes its close combat attacks, you can attack with its mount. Make 3 additional attacks, using this weapon profile.

WARGEAR OPTIONS	• Any model may replace its chainsword with an item from the *Space Wolves Melee Weapons* list. • Any model may replace its bolt pistol with a storm shield, boltgun or plasma pistol.

ABILITIES	**And They Shall Know No Fear** (pg 130)	**Storm Shield:** A model equipped with a storm shield has a 3+ invulnerable save.

FACTION KEYWORDS	**IMPERIUM, ADEPTUS ASTARTES, SPACE WOLVES**

KEYWORDS	**CAVALRY, WOLF GUARD, THUNDERWOLF CAVALRY**

FENRISIAN WOLVES

2 POWER

NAME	M	WS	BS	S	T	W	A	Ld	Sv
Fenrisian Wolf	10"	3+	-	4	4	1	2	4	6+
Cyberwolf	10"	3+	-	4	4	2	3	4	4+

This unit contains 5 Fenrisian Wolves. It can include up to 5 additional Fenrisian Wolves (**Power Rating +2**) or up to 10 additional Fenrisian Wolves (**Power Rating +4**). It can also include 1 Cyberwolf (**Power Rating +1**). Each model attacks with its teeth and claws.

WEAPON	RANGE	TYPE	S	AP	D	ABILITIES
Teeth and claws	Melee	Melee	User	-1	1	-

ABILITIES	**Pack Mentality:** Add 1 to this unit's Leadership if it contains 6 or more models, or add 2 instead if the unit contains 10 or more models.	**Swift Hunters:** You can re-roll failed charge rolls for this unit.

FACTION KEYWORDS	**IMPERIUM, ADEPTUS ASTARTES, SPACE WOLVES**

KEYWORDS	**BEAST, FENRISIAN WOLVES**

SKYCLAWS

5 POWER

NAME	M	WS	BS	S	T	W	A	Ld	Sv
Skyclaw	12"	3+	4+	4	4	1	1	7	3+
Skyclaw Pack Leader	12"	3+	4+	4	4	1	2	7	3+
Wolf Guard Sky Leader	12"	3+	3+	4	4	1	2	8	3+

This unit contains 1 Skyclaw Pack Leader and 4 Skyclaws. It can include up to 5 additional Skyclaws (**Power Rating +4**). It can also include a Wolf Guard Sky Leader (**Power Rating +2**). Each model is armed with a chainsword, bolt pistol, frag grenades and krak grenades.

WEAPON	RANGE	TYPE	S	AP	D	ABILITIES
Bolt pistol	12"	Pistol 1	4	0	1	-
Plasma pistol	When attacking with this weapon, choose one of the profiles below.					
- Standard	12"	Pistol 1	7	-3	1	-
- Supercharge	12"	Pistol 1	8	-3	2	On a hit roll of 1, the bearer is slain.
Chainsword	Melee	Melee	User	0	1	Each time the bearer fights, it can make 1 additional attack with this weapon.
Frag grenade	6"	Grenade D6	3	0	1	-
Krak grenade	6"	Grenade 1	6	-1	D3	-

WARGEAR OPTIONS	• Up to two models may replace their bolt pistol with a plasma pistol or an item from the *Space Wolves Special Weapons* list. • The Skyclaw Pack Leader may replace his chainsword with an item from the *Space Wolves Melee Weapons* list. • The Wolf Guard Sky Leader may replace his chainsword with an item from the *Space Wolves Melee Weapons* list; he may also replace his bolt pistol with a plasma pistol or an item from the *Space Wolves Combi-weapons* list.
ABILITIES	**And They Shall Know No Fear** (pg 130) **Jump Pack Assault:** When you set this unit up during deployment, it can be set up high in the skies, ready to strike, instead of being placed on the battlefield. If it is, it can make a sudden assault to arrive on the battlefield at the end of any of your Movement phases; when it does so set it up anywhere that is more than 9" from any enemy models.	**Berserk Charge:** On a turn in which they make a successful charge, you can make 1 additional attack in the Fight phase with all models in the unit. **Headstrong:** Unless this unit contains a Wolf Guard Sky Leader, or is within 6" of a friendly **WOLF GUARD**, it must declare a charge in its Charge phase if it is possible to do so.
FACTION KEYWORDS	**IMPERIUM, ADEPTUS ASTARTES, SPACE WOLVES**
KEYWORDS	**INFANTRY, BLOOD CLAW, JUMP PACK, FLY, SKYCLAWS**

Headstrong and spirited, Skyclaws surge into battle without a thought for their own safety, seeking slaughter and glory at any price.

STORMFANG GUNSHIP

A Stormfang Gunship is a single model armed with a helfrost destructor, two twin heavy bolters and a two stormstrike missile launchers.

NAME	M	WS	BS	S	T	W	A	Ld	Sv
Stormfang Gunship	*	6+	*	8	7	14	3	8	3+

DAMAGE

Some of this model's characteristics change as it suffers damage, as shown below:

REMAINING W	M	BS
8-14+	20-50"	3+
4-7	20-35"	4+
1-3	20"	5+

WEAPON	RANGE	TYPE	S	AP	D	ABILITIES
Helfrost destructor		When attacking with this weapon, choose one of the profiles below. If a model suffers any unsaved wounds from this weapon but is not slain, roll a D6; on a 6, the target suffers a mortal wound.				
- Dispersed beam	24"	Heavy 3D3	6	-2	2	-
- Focused beam	24"	Heavy 3	8	-4	D6	-
Lascannon	48"	Heavy 1	9	-3	D6	-
Skyhammer missile launcher	60"	Heavy 3	7	-1	D3	Add 1 to all hit rolls made for this weapon against targets that can **FLY**. Subtract 1 from the hit rolls made for this weapon against all other targets.
Stormstrike missile launcher	72"	Heavy 1	8	-3	3	-
Twin heavy bolter	36"	Heavy 6	5	-1	1	-
Twin multi-melta	24"	Heavy 2	8	-4	D6	If the target is within half range of this weapon, roll two dice when inflicting damage with it and discard the lowest result.

WARGEAR OPTIONS	• This model may replace its twin heavy bolters with two twin multi-meltas or a skyhammer missile launcher. • This model may replace its stormstrike missile launchers with two lascannons.
ABILITIES	**Crash and Burn:** If this model is reduced to 0 wounds, roll a D6 before removing it from the battlefield and before any embarked models disembark. On a 6 it crashes in a fiery explosion and each unit within 6" suffers D6 mortal wounds. **Hover Jet:** Before this model moves in your Movement phase, you can declare it will hover. Its Move characteristic becomes 20" until the end of the phase, and it loses the Airborne, Hard to Hit and Supersonic abilities until the beginning of your next Movement phase. **Power of the Machine Spirit:** This model can move and fire Heavy weapons without suffering the penalty to its hit rolls.	**Airborne:** This model cannot charge, can only be charged by units that can Fly, and can only attack or be attacked in the Fight phase by units that can Fly. **Hard to Hit:** Your opponent must subtract 1 from hit rolls for attacks that target this model in the Shooting phase. **Supersonic:** Each time this model moves, first pivot it on the spot up to 90° (this does not contribute to how far the model moves), and then move the model straight forwards. Note that it cannot pivot again after the initial pivot. When this model Advances, increase its Move characteristic by 20" until the end of the phase – do not roll a dice.
TRANSPORT	This model can transport 6 **SPACE WOLVES INFANTRY** models. Each **TERMINATOR**, **JUMP PACK** or Wulfen model takes the space of two other models. It may not transport **PRIMARIS** models.
FACTION KEYWORDS	**IMPERIUM, ADEPTUS ASTARTES, SPACE WOLVES**
KEYWORDS	**VEHICLE, TRANSPORT, FLY, STORMFANG GUNSHIP**

LONG FANGS

7 POWER

NAME	M	WS	BS	S	T	W	A	Ld	Sv
Long Fang	6"	3+	3+	4	4	1	1	8	3+
Long Fang Pack Leader	6"	3+	3+	4	4	1	2	8	3+
Wolf Guard Pack Leader	6"	3+	3+	4	4	1	2	8	3+
Wolf Guard Pack Leader in Terminator Armour	5"	3+	3+	4	4	2	2	8	2+

This unit contains 1 Long Fang Pack Leader and 4 Long Fangs. It can include 1 additional Long Fang (**Power Rating +1**). It can also include either a Wolf Guard Pack Leader (**Power Rating +2**) or a Wolf Guard Pack Leader in Terminator Armour (**Power Rating +3**).
- The Long Fangs and the Long Fang Pack Leader are each armed with a boltgun, bolt pistol, frag grenades and krak grenades. The Long Fang Pack Leader is also armed with a chainsword.
- A Wolf Guard Pack Leader is armed with a chainsword, bolt pistol, frag grenades and krak grenades.
- A Wolf Guard Pack Leader in Terminator Armour is armed with a power sword and storm bolter.

WEAPON	RANGE	TYPE	S	AP	D	ABILITIES
Bolt pistol	12"	Pistol 1	4	0	1	-
Boltgun	24"	Rapid Fire 1	4	0	1	-
Plasma pistol	When attacking with this weapon, choose one of the profiles below.					
- Standard	12"	Pistol 1	7	-3	1	-
- Supercharge	12"	Pistol 1	8	-3	2	On a hit roll of 1, the bearer is slain.
Storm bolter	24"	Rapid Fire 2	4	0	1	-
Chainsword	Melee	Melee	User	0	1	Each time the bearer fights, it can make 1 additional attack with this weapon.
Power sword	Melee	Melee	User	-3	1	-
Frag grenade	6"	Grenade D6	3	0	1	-
Krak grenade	6"	Grenade 1	6	-1	D3	-

WARGEAR OPTIONS
- Any Long Fang may replace his boltgun with an item from the *Space Wolves Heavy Weapons* list.
- The Long Fang Pack Leader may replace his boltgun and bolt pistol with a plasma pistol or an item from the *Space Wolves Special Weapons* list.
- The Long Fang Pack Leader may replace his chainsword with an item from the *Space Wolves Melee Weapons* list.
- The Wolf Guard Pack Leader may replace his chainsword with an item from the *Space Wolves Melee Weapons* list; he may also replace his bolt pistol with a plasma pistol or an item from the *Space Wolves Combi-weapons* list.
- The Wolf Guard Pack Leader in Terminator Armour may replace his power sword with an item from the *Space Wolves Terminator Melee Weapons* list; he may also replace his storm bolter with an item from the *Space Wolves Combi-weapons* or *Terminator Heavy Weapons* list.

ABILITIES

And They Shall Know No Fear (pg 130)

Crux Terminatus: A Wolf Guard Pack Leader in Terminator Armour has a 5+ invulnerable save.

Fire Discipline: At the start of each of your Shooting phases, pick one enemy unit on the battlefield. You can re-roll hit rolls of 1 for any models from this unit that target the enemy unit you picked that phase.

FACTION KEYWORDS | IMPERIUM, ADEPTUS ASTARTES, SPACE WOLVES

KEYWORDS | INFANTRY, LONG FANGS

DEATHWATCH

Armed with the most advanced weapons and technology at the Imperium's disposal, the Deathwatch is Humanity's shield against the xenos horrors that threaten to overrun it on all fronts.

With members hailing from across the Space Marine Chapters, the Deathwatch is a brotherhood of warriors sworn to the safeguarding of Mankind against the alien menace. They have access to the very finest artefacts, weapons and equipment available in the Imperium, for they are outnumbered a billion times over by the seething hordes and cruel warbands of the xenos. It is a mark of the devastating skill and precision tactics of these deadly warriors that they stand strong against this hateful tide, never faltering for a moment. Theirs is the long watch, and without their ceaseless vigilance the Imperium would have fallen long ago.

> *'Such things I have seen. Shapeless horrors, their twisted, lumpen forms devoid of all logic, drifting forth from the space beyond the stars to infect our galaxy with their dreaming madness. An ocean of swarming, writhing alien shapes, pressed thick enough to smother the light from a sun. Creatures so unimaginably vast that our strike cruisers were naught but a speck of grit upon their eye. If the common man knew, brother. If he had even an inkling. Throne of Terra, the entire Imperium would be lost to madness and terror.'*
>
> *- Sergeant Vietrach, 2nd Company Howling Griffons, formerly assigned to Deathwatch Kill Team Chaeros*

Much as the Space Marines are recruited from the very finest specimens of Humanity, the Deathwatch draws its warriors from the elite of the Adeptus Astartes. Battle-brothers of the Deathwatch may hail from any Chapter, but to be chosen for such an honour they must already have displayed a particular talent for the eradication of xenos. With the assent of his superiors and the Chapter Master himself, the chosen warrior departs for the watch fortress that will be his home for the length of his vigil. Scattered across the galaxy, and commanded by the strategic masterminds known as Watch Masters, these fortified bastions stand guard against unimaginable horrors from amidst the stars and beyond. They also act as training grounds for the next generation of Deathwatch warriors.

New recruits are forced to endure gruelling regimes of physical and mental excoriation, supplemented by hypno-indoctrination courses that hammer all manner of xeno-biological knowledge into the subject's subconscious mind. By the time the recruit is ready to join a Kill Team – a squad comprised of fellow acolytes taken from as many as ten different Chapters – he is intimately familiar with the vulnerabilities and unique strengths of every alien species the Deathwatch has ever encountered. Bolstering this new-found knowledge, and the personal battle experience the warrior has accumulated during his own years of combat, are the disparate skills of his fellow warriors. While there is often inter-squad friction between the disparate Chapters, each warrior brings to the Deathwatch his own specialties, cultural beliefs and insights. Each Kill Team bonds in the heat of battle, learning to combine its varied talents into a fighting force that is both versatile and furiously potent.

The Deathwatch fight with predatory precision, identifying key weak points to exploit and overwhelming their foe with a single, deadly strike. Where a Tyranid swarm threatens to overwhelm a helpless frontier world, a Kill Team is dispatched to eliminate the synapse creatures that hold it together. Should an Ork gathering threaten an entire sector with the prospect of a Waaagh!, strike teams will swoop down within heavily armed Corvus Blackstars to eliminate the threat. The heavy assault cannons and cluster missiles of these swift gunships unleash a storm of flesh-rending fire, while their post-human occupants spill out to cut the heads from the snake, mowing the greenskin leaders down with a volley of hellfire bolter rounds that douse them in voracious acids. Evasive foes such as the capricious Aeldari are hunted down by packs of speeding bikers, while Terminators and hulking Dreadnoughts provide a heavy counter-punch should a Deathwatch detachment find itself facing monstrous, bio-organic horrors or alien mechs.

There is no xenos threat that these black-clad warriors cannot conquer, and no lengths to which they will not go to fulfil their vows. They utilise every weapon and warrior at their disposal and so, as the new influx of Primaris Space Marines flows out to the Emperor's embattled Chapters, the Watch Masters observe with interest, and draw up revised plans of their own.

THE BLACK SHIELDS

There are those amongst the ranks of the Deathwatch who forgo the right to wear their Chapter's heraldry upon their right shoulder. These enigmatic figures have abandoned their true names and removed from their armour any icons or honour-scrolls that might once have identified them. They come to the watch fortresses of the Deathwatch in supplication, pleading with the resident Watch Master for a chance to join the ranks of the alien hunters. So few are the Deathwatch that such requests are rarely turned down. None know the reasons why these warriors – known as Black Shields by their fellow battle-brothers – have denied their heritage, and it is an unspoken rule amongst the Deathwatch that none shall ask. Perhaps they are the last of a lost Chapter, destroyed by xenos raiders. It may be that they seek atonement for a grievous sin or failure of duty committed in their past. All that matters is that they fight with a furious determination to prove their loyalty to the Imperium.

DEATHWATCH ARMY LIST

This section contains all of the datasheets that you will need in order to fight battles with your Deathwatch miniatures. Each datasheet includes the characteristics profiles of the unit it describes, as well as any wargear and special abilities it may have. Some abilities are common to several Deathwatch units, in which case they are described below and referenced on the datasheets themselves.

ABILITIES
The following abilities are common to several Deathwatch units:

And They Shall Know No Fear
You can re-roll failed Morale tests for this unit.

Special Issue Ammunition
When this unit fires a bolt pistol, boltgun, twin boltgun, stalker pattern boltgun or a guardian spear, you can choose for it to fire special issue ammunition. If you do so, choose one kind of ammunition from the following list, and apply the corresponding modifier.

SPECIAL ISSUE AMMUNITION	
AMMUNITION	**MODIFIER**
Dragonfire bolt	Add 1 to the hit rolls for this weapon when targeting a unit that is in cover.
Hellfire round	This weapon always wounds on a 2+ (except against Vehicles).
Kraken bolt	Add 3" to the range of this weapon if it is a bolt pistol, or 6" otherwise, and improve the AP of the attack by 1 (e.g. an AP of 0 becomes -1).
Vengeance round	Subtract 3" from the range of this weapon if it is a bolt pistol, or 6" otherwise, and improve the AP of the attack by 2 (e.g. an AP of 0 becomes -2).

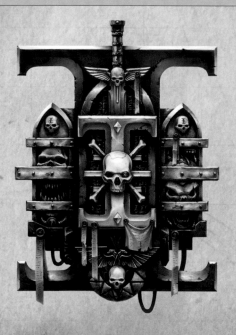

DEATHWATCH CHAPTER

The following Space Marines datasheets can be from the Deathwatch. Those that are replace the <Chapter> keyword on their datasheet in all instances with **DEATHWATCH**. If a Space Marines unit does not appear on the list below, it cannot be from the Deathwatch, and so cannot have the **DEATHWATCH** Faction keyword.

- Chaplain (pg 19)
- Dreadnought (pg 35)
- Drop Pod (pg 48)
- Land Raider (pg 58)
- Land Raider Crusader (pg 59)
- Land Raider Redeemer (pg 60)
- Librarian (pg 14)
- Librarian in Terminator Armour (pg 15)
- Razorback (pg 48)
- Rhino (pg 46)
- Venerable Dreadnought (pg 36)
- Watch Captain – use the Captain datasheet (pg 12)
- Watch Captain in Terminator Armour – use the Captain in Terminator Armour datasheet (pg 12)

DEATHWATCH WARGEAR

The Deathwatch favour different weapons to other Space Marine Chapters.

Add the following weapons to the *Pistols* list (pg 11) when equipping **DEATHWATCH** units:

- Inferno pistol
- Hand flamer

Remove the following weapon from the *Combi-weapons* lists (pg 11) when equipping **DEATHWATCH** units:

- Combi-grav

Use the *Deathwatch Dreadnought Heavy Weapons* list instead of the Space Marines *Dreadnought Heavy Weapons* list when equipping **DEATHWATCH DREADNOUGHTS**. In addition, **DEATHWATCH DREADNOUGHTS** cannot replace their Dreadnought combat weapon and storm bolter with a twin autocannon.

A **DEATHWATCH** Captain may replace his chainsword with a xenophase blade.

The only change a **DEATHWATCH** Captain in Terminator Armour can make to their default equipment is to replace their power sword with a relic blade.

DEATHWATCH Librarians and Chaplains may not be equipped with jump packs.

A **DEATHWATCH** Chaplain may not be equipped with a power fist.

A **DEATHWATCH** Librarian in Terminator Armour may not be equipped with a storm shield.

A **DEATHWATCH** Razorback cannot be equipped with a twin heavy flamer or a lascannon and twin plasma gun.

WARGEAR

Many of the units you will find on the following pages reference one or more of the following wargear lists. When this is the case, the unit may take any item from the appropriate list below. The profiles for the weapons in these lists can be found in the appendix (pg 206-209 and 221).

DEATHWATCH EQUIPMENT

Up to two items can be chosen from the following list:
- Bolt pistol
- Chainsword
- Grav-pistol
- Inferno pistol
- Hand flamer
- Lightning claw
- Plasma pistol
- Power axe
- Power fist
- Power lance
- Power maul
- Power sword
- Storm shield
- Thunder hammer
- Xenophase blade [1]

[1] *Watch Sergeant only*

One weapon can be chosen from the following list:
- Boltgun
- Combi-flamer
- Combi-melta
- Combi-plasma
- Deathwatch shotgun
- Flamer
- Grav-gun
- Meltagun
- Plasma gun
- Stalker pattern boltgun
- Storm bolter

DEATHWATCH HEAVY WEAPONS

- Deathwatch frag cannon
- Heavy bolter
- Heavy flamer
- Infernus heavy bolter
- Missile launcher

DEATHWATCH VANGUARD EQUIPMENT

- Bolt pistol
- Chainsword
- Grav-pistol
- Inferno pistol
- Hand flamer
- Lightning claw
- Plasma pistol
- Power axe
- Power fist
- Power lance
- Power maul
- Power sword
- Storm shield
- Thunder hammer

DEATWATCH TERMINATOR MELEE WEAPONS

- Chainfist
- Power axe
- Power lance
- Power maul
- Power sword
- Power fist & meltagun

DEATHWATCH TERMINATOR HEAVY WEAPONS

- Heavy flamer
- Assault cannon
- Cyclone missile launcher & storm bolter

DEATHWATCH DREADNOUGHT HEAVY WEAPONS

- Twin lascannon
- Assault cannon
- Plasma cannon

WATCH MASTER

7 POWER

NAME	M	WS	BS	S	T	W	A	Ld	Sv
Watch Master	6"	2+	2+	4	4	6	4	9	2+

A Watch Master is a single model armed with a guardian spear, frag grenades and krak grenades.

WEAPONS	RANGE	TYPE	S	AP	D	ABILITIES
Guardian spear (shooting)	24"	Rapid Fire 1	4	-1	2	-
Guardian spear (melee)	Melee	Melee	+1	-3	D3	-
Frag grenade	6"	Grenade D6	3	0	1	-
Krak grenade	6"	Grenade 1	6	-1	D3	-

ABILITIES	And They Shall Know No Fear, Special Issue Ammunition (pg 170)	**Watch Master:** You can re-roll failed hit rolls for friendly DEATHWATCH units within 6" of this model.
	Iron Halo: This model has a 4+ invulnerable save.	

FACTION KEYWORDS	IMPERIUM, ADEPTUS ASTARTES, DEATHWATCH
KEYWORDS	INFANTRY, CHARACTER, WATCH MASTER

WATCH CAPTAIN ARTEMIS

7 POWER

NAME	M	WS	BS	S	T	W	A	Ld	Sv
Watch Captain Artemis	6"	2+	2+	4	4	5	4	9	3+

Watch Captain Artemis is a single model armed with a power sword, Hellfire Extremis, frag grenades, krak grenades and a stasis bomb. Only one of this model may be included in your army.

WEAPONS	RANGE	TYPE	S	AP	D	ABILITIES
Hellfire Extremis	When attacking with this weapon, choose one or both of the profiles below. If you choose both, subtract 1 from all hit rolls made for this weapon.					
- Hellfire flamer	8"	Assault D6	*	0	1	This weapon automatically hits its target. This weapon wounds on a 4+, unless it is targeting a VEHICLE, in which case it wounds on a 6+.
- Boltgun	24"	Rapid Fire 1	4	0	1	-
Power sword	Melee	Melee	User	-3	1	-
Frag grenade	6"	Grenade D6	3	0	1	-
Krak grenade	6"	Grenade 1	6	-1	D3	-
Stasis bomb	6"	Grenade 1	-	-	-	This weapon can only be used once per battle. If the attack hits, deal D6 mortal wounds to your target. If it misses, Watch Captain Artemis suffers D6 mortal wounds.

ABILITIES	And They Shall Know No Fear, Special Issue Ammunition (pg 170)	**Unstoppable Champion:** Roll a D6 whenever Watch Captain Artemis loses a wound. On a 6, he does not lose that wound.
	Rites of Battle: You can re-roll hit rolls of 1 made for friendly DEATHWATCH units within 6" of Watch Captain Artemis.	**Iron Halo:** Watch Captain Artemis has a 4+ invulnerable save.

FACTION KEYWORDS	IMPERIUM, ADEPTUS ASTARTES, DEATHWATCH
KEYWORDS	INFANTRY, CHARACTER, CAPTAIN, ARTEMIS

DEATHWATCH KILL TEAM

NAME	M	WS	BS	S	T	W	A	Ld	Sv
Deathwatch Veteran	6"	3+	3+	4	4	1	2	8	3+
Watch Sergeant	6"	3+	3+	4	4	1	3	9	3+
Black Shield	6"	3+	3+	4	4	1	3	8	3+
Deathwatch Terminator	5"	3+	3+	4	4	2	2	8	2+
Deathwatch Biker	14"	3+	3+	4	5	2	2	8	3+
Deathwatch Vanguard Veteran	12"	3+	3+	4	4	1	2	8	3+

This unit contains 5 Deathwatch Veterans. A Watch Sergeant can take the place of one Deathwatch Veteran. A Black Shield can take the place of one Deathwatch Veteran. It can include up to 5 additional models in any combination of Deathwatch Veterans (**Power Rating +2 per model**), Deathwatch Terminators (**Power Rating +3 per model**), Deathwatch Bikers (**Power Rating +2 per model**) and Deathwatch Vanguard Veterans (**Power Rating +2 per model**).
- Each Deathwatch Veteran, Watch Sergeant and Black Shield is equipped with a boltgun, frag grenades and krak grenades.
- Each Deathwatch Terminator is armed with a storm bolter and power fist.
- Each Deathwatch Vanguard Veteran is equipped with a bolt pistol, chainsword, frag grenades and krak grenades.
- Each Deathwatch Biker is armed with frag grenades and krak grenades, and rides into battle on a Space Marine bike equipped with a twin boltgun.

WEAPON	RANGE	TYPE	S	AP	D	ABILITIES
Bolt pistol	12"	Pistol 1	4	0	1	-
Boltgun	24"	Rapid Fire 1	4	0	1	-
Storm bolter	24"	Rapid Fire 2	4	0	1	-
Chainsword	Melee	Melee	User	0	1	Each time the bearer fights, it can make 1 additional attack with this weapon.
Power fist	Melee	Melee	x2	-3	D3	When attacking with this weapon, you must subtract 1 from the hit roll.
Twin boltgun	24"	Rapid fire 2	4	0	1	-
Frag grenade	6"	Grenade D6	3	0	1	-
Krak grenade	6"	Grenade 1	6	-1	D3	-

WARGEAR OPTIONS
- Any Deathwatch Veteran, Watch Sergeant or Black Shield may replace their boltgun with two items from the *Deathwatch Equipment* list.
- Up to 4 Deathwatch Veterans may replace their boltgun with an item from the *Deathwatch Heavy Weapons* list.
- Any Deathwatch Veteran may replace their boltgun with a heavy thunder hammer (pg 221).
- A Watch Sergeant may take a combat shield (pg 209).
- Any Deathwatch Vanguard Veteran may replace their bolt pistol and chainsword with a heavy thunder hammer (pg 221) or two items chosen from the *Deathwatch Vanguard Equipment* list.

- Up to 3 Deathwatch Terminators may replace their storm bolter with a weapon from the *Deathwatch Terminator Heavy Weapons* list.
- Any Deathwatch Terminator may replace its power fist with a weapon from the *Deathwatch Terminator Melee Weapons* list.
- Any Deathwatch Terminator may replace its storm bolter and power fist with two lightning claws (pg 209) or a thunder hammer (pg 209) and storm shield (pg 209).
- Any Deathwatch Biker may take a power axe (pg 209), power maul (pg 209) or power sword (pg 209).
- One Deathwatch Biker may take a Deathwatch teleport homer.

ABILITIES

And They Shall Know No Fear, Special Issue Ammunition (pg 170)

Mixed Unit: A Deathwatch Kill Team can contain models with different Toughness characteristics. If this is the case, use the Toughness characteristic of the majority of the models in the unit when the enemy makes wound rolls against it. If there is no majority, the Deathwatch player may choose which of the values is used. Whilst the unit includes any Deathwatch Terminators, it has the **TERMINATOR** keyword; whilst it includes any Deathwatch Bikers, it has the **BIKER** keyword; whilst is includes any Deathwatch Vanguard Veterans, it has the **JUMP PACK** keyword.

Unflinching: This unit automatically passes Morale tests if it contains any Deathwatch Terminators.

Crux Terminatus: Deathwatch Terminators have a 5+ invulnerable save.

Vanguard Strike: When a Kill Team that includes any Vanguard Veterans Falls Back, it can shoot later that turn as if it could **FLY**.

Atonement Through Honour: A unit that contains a Black Shield can make Heroic Interventions as if it were a **CHARACTER**, and must do so if able to.

Relentless Assault: When a Kill Team that includes any Deathwatch Bikers Falls Back, it can charge later that turn.

Deathwatch Teleport Homer: If this unit has a Deathwatch teleport homer, place it anywhere in your deployment zone when your army deploys. If an enemy model is ever within 9" of the Deathwatch teleport homer, it is deactivated and removed from the battlefield. Whilst there are any friendly Deathwatch teleport homers on the battlefield, a unit that contains one or more Deathwatch Terminators can perform an emergency teleport instead of moving in its Movement phase. At the end of the Movement phase, remove the unit and then set it up with all models within 6" of a friendly Deathwatch teleport homer. That Deathwatch teleport homer then shorts out and is removed from the battlefield.

FACTION KEYWORDS	IMPERIUM, ADEPTUS ASTARTES, DEATHWATCH
KEYWORDS	INFANTRY, KILL TEAM

DEATHWATCH TERMINATORS

17 POWER

NAME	M	WS	BS	S	T	W	A	Ld	Sv
Deathwatch Terminator	5"	3+	3+	4	4	2	2	8	2+
Deathwatch Terminator Sergeant	5"	3+	3+	4	4	2	3	9	2+

This unit contains 1 Deathwatch Terminator Sergeant and 4 Deathwatch Terminators. It can include up to 5 additional Deathwatch Terminators **(Power Rating +13)**.
- Each Deathwatch Terminator is armed with a storm bolter and power fist.
- The Deathwatch Terminator Sergeant is armed with a storm bolter and power sword.

WEAPONS	RANGE	TYPE	S	AP	D	ABILITIES
Storm bolter	24"	Rapid Fire 2	4	0	1	-
Lightning claw	Melee	Melee	User	-2	1	You can re-roll failed wound rolls for this weapon. If a model is armed with two lightning claws, each time it fights it can make 1 additional attack with them.
Power fist	Melee	Melee	x2	-3	D3	When attacking with this weapon, you must subtract 1 from the hit roll.
Power sword	Melee	Melee	User	-3	1	-
Thunder hammer	Melee	Melee	x2	-3	3	When attacking with this weapon, you must subtract 1 from the hit roll.

WARGEAR OPTIONS	
	• Up to 3 Deathwatch Terminators may replace their storm bolter with a weapon from the *Deathwatch Terminator Heavy Weapons* list. • Any model may replace its power fist or power sword with a weapon from the *Deathwatch Terminator Melee Weapons* list. • Any model may replace its storm bolter and power fist with two lightning claws or a thunder hammer and storm shield (pg 209).

ABILITIES	
	And They Shall Know No Fear (pg 170) **Crux Terminatus:** Terminators have a 5+ invulnerable save. **Unflinching:** This unit automatically passes Morale tests.	**Teleport Strike:** During deployment, you can set up this unit in a teleportarium chamber instead of placing it on the battlefield. At the end of any of your Movement phases this unit can use a teleport strike to arrive on the battlefield – set it up anywhere on the battlefield that is more than 9" away from any enemy models.

FACTION KEYWORDS	**IMPERIUM, ADEPTUS ASTARTES, DEATHWATCH**
KEYWORDS	**INFANTRY, TERMINATORS**

Clad in ancient armour and wielding the most devastating weaponry, Terminators are walking symbols of the Imperium's might.

DEATHWATCH VANGUARD VETERANS

10 POWER

NAME	M	WS	BS	S	T	W	A	Ld	Sv
Deathwatch Vanguard Veteran	12"	3+	3+	4	4	1	2	8	3+
Deathwatch Vanguard Sergeant	12"	3+	3+	4	4	1	3	9	3+

This unit contains 1 Deathwatch Vanguard Sergeant and 4 Deathwatch Vanguard Veterans. It can include up to 5 additional Deathwatch Vanguard Veterans (**Power Rating +10**). Each model is equipped with a bolt pistol, chainsword, frag grenades and krak grenades.

WEAPONS	RANGE	TYPE	S	AP	D	ABILITIES
Bolt pistol	12"	Pistol 1	4	0	1	-
Chainsword	Melee	Melee	User	0	1	Each time the bearer fights, it can make 1 additional attack with this weapon.
Heavy thunder hammer	Melee	Melee	x2	-3	D6	When attacking with this weapon, you must subtract 1 from the hit roll. Each time you make a wound roll of 6+ with this weapon, that hit is resolved with a Damage of 6.
Frag grenade	6"	Grenade D6	3	0	1	-
Krak grenade	6"	Grenade 1	6	-1	D3	-

WARGEAR OPTIONS	• Any model may replace their bolt pistol and chainsword with two items from the *Deathwatch Vanguard Equipment* list. • Any Deathwatch Vanguard Veteran may replace their bolt pistol and chainsword with a heavy thunder hammer.
ABILITIES	**And They Shall Know No Fear, Special Issue Ammunition** (pg 170) **Jump Pack Assault:** During deployment, you can set up this unit high in the skies instead of placing it on the battlefield. At the end of any of your Movement phases this unit can assault from above – set it up anywhere on the battlefield that is more than 9" away from any enemy models.
FACTION KEYWORDS	**IMPERIUM, ADEPTUS ASTARTES, DEATHWATCH**
KEYWORDS	**INFANTRY, JUMP PACK, FLY, VANGUARD VETERANS**

Vanguard Veterans specialise in pinpoint strikes, stabbing from the sky directly into the heart of the enemy's ranks.

DEATHWATCH BIKERS

5 POWER

NAME	M	WS	BS	S	T	W	A	Ld	Sv
Deathwatch Biker	14"	3+	3+	4	5	2	2	8	3+
Deathwatch Biker Sergeant	14"	3+	3+	4	5	2	3	9	3+

This unit contains 1 Deathwatch Biker Sergeant and 2 Deathwatch Bikers. It can include up to 3 additional Deathwatch Bikers (**Power Rating +5**). Each model is armed with frag grenades and krak grenades, and rides into battle on a Space Marine bike equipped with a twin boltgun.

WEAPONS	RANGE	TYPE	S	AP	D	ABILITIES
Twin boltgun	24"	Rapid fire 2	4	0	1	-
Power axe	Melee	Melee	+1	-2	1	-
Power maul	Melee	Melee	+2	-1	1	-
Power sword	Melee	Melee	User	-3	1	-
Frag grenade	6"	Grenade D6	3	0	1	-
Krak grenade	6"	Grenade 1	6	-1	D3	-

WARGEAR OPTIONS	
	• Any model may take a power axe, power maul or power sword.
	• One Deathwatch Biker may take a Deathwatch teleport homer.

ABILITIES	
	And They Shall Know No Fear, Special Issue Ammunition (pg 170)

Relentless Assault: When this unit Falls Back, it can charge later that turn.

Turbo-boost: When this unit Advances, add 6" to its Move characteristic for that Movement phase instead of rolling a dice.

Deathwatch Teleport Homer: If this unit has a Deathwatch teleport homer, place it anywhere in your deployment zone when your army deploys. If an enemy model is ever within 9" of the Deathwatch teleport homer, it is deactivated and removed from the battlefield. Whilst there are any friendly Deathwatch teleport homers on the battlefield, a unit that contains one or more Deathwatch Terminators can perform an emergency teleport instead of moving in its Movement phase. At the end of the Movement phase, remove the unit and then set it up with all models within 6" of a friendly Deathwatch teleport homer. That Deathwatch teleport homer then shorts out and is removed from the battlefield.

FACTION KEYWORDS	IMPERIUM, ADEPTUS ASTARTES, DEATHWATCH
KEYWORDS	BIKERS

The deafening roar of engines and boltgun fire fills the air as the Bikers of the Deathwatch run their quarry to ground.

CORVUS BLACKSTAR

DAMAGE

Some of this model's characteristics change as it suffers damage, as shown below:

REMAINING W	M	BS	A
8-14+	20-45"	3+	3
4-7	20-30"	4+	D3
1-3	20"	5+	1

NAME	M	WS	BS	S	T	W	A	Ld	Sv
Corvus Blackstar	*	6+	*	8	7	14	*	8	3+

A Corvus Blackstar is a single model equipped with a twin assault cannon and two stormstrike missile launchers.

WEAPONS	RANGE	TYPE	S	AP	D	ABILITIES
Blackstar rocket launcher	When attacking with this weapon, choose one of the profiles below.					
- Corvid warhead	30"	Heavy D6	6	-1	1	Add 1 to hit rolls for this weapon when targeting a unit that can FLY.
- Dracos warhead	30"	Heavy D6	4	0	1	Add 1 to hit rolls for this weapon when targeting a unit that is in cover.
Hurricane bolter	24"	Rapid Fire 6	4	0	1	-
Stormstrike missile launcher	72"	Heavy 1	8	-3	3	-
Twin assault cannon	24"	Heavy 12	6	-1	1	-
Twin lascannon	48"	Heavy 2	9	-3	D6	-

WARGEAR OPTIONS	
	• This model may replace its twin assault cannon with a twin lascannon. • This model may replace its two stormstrike missile launchers with two Blackstar rocket launchers. • This model may take a hurricane bolter. • This model may take an infernum halo-launcher or an auspex array.

ABILITIES

Hover Jet: Before this model moves in your Movement phase, you can declare it will hover. Its Move characteristic becomes 20" until the end of the phase, and it loses the Airborne, Hard to Hit and Supersonic abilities until the beginning of your next Movement phase.

Airborne: This model cannot charge, can only be charged by units that can FLY, and can only attack or be attacked in the Fight phase by units that can FLY.

Hard to Hit: Your opponent must subtract 1 from hit rolls for attacks that target this model in the Shooting phase.

Supersonic: Each time this model moves, first pivot it on the spot up to 90° (this does not contribute to how far the model moves), and then move the model straight forwards. Note that it cannot pivot again after the initial pivot. When this model Advances, increase its Move characteristic by 20" until the end of the phase – do not roll a dice.

Crash and Burn: If this model is reduced to 0 wounds, roll a D6 before removing it from the battlefield and before any embarked models disembark. On a 6 it crashes in a fiery explosion and each unit within 6" suffers D6 mortal wounds.

Blackstar Cluster Launcher: This model can fire its Blackstar cluster launcher as it flies over enemy units in its Movement phase. To do so, after this model has moved, pick one enemy unit that it flew over. Then, roll one D6 for each model in the enemy unit (up to a maximum of 10 D6). Each time you roll a 6 the unit being bombed suffers 1 mortal wound.

Auspex Array: You can re-roll hit rolls of 1 for a model with an auspex array when targeting an enemy in the Shooting phase that cannot FLY.

Infernum Halo-launcher: If an enemy unit that can FLY targets a supersonic model with an infernum halo-launcher in the Shooting phase, your opponent must subtract 1 from the subsequent hit rolls.

TRANSPORT	This model can transport 12 DEATHWATCH INFANTRY models. Each JUMP PACK or TERMINATOR model takes the space of two other models. It can also transport DEATHWATCH BIKER models – each takes up the space of three other models.
FACTION KEYWORDS	IMPERIUM, ADEPTUS ASTARTES, DEATHWATCH
KEYWORDS	VEHICLE, TRANSPORT, FLY, CORVUS BLACKSTAR

GREY KNIGHTS

An ancient order of champions shrouded in mystery and legend, the Grey Knights are Humanity's greatest defence against the threat of Daemonkind. Though the common folk of the Imperium will never know of their sacrifice and courage, it is only by their hand that the untold perils of the warp are kept at bay.

Within the warp – that roiling, ever-mutable dimension in which the accumulated sins and fears of the mortal races take terrible form – lurk the greatest threats to Humanity's survival. Creatures of unnatural horror and awful might, the Daemons of Chaos ever hunger for mortal souls, and strain constantly against the fabric of reality in their desperation to break through into realspace and commit their manifold atrocities upon Mankind. The Emperor, in his infinite wisdom, recognised this grave peril, and created a unique order of Space Marines whose entire purpose was to combat the daemonic threat. Thus were the Grey Knights founded, the ultimate weapon against the Dark Powers.

If only a fraction of Humanity possess the strength and will to become a Space Marine, that number is even lower for those chosen to take up the ceaseless vigil of a Grey Knight. Of the millions of recruits who are brought to the Knights' secret citadel upon Titan for testing, only a handful survive the vicious physical and mental torment inflicted upon them by their pitiless handlers. The brutality of this training is necessary. The Grey Knights fight on the forefront of a war that will decide the fate of the Imperium, and the hideous threats they face would shatter the minds of the unworthy. It is for this very reason that every Grey Knight is psychically active – there is no greater weapon against the creatures of the immaterium than to turn the power of the warp against them. Even amongst the Librarians of the Adeptus Astartes, this constant exposure to the horrors of Daemonkind would risk the insidious threat of possession, but every brother of the Grey Knights is incorruptible and utterly pure of soul. When they gaze into the warp, the shapeless malice within recoils to witness such strength of will.

Due to their unique mission, the Grey Knights do not adhere to the Codex Astartes. The Chapter is instead organised into brotherhoods – roughly comparably to the companies of the Space Marines – and armed with a variety of unique and esoteric weaponry and equipment focused towards the slaying of Daemons. Grey Knights learn to master all of these weapons during their vigil; a brother may begin his service in a lightly-armoured Strike Squad, before shifting into a heavily-armed Terminator Squad or taking up the storm bolter of a Purgator. Terminators form the backbone of a brotherhood's fighting force. It is a mark of the elite nature of the Grey Knights that their battle line troops are armed and armoured with the most powerful technology in the Imperium. They wield Nemesis force weapons, psychically active artefacts inscribed with runes of Daemon-slaying and bearing advanced power-field generators. These wondrous blades can carve through the unnaturally thick hide of a warp-spawned monstrosity as if it were naught but leprous skin.

When a daemonic threat emerges to threaten the Imperium, the Grey Knights strike with the fury of the Emperor, teleporting into the thick of the enemy force in a terrifying eruption of psychic might and blistering firepower. They know they must banish or slaughter their daemonic foes quickly, lest the incursion spread further and further, and more wretched abominations crawl forth from the immaterium. Terminators lumber forward, unleashing the thunderous percussion of their storm bolters. Scores of Daemons are shredded and blasted apart as bolter rounds inscribed with ancient runes of warding strike home. Before the monstrous ranks can react, the Grey Knights are amongst them, slashing and slicing with their Nemesis blades, purifying the taint of Daemonkind with bolter and flamer. Towering Nemesis Dreadknights stalk through the carnage, crushing foes to bloody paste with their energised fists, sending great thunderstorms of psycannon rounds into the thick of the Daemon ranks.

Whatever creature leads this army of the damned, whether it be Daemon Prince or mortal sorcerer, is hunted down and obliterated utterly, its psychic essence sent screaming into the warp. Shorn of their anchor to the material plane, the summoner's daemonic minions are sent howling back into the nightmare dimension they call home. A single battle in the eternal war is won, and yet there is barely a moment of respite for the Grey Knights. Upon the moon of Saturn, in the Citadel of Titan, the psychics known as Prognosticars read and interpret the twisting skeins of the warp using the Emperor's Tarot, constantly searching for new threats. Few as they are, the warriors of Titan cannot address every daemonic incursion, and so the Prognosticars seek the gravest, most terrible gatherings of Daemonkind, those manifestations that threaten entire sectors of the Imperium. There the Grey Knights strike with the light of the Emperor blazing in their souls, fighting and dying on behalf of a galaxy that will never know the magnitude of their sacrifice.

THE SECRET WAR

The wider Imperium has never heard of the Grey Knights. The truth of the warp and its infinite horrors is kept from the Imperium's citizens, for if Humanity was to truly recognise the nightmare that threatens to envelop it, the consequences would be grave indeed. Any reports of daemonic activity are quickly and ruthlessly censored by the Inquisition, which maintains close ties with the Grey Knights, often aiding or facilitating their campaigns of eradication.

Only the Grey Knights are truly immune to the taint of Chaos, and so any other Imperial force that aids them in the destruction of warp entities is in grave danger of being corrupted. Even the smallest chance this has occurred cannot be tolerated; entire armies of Guardsmen are put to the sword or subjected to telepathic scouring that renders them little more than mindless servitors. Space Marines are too valuable for such brutal methods, and so are instead mind-wiped or sworn to secrecy under threat of excommunication. Thus the Grey Knights remain nothing but a myth, a legend told in whispers amongst the very rarest of scholars.

ABILITIES

The following abilities are common to several Grey Knights units:

And They Shall Know No Fear

You can re-roll failed Morale tests for this unit.

Daemon Hunters

If this unit attacks any DAEMONS in the Fight phase, you can re-roll failed wound rolls for those attacks.

Rites of Banishment

When this unit manifests the *Smite* psychic power, it has a range of 12" rather than 18". Additionally, the target unit suffers only 1 mortal wound rather than D3 (whether or not the result of the Psychic test is more than 10) – unless the target unit is a DAEMON, in which case it suffers 3 mortal wounds instead of D3.

Teleport Strike

During deployment, you can set up this unit in a teleportarium chamber instead of placing it on the battlefield. At the end of any of your Movement phases this unit can teleport into battle – set it up anywhere on the battlefield that is more than 9" away from any enemy models.

GREY KNIGHTS CHAPTER

The following Space Marines datasheets, can be from the Grey Knights Chapter. Those that are replace the <CHAPTER> keyword on their datasheet in all instances with GREY KNIGHTS. If a Space Marines unit does not appear on the list below, it cannot be from the Grey Knights Chapter, and so cannot have the GREY KNIGHTS faction keyword. GREY KNIGHTS PSYKERS generate their psychic powers from the Sanctic discipline (right) instead of the Librarius discipline.

- Dreadnought [1] (pg 35)
- Land Raider (pg 58)
- Land Raider Crusader (pg 59)
- Land Raider Redeemer (pg 60)
- Librarian in Terminator Armour [2, 3] (pg 15)
- Razorback (pg 48)
- Rhino (pg 46)
- Servitors (pg 16)
- Stormraven Gunship (pg 57)
- Techmarine [1, 3, 4] (pg 16)
- Venerable Dreadnought [1] (pg 36)

[1] These units gain the PSYKER keyword and the Daemon Hunters and Rites of Banishment abilities. They can attempt to manifest one psychic power in each friendly Psychic phase, and attempt to deny one psychic power in each enemy Psychic phase. They know the *Smite* psychic power.

[2] This unit is armed with frag grenades and krak grenades. He is also armed with a Nemesis warding stave instead of a force stave, which he can replace with an item from the *Grey Knights Melee Weapons* list.

[3] These units are armed with psyk-out grenades.

[4] This unit must take a servo-harness.

SANCTIC DISCIPLINE

Before the battle, generate the psychic powers for PSYKERS that can use powers from the Sanctic discipline using the table below. You can either roll a D3 to generate their powers randomly (re-roll any duplicate results), or you can select the psychic powers you wish the psyker to have.

SANCTIC DISCIPLINE	
D3	**PSYCHIC POWER**
1	**Purge Soul** *Purge Soul* has a warp charge value of 5. If manifested, pick a visible enemy unit within 12" of the psyker. Both controlling players roll a dice and add their respective unit's highest Leadership value. If the target's total is equal to or greater than the psyker's total, nothing happens. If the psyker's total is greater than the target's total, the target unit suffers a number of mortal wounds equal to the difference.
2	**Gate of Infinity** *Gate of Infinity* has a warp charge value of 6. If manifested, pick a friendly GREY KNIGHTS unit within 12" of the psyker. Remove that unit from the battlefield and immediately set it up anywhere on the battlefield that is more than 9" from any enemy models.
3	**Hammerhand** *Hammerhand* has a warp charge value of 6. If manifested, pick a friendly GREY KNIGHTS unit within 12" of the psyker. Add 1 to any wound rolls you make for that unit's Melee weapons until the start of your next Psychic phase.

WARGEAR

Many of the units you will find on the following pages reference one or more wargear lists. When this is the case, the unit may take any item from the appropriate list on pg 11 or below. The profiles for the weapons in these lists can be found in the appendix (pg 223).

GREY KNIGHTS MELEE WEAPONS

- Nemesis Daemon hammer
- Nemesis force halberd
- Nemesis force sword
- Nemesis warding stave
- Two Nemesis falchions [1]

GREY KNIGHTS SPECIAL WEAPONS

- Incinerator
- Psilencer
- Psycannon

[1] May not be taken by an Apothecary.

LORD KALDOR DRAIGO

12 POWER

NAME	M	WS	BS	S	T	W	A	Ld	Sv
Lord Kaldor Draigo	5"	2+	2+	4	4	7	5	9	2+

Lord Kaldor Draigo is a single model armed with the Titansword, a storm shield, a storm bolter, frag grenades, krak grenades and psyk-out grenades. Only one of this model may be included in your army.

WEAPON	RANGE	TYPE	S	AP	D	ABILITIES
Storm bolter	24"	Rapid Fire 2	4	0	1	-
The Titansword	Melee	Melee	+4	-4	3	-
Frag grenade	6"	Grenade D6	3	0	1	-
Krak grenade	6"	Grenade 1	6	-1	D3	-
Psyk-out grenade	6"	Grenade D3	2	0	1	Each time you roll a hit roll of 6+ for this weapon when targeting a **PSYKER** or **DAEMON**, the target suffers a mortal wound instead of the normal damage.

ABILITIES	And They Shall Know No Fear, Daemon Hunters, Rites of Banishment (pg 181) **Bane of Evil:** When a friendly **GREY KNIGHTS** unit within 6" of Lord Kaldor Draigo makes an attack against a **DAEMON** unit in the Fight phase, you can re-roll damage rolls for that unit. **Storm Shield:** Lord Kaldor Draigo has a 3+ invulnerable save.	**Chapter Master:** You can re-roll failed hit rolls for friendly **GREY KNIGHTS** units that are within 6" of Lord Kaldor Draigo. **Warp Emergence:** During deployment, you can set up Lord Kaldor Draigo in the warp instead of placing him on the battlefield. At the end of any of your Movement phases Lord Kaldor Draigo can emerge from the warp – set him up anywhere on the battlefield that is more than 9" away from any enemy models.
PSYKER	Lord Kaldor Draigo can attempt to manifest two psychic powers in each friendly Psychic phase, and attempt to deny two psychic powers in each enemy Psychic phase. He knows the *Smite* psychic power and two psychic powers from the Sanctic discipline (pg 181).	
FACTION KEYWORDS	**IMPERIUM, ADEPTUS ASTARTES, GREY KNIGHTS**	
KEYWORDS	**CHARACTER, INFANTRY, GRAND MASTER, TERMINATOR, PSYKER, LORD KALDOR DRAIGO**	

Kaldor Draigo, Supreme Grand Master of the Grey Knights, strides from the empyrean to smite his foes.

GRAND MASTER VOLDUS

10 POWER

NAME	M	WS	BS	S	T	W	A	Ld	Sv
Grand Master Voldus	5"	2+	2+	4	4	6	5	9	2+

Grand Master Voldus is a single model armed with Malleus Argyrum, a storm bolter, frag grenades, krak grenades and psyk-out grenades. Only one of this model may be included in your army.

WEAPON	RANGE	TYPE	S	AP	D	ABILITIES
Storm bolter	24"	Rapid Fire 2	4	0	1	-
Malleus Argyrum	Melee	Melee	x2	-3	3	-
Frag grenade	6"	Grenade D6	3	0	1	-
Krak grenade	6"	Grenade 1	6	-1	D3	-
Psyk-out grenade	6"	Grenade D3	2	0	1	Each time you roll a hit roll of 6+ for this weapon when targeting a **Psyker** or **Daemon**, the target suffers a mortal wound instead of the normal damage.

ABILITIES	**And They Shall Know No Fear, Daemon Hunters, Rites of Banishment, Teleport Strike** (pg 181) **Iron Halo:** Grand Master Voldus has a 4+ invulnerable save.	**Rites of Battle:** You can re-roll hit rolls of 1 for friendly **Grey Knights** units within 6" of Grand Master Voldus.
PSYKER	Grand Master Voldus can attempt to manifest three psychic powers in each friendly Psychic phase, and attempt to deny three psychic powers in each enemy Psychic phase. He knows the *Smite* psychic power and three psychic powers from the Sanctic discipline (pg 181).	
FACTION KEYWORDS	**Imperium, Adeptus Astartes, Grey Knights**	
KEYWORDS	**Character, Infantry, Grand Master, Terminator, Psyker, Voldus**	

GRAND MASTER

10 POWER

NAME	M	WS	BS	S	T	W	A	Ld	Sv
Grand Master	5"	2+	2+	4	4	6	5	9	2+

A Grand Master is a single model armed with a Nemesis force halberd, storm bolter, frag grenades, krak grenades and psyk-out grenades.

WEAPON	RANGE	TYPE	S	AP	D	ABILITIES
Storm bolter	24"	Rapid Fire 2	4	0	1	-
Nemesis force halberd	Melee	Melee	+1	-2	D3	-
Frag grenade	6"	Grenade D6	3	0	1	-
Krak grenade	6"	Grenade 1	6	-1	D3	-
Psyk-out grenade	6"	Grenade D3	2	0	1	Each time you roll a hit roll of 6+ for this weapon when targeting a **Psyker** or **Daemon**, the target suffers a mortal wound instead of the normal damage.

WARGEAR OPTIONS	• This model may replace his Nemesis force halberd with an item from the *Grey Knights Melee Weapons* list. • This model may replace his storm bolter with an item from the *Grey Knights Special Weapons* list.	
ABILITIES	**And They Shall Know No Fear, Daemon Hunters, Rites of Banishment, Teleport Strike** (pg 181) **Iron Halo:** This model has a 4+ invulnerable save.	**Rites of Battle:** You can re-roll hit rolls of 1 for friendly **Grey Knights** units within 6" of this model.
PSYKER	This model can attempt to manifest two psychic powers in each friendly Psychic phase, and attempt to deny one psychic power in each enemy Psychic phase. It knows the *Smite* psychic power and one psychic power from the Sanctic discipline (pg 181).	
FACTION KEYWORDS	**Imperium, Adeptus Astartes, Grey Knights**	
KEYWORDS	**Character, Infantry, Terminator, Psyker, Grand Master**	

BROTHER-CAPTAIN

NAME	M	WS	BS	S	T	W	A	Ld	Sv
Brother-Captain	5"	2+	2+	4	4	6	4	9	2+

A Brother-Captain is a single model armed with a Nemesis force halberd, storm bolter, frag grenades, krak grenades and psyk-out grenades.

WEAPON	RANGE	TYPE	S	AP	D	ABILITIES
Storm bolter	24"	Rapid Fire 2	4	0	1	-
Nemesis force halberd	Melee	Melee	+1	-2	D3	-
Frag grenade	6"	Grenade D6	3	0	1	-
Krak grenade	6"	Grenade 1	6	-1	D3	-
Psyk-out grenade	6"	Grenade D3	2	0	1	Each time you roll a hit roll of 6+ for this weapon when targeting a **PSYKER** or **DAEMON**, the target suffers a mortal wound instead of the normal damage.

WARGEAR OPTIONS	• This model may replace his Nemesis force halberd with an item from the *Grey Knights Melee Weapons* list. • This model may replace his storm bolter with an item from the *Grey Knights Special Weapons* list.	
ABILITIES	**And They Shall Know No Fear, Daemon Hunters, Rites of Banishment, Teleport Strike** (pg 181) **Iron Halo:** This model has a 4+ invulnerable save.	**Psychic Locus:** When a friendly **GREY KNIGHTS** unit within 6" of any **BROTHER-CAPTAINS** manifests the *Smite* power, double its range.
PSYKER	This model can attempt to manifest one psychic power in each friendly Psychic phase, and attempt to deny one psychic power in each enemy Psychic phase. It knows the *Smite* psychic power and one psychic power from the Sanctic discipline (pg 181).	
FACTION KEYWORDS	**IMPERIUM, ADEPTUS ASTARTES, GREY KNIGHTS**	
KEYWORDS	**CHARACTER, INFANTRY, TERMINATOR, PSYKER, BROTHER-CAPTAIN**	

Storm bolter blazing, this Brother-Captain of the Grey Knights is an inviolable bastion against the malefic and daemonic.

BROTHER-CAPTAIN STERN

8 POWER

NAME	M	WS	BS	S	T	W	A	Ld	Sv
Brother-Captain Stern	5"	2+	2+	4	4	6	4	9	2+

Brother-Captain Stern is a single model armed with a Nemesis force sword, storm bolter, frag grenades, krak grenades and psyk-out grenades. Only one of this model may be included in your army.

WEAPON	RANGE	TYPE	S	AP	D	ABILITIES
Storm bolter	24"	Rapid Fire 2	4	0	1	-
Nemesis force sword	Melee	Melee	User	-3	D3	-
Frag grenade	6"	Grenade D6	3	0	1	-
Krak grenade	6"	Grenade 1	6	-1	D3	-
Psyk-out grenade	6"	Grenade D3	2	0	1	Each time you roll a hit roll of 6+ for this weapon when targeting a **PSYKER** or **DAEMON**, the target suffers a mortal wound instead of the normal damage.

ABILITIES	And They Shall Know No Fear, Daemon Hunters, Teleport Strike (pg 181) **The Strands of Fate:** In each of your turns, you can choose to re-roll a single failed hit or wound roll, or a single failed saving throw for Brother-Captain Stern. However, if you do so, your opponent can re-roll a single failed hit or wound roll, or a single failed saving throw for one of their models in their next turn. **Iron Halo:** Brother-Captain Stern has a 4+ invulnerable save.	**Psychic Locus:** When a friendly **GREY KNIGHTS** unit within 6" of any **BROTHER-CAPTAINS** manifests the *Smite* power, double its range. **Zone of Banishment:** When Brother-Captain Stern manifests the *Smite* psychic power, it has a range of 6" rather than 18". Additionally, the target unit suffers only 1 mortal wound rather than D3 (whether or not the result of the Psychic test is more than 10) – unless the target is a **DAEMON**, in which case it suffers 3 mortal wounds instead of D3 – and all **DAEMON** units within 6" of Brother-Captain Stern also suffer a mortal wound.
PSYKER	Brother-Captain Stern can attempt to manifest two psychic powers in each friendly Psychic phase, and attempt to deny one psychic power in each enemy Psychic phase. He knows the *Smite* psychic power and one psychic power from the Sanctic discipline (pg 181).
FACTION KEYWORDS	**IMPERIUM, ADEPTUS ASTARTES, GREY KNIGHTS**
KEYWORDS	**CHARACTER, INFANTRY, BROTHER-CAPTAIN, TERMINATOR, PSYKER, STERN**

BROTHERHOOD ANCIENT

NAME	M	WS	BS	S	T	W	A	Ld	Sv
Brotherhood Ancient	5"	3+	3+	4	4	5	3	8	2+

A Brotherhood Ancient is a single model armed with a storm bolter, frag grenades, krak grenades and psyk-out grenades.

WEAPON	RANGE	TYPE	S	AP	D	ABILITIES
Storm bolter	24"	Rapid Fire 2	4	0	1	-
Nemesis falchion	Melee	Melee	User	-2	D3	-
Frag grenade	6"	Grenade D6	3	0	1	-
Krak grenade	6"	Grenade 1	6	-1	D3	-
Psyk-out grenade	6"	Grenade D3	2	0	1	Each time you roll a hit roll of 6+ for this weapon when targeting a PSYKER or DAEMON, the target suffers a mortal wound instead of the normal damage.

WARGEAR OPTIONS	• This model may take a Nemesis falchion.

ABILITIES	**And They Shall Know No Fear, Daemon Hunters, Rites of Banishment, Teleport Strike** (pg 181) **Crux Terminatus:** This model has a 5+ invulnerable save.	**Sacred Banner:** Friendly GREY KNIGHTS units within 6" of any sacred banners add 1 to their Leadership characteristic. In addition, models from friendly GREY KNIGHTS INFANTRY units that are within 6" of any sacred banners when they fight can make 1 additional attack that phase.

PSYKER	This model can attempt to manifest one psychic power in each friendly Psychic phase, and attempt to deny one psychic power in each enemy Psychic phase. It knows the *Smite* psychic power and one psychic power from the Sanctic discipline (pg 181).

FACTION KEYWORDS	**IMPERIUM, ADEPTUS ASTARTES, GREY KNIGHTS**

KEYWORDS	**CHARACTER, INFANTRY, TERMINATOR, PSYKER, ANCIENT, BROTHERHOOD ANCIENT**

BROTHERHOOD CHAMPION

6 POWER

NAME	M	WS	BS	S	T	W	A	Ld	Sv
Brotherhood Champion	6"	2+	2+	4	4	4	4	8	2+

A Brotherhood Champion is a single model armed with a Nemesis force sword, storm bolter, frag grenades, krak grenades and psyk-out grenades.

WEAPON	RANGE	TYPE	S	AP	D	ABILITIES
Storm bolter	24"	Rapid Fire 2	4	0	1	-
Nemesis force sword	Melee	Melee	User	-3	D3	-
Frag grenade	6"	Grenade D6	3	0	1	-
Krak grenade	6"	Grenade 1	6	-1	D3	-
Psyk-out grenade	6"	Grenade D3	2	0	1	Each time you roll a hit roll of 6+ for this weapon when targeting a **PSYKER** or **DAEMON**, the target suffers a mortal wound instead of the normal damage.

ABILITIES	**And They Shall Know No Fear, Daemon Hunters, Rites of Banishment** (pg 181) **Heroic Sacrifice:** If this model is slain in the Fight phase, he can immediately pile in and attack before being removed as a casualty. **Iron Halo:** This model has a 4+ invulnerable save.	**The Perfect Warrior:** At the start of each Fight phase, you must choose a combat stance for this model to adopt for the duration of that phase – either the Sword Strike stance or the Blade Shield stance. If you choose the Sword Strike stance, add 1 to this model's wound rolls for that phase. If you choose the Blade Shield stance, add 1 to this model's saving throws for that phase.
PSYKER	This model can attempt to manifest one psychic power in each friendly Psychic phase, and attempt to deny one psychic power in each enemy Psychic phase. It knows the *Smite* psychic power and one psychic power from the Sanctic discipline (pg 181).	
FACTION KEYWORDS	**IMPERIUM, ADEPTUS ASTARTES, GREY KNIGHTS**	
KEYWORDS	**CHARACTER, INFANTRY, PSYKER, BROTHERHOOD CHAMPION**	

The Brotherhood Champion is a masterful bladesman, sublimely skilled in the arts of single combat.

CASTELLAN CROWE

7 POWER

NAME	M	WS	BS	S	T	W	A	Ld	Sv
Castellan Crowe	6"	2+	2+	4	4	5	5	8	2+

Castellan Crowe is a single model armed with the Black Blade of Antwyr, a storm bolter, frag grenades, krak grenades and psyk-out grenades. Only one of this model may be included in your army.

WEAPON	RANGE	TYPE	S	AP	D	ABILITIES
Storm bolter	24"	Rapid Fire 2	4	0	1	-
The Black Blade of Antwyr	Melee	Melee	User	0	1	-
Frag grenade	6"	Grenade D6	3	0	1	-
Krak grenade	6"	Grenade 1	6	-1	D3	-
Psyk-out grenade	6"	Grenade D3	2	0	1	Each time you roll a hit roll of 6+ for this weapon when targeting a **Psyker** or **Daemon**, the target suffers a mortal wound instead of the normal damage.

ABILITIES	And They Shall Know No Fear, Daemon Hunters (pg 181)	Iron Halo: Castellan Crowe has a 4+ invulnerable save.
	Heroic Sacrifice: If Castellan Crowe is slain in the Fight phase, he can immediately pile in and attack before being removed as a casualty. **Purifying Flame:** When Castellan Crowe manifests the *Smite* psychic power, it only has a range of 3", but it inflicts D6 mortal wounds instead of D3 (whether or not the result of the Psychic test is more than 10).	**Master Swordsman:** You can re-roll failed hit and wound rolls for Castellan Crowe in the Fight phase. In addition, each time you make a successful wound roll for Castellan Crowe in the Fight phase, you can immediately make another attack with the Black Blade of Antwyr, though these additional attacks cannot generate any further attacks.

PSYKER	Castellan Crowe can attempt to manifest two psychic powers in each friendly Psychic phase, and attempt to deny one psychic power in each enemy Psychic phase. He knows the *Smite* psychic power and one psychic power from the Sanctic discipline (pg 181).
FACTION KEYWORDS	**IMPERIUM, ADEPTUS ASTARTES, GREY KNIGHTS**
KEYWORDS	**CHARACTER, INFANTRY, BROTHERHOOD CHAMPION, PSYKER, CASTELLAN CROWE**

STRIKE SQUAD

NAME	M	WS	BS	S	T	W	A	Ld	Sv
Grey Knight	6"	3+	3+	4	4	1	1	7	3+
Justicar	6"	3+	3+	4	4	1	2	8	3+

This unit contains 1 Justicar and 4 Grey Knights. It can include up to 5 additional Grey Knights (**Power Rating +7**). Each model is armed with a Nemesis force sword, storm bolter, frag grenades, krak grenades and psyk-out grenades.

WEAPON	RANGE	TYPE	S	AP	D	ABILITIES
Storm bolter	24"	Rapid Fire 2	4	0	1	-
Nemesis force sword	Melee	Melee	User	-3	D3	-
Frag grenade	6"	Grenade D6	3	0	1	-
Krak grenade	6"	Grenade 1	6	-1	D3	-
Psyk-out grenade	6"	Grenade D3	2	0	1	Each time you roll a hit roll of 6+ for this weapon when targeting a **Psyker** or **Daemon**, the target suffers a mortal wound instead of the normal damage.

WARGEAR OPTIONS	• Any model may replace his Nemesis force sword with an item from the *Grey Knights Melee Weapons* list. • For every five models in the unit, one Grey Knight may replace his Nemesis force sword and storm bolter with an item from the *Grey Knights Special Weapons* list.	
ABILITIES	**And They Shall Know No Fear, Daemon Hunters, Rites of Banishment, Teleport Strike** (pg 181)	**Combat Squads:** Before any models are deployed at the start of the game, a Strike Squad containing 10 models may be split into two units, each containing 5 models.
PSYKER	This unit can attempt to manifest one psychic power in each friendly Psychic phase, and attempt to deny one psychic power in each enemy Psychic phase. It knows the *Smite* psychic power and one psychic power from the Sanctic discipline (pg 181).	When manifesting or denying a psychic power, first select a model in the unit – measure range, visibility, etc. from this model. If this unit suffers Perils of the Warp, it suffers D3 mortal wounds as described in the core rules, but units within 6" will only suffer damage if the Perils of the Warp cause the last model in the manifesting unit to be slain.
FACTION KEYWORDS	**IMPERIUM, ADEPTUS ASTARTES, GREY KNIGHTS**	
KEYWORDS	**INFANTRY, PSYKER, STRIKE SQUAD**	

With Nemesis blade, boltgun and psycannon, the Grey Knights Strike Squad purges its foes.

TERMINATOR SQUAD

NAME	M	WS	BS	S	T	W	A	Ld	Sv
Grey Knight Terminator	5"	3+	3+	4	4	2	2	7	2+
Terminator Justicar	5"	3+	3+	4	4	2	3	8	2+

This unit contains 1 Terminator Justicar and 4 Grey Knight Terminators. It can include up to 5 additional Grey Knight Terminators (**Power Rating +13**). Each model is armed with a Nemesis force sword, storm bolter, frag grenades, krak grenades and psyk-out grenades.

WEAPON	RANGE	TYPE	S	AP	D	ABILITIES
Storm bolter	24"	Rapid Fire 2	4	0	1	-
Nemesis force sword	Melee	Melee	User	-3	D3	-
Frag grenade	6"	Grenade D6	3	0	1	-
Krak grenade	6"	Grenade 1	6	-1	D3	-
Psyk-out grenade	6"	Grenade D3	2	0	1	Each time you roll a hit roll of 6+ for this weapon when targeting a **PSYKER** or **DAEMON**, the target suffers a mortal wound instead of the normal damage.

WARGEAR OPTIONS	• Any model may replace his Nemesis force sword with an item from the *Grey Knights Melee Weapons* list. • For every five models in the unit, one Grey Knight Terminator may replace his storm bolter with an item from the *Grey Knights Special Weapons* list.

ABILITIES	**And They Shall Know No Fear, Daemon Hunters, Rites of Banishment, Teleport Strike** (pg 181) **Crux Terminatus:** All models in this unit have a 5+ invulnerable save.	**Combat Squads:** Before any models are deployed at the start of the game, a Terminator Squad containing 10 models may be split into two units, each containing 5 models.

PSYKER	This unit can attempt to manifest one psychic power in each friendly Psychic phase, and attempt to deny one psychic power in each enemy Psychic phase. It knows the *Smite* psychic power and one psychic power from the Sanctic discipline (pg 181).	When manifesting or denying a psychic power, first select a model in the unit – measure range, visibility, etc. from this model. If this unit suffers Perils of the Warp, it suffers D3 mortal wounds as described in the core rules, but units within 6" will only suffer damage if the Perils of the Warp cause the last model in the manifesting unit to be slain.

FACTION KEYWORDS	**IMPERIUM, ADEPTUS ASTARTES, GREY KNIGHTS**
KEYWORDS	**INFANTRY, TERMINATOR, PSYKER, TERMINATOR SQUAD**

Grey Knight Terminators are mighty heroes all, each a resilient, powerful and deadly warrior.

PURIFIER SQUAD

NAME	M	WS	BS	S	T	W	A	Ld	Sv
Purifier	6"	3+	3+	4	4	1	1	8	3+
Knight of the Flame	6"	3+	3+	4	4	1	2	9	3+

This unit contains 1 Knight of the Flame and 4 Purifiers. It can include up to 5 additional Purifiers (**Power Rating +9**). Each model is armed with a Nemesis force sword, storm bolter, frag grenades, krak grenades and psyk-out grenades.

WEAPON	RANGE	TYPE	S	AP	D	ABILITIES
Storm bolter	24"	Rapid Fire 2	4	0	1	-
Nemesis force sword	Melee	Melee	User	-3	D3	-
Frag grenade	6"	Grenade D6	3	0	1	-
Krak grenade	6"	Grenade 1	6	-1	D3	-
Psyk-out grenade	6"	Grenade D3	2	0	1	Each time you roll a hit roll of 6+ for this weapon when targeting a **PSYKER** or **DAEMON**, the target suffers a mortal wound instead of the normal damage.

WARGEAR OPTIONS	• Any model may replace his Nemesis force sword with an item from the *Grey Knights Melee Weapons* list. • For every five models in the unit, two Purifiers may replace their Nemesis force sword and storm bolter with an item from the *Grey Knights Special Weapons* list.

ABILITIES	**And They Shall Know No Fear, Daemon Hunters** (pg 181) **Purifying Flame:** When this unit manifests the *Smite* psychic power, it only has a range of 3", but it inflicts D6 mortal wounds instead of D3 (whether or not the result of the Psychic test is more than 10).	**Combat Squads:** Before any models are deployed at the start of the game, a Purifier Squad containing 10 models may be split into two units, each containing 5 models.

PSYKER	This unit can attempt to manifest one psychic power in each friendly Psychic phase, and attempt to deny one psychic power in each enemy Psychic phase. It knows the *Smite* psychic power and one psychic power from the Sanctic discipline (pg 181).	When manifesting or denying a psychic power, first select a model in the unit – measure range, visibility, etc. from this model. If this unit suffers Perils of the Warp, it suffers D3 mortal wounds as described in the core rules, but units within 6" will only suffer damage if the Perils of the Warp cause the last model in the manifesting unit to be slain.

FACTION KEYWORDS	**IMPERIUM, ADEPTUS ASTARTES, GREY KNIGHTS**
KEYWORDS	**INFANTRY, PSYKER, PURIFIER SQUAD**

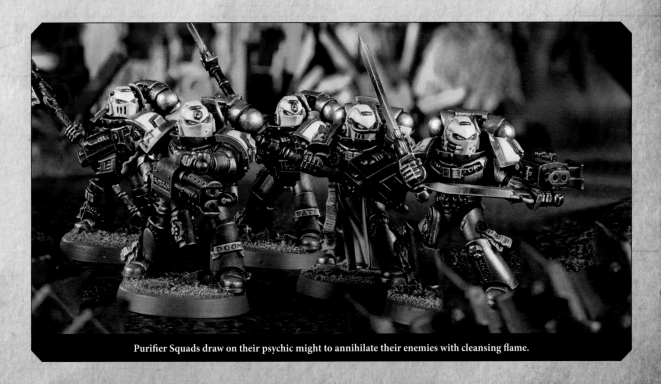

Purifier Squads draw on their psychic might to annihilate their enemies with cleansing flame.

PALADIN SQUAD

NAME	M	WS	BS	S	T	W	A	Ld	Sv
Paladin	5"	3+	3+	4	4	3	3	8	2+
Paragon	5"	2+	3+	4	4	3	3	9	2+

This unit contains 1 Paragon and 2 Paladins. It can include up to 2 additional Paladins (**Power Rating +9**), or up to 7 additional Paladins (**Power Rating +22**). Each model is armed with a Nemesis force sword, storm bolter, frag grenades, krak grenades and psyk-out grenades.

WEAPON	RANGE	TYPE	S	AP	D	ABILITIES
Storm bolter	24"	Rapid Fire 2	4	0	1	-
Nemesis force sword	Melee	Melee	User	-3	D3	-
Frag grenade	6"	Grenade D6	3	0	1	-
Krak grenade	6"	Grenade 1	6	-1	D3	-
Psyk-out grenade	6"	Grenade D3	2	0	1	Each time you roll a hit roll of 6+ for this weapon when targeting a **PSYKER** or **DAEMON**, the target suffers a mortal wound instead of the normal damage.

WARGEAR OPTIONS	• Any model may replace his Nemesis force sword with an item from the *Grey Knights Melee Weapons* list. • For every five models in the unit, two Paladins may replace their storm bolter with an item from the *Grey Knights Special Weapons* list.

ABILITIES	**And They Shall Know No Fear, Daemon Hunters, Rites of Banishment, Teleport Strike** (pg 181) **Crux Terminatus:** Models in this unit have a 5+ invulnerable save.	**Combat Squads:** Before any models are deployed at the start of the game, a Paladin Squad containing 10 models may be split into two units, each containing 5 models.

PSYKER	This unit can attempt to manifest one psychic power in each friendly Psychic phase, and attempt to deny one psychic power in each enemy Psychic phase. It knows the *Smite* psychic power and one psychic power from the Sanctic discipline (pg 181).	When manifesting or denying a psychic power, first select a model in the unit – measure range, visibility, etc. from this model. If this unit suffers Perils of the Warp, it suffers D3 mortal wounds as described in the core rules, but units within 6" will only suffer damage if the Perils of the Warp cause the last model in the manifesting unit to be slain.

FACTION KEYWORDS	**IMPERIUM, ADEPTUS ASTARTES, GREY KNIGHTS**
KEYWORDS	**INFANTRY, PALADIN, TERMINATOR, PSYKER, PALADIN SQUAD**

Even amongst the rarefied ranks of the Grey Knights, Paladins are magnificent Imperial champions.

PALADIN ANCIENT

7 POWER

NAME	M	WS	BS	S	T	W	A	Ld	Sv
Paladin Ancient	5"	2+	3+	4	4	5	4	8	2+

A Paladin Ancient is a single model armed with a storm bolter, frag grenades, krak grenades and psyk-out grenades.

WEAPON	RANGE	TYPE	S	AP	D	ABILITIES
Storm bolter	24"	Rapid Fire 2	4	0	1	-
Nemesis falchion	Melee	Melee	User	-2	D3	-
Frag grenade	6"	Grenade D6	3	0	1	-
Krak grenade	6"	Grenade 1	6	-1	D3	-
Psyk-out grenade	6"	Grenade D3	2	0	1	Each time you roll a hit roll of 6+ for this weapon when targeting a **PSYKER** or **DAEMON**, the target suffers a mortal wound instead of the normal damage.

WARGEAR OPTIONS	• This model may take a Nemesis falchion or replace its storm bolter with an item from the *Grey Knights Special Weapons* list.

ABILITIES	**And They Shall Know No Fear, Daemon Hunters, Rites of Banishment, Teleport Strike** (pg 181) **Crux Terminatus:** This model has a 5+ invulnerable save.	**Sacred Banner:** Friendly **GREY KNIGHTS** units within 6" of any sacred banners add 1 to their Leadership characteristic. In addition, models from friendly **GREY KNIGHTS INFANTRY** units that are within 6" of any sacred banners when they fight can make 1 additional attack that phase.

PSYKER	This model can attempt to manifest one psychic power in each friendly Psychic phase, and attempt to deny one psychic power in each enemy Psychic phase. It knows the *Smite* psychic power and one psychic power from the Sanctic discipline (pg 181).

FACTION KEYWORDS	**IMPERIUM, ADEPTUS ASTARTES, GREY KNIGHTS**

KEYWORDS	**CHARACTER, INFANTRY, PALADIN, TERMINATOR, PSYKER, ANCIENT**

APOTHECARY

NAME	M	WS	BS	S	T	W	A	Ld	Sv
Apothecary	5"	2+	3+	4	4	5	4	8	2+

An Apothecary is a single model armed with a Nemesis force sword, frag grenades, krak grenades and psyk-out grenades.

WEAPON	RANGE	TYPE	S	AP	D	ABILITIES
Nemesis falchion	Melee	Melee	User	-2	D3	-
Nemesis force sword	Melee	Melee	User	-3	D3	-
Frag grenade	6"	Grenade D6	3	0	1	-
Krak grenade	6"	Grenade 1	6	-1	D3	-
Psyk-out grenade	6"	Grenade D3	2	0	1	Each time you roll a hit roll of 6+ for this weapon when targeting a **PSYKER** or **DAEMON**, the target suffers a mortal wound instead of the normal damage.

WARGEAR OPTIONS	• This model may replace its Nemesis force sword with a Nemesis falchion or an item from the *Grey Knights Melee Weapons* list.
ABILITIES	**And They Shall Know No Fear, Daemon Hunters, Rites of Banishment, Teleport Strike** (pg 181) **Crux Terminatus:** This model has a 5+ invulnerable save. **Narthecium:** At the end of any of your Movement phases, the Apothecary can attempt to heal or revive a single model. Select a friendly **GREY KNIGHTS INFANTRY** unit within 3" of the Apothecary. If that unit contains a wounded model, it immediately regains D3 lost wounds. If the chosen unit contains no wounded models but one or more of its models have been slain during the battle, roll a D6. On a 4+ a single slain model is returned to the unit with 1 wound remaining. If an Apothecary fails to revive a model in this manner he can do nothing else for the remainder of the turn (shoot, charge, fight etc.) as he recovers the gene-seed of the fallen warrior. A unit can only be the target of the Narthecium ability once in each turn.
PSYKER	This model can attempt to manifest one psychic power in each friendly Psychic phase, and attempt to deny one psychic power in each enemy Psychic phase. It knows the *Smite* psychic power and one psychic power from the Sanctic discipline (pg 181).
FACTION KEYWORDS	**IMPERIUM, ADEPTUS ASTARTES, GREY KNIGHTS**
KEYWORDS	**CHARACTER, INFANTRY, TERMINATOR, PSYKER, APOTHECARY**

INTERCEPTOR SQUAD

8 POWER

NAME	M	WS	BS	S	T	W	A	Ld	Sv
Interceptor	12"	3+	3+	4	4	1	1	7	3+
Interceptor Justicar	12"	3+	3+	4	4	1	2	8	3+

This unit contains 1 Interceptor Justicar and 4 Interceptors. It can include up to 5 additional Interceptors (**Power Rating +8**). Each model is armed with a Nemesis force sword, storm bolter, frag grenades, krak grenades and psyk-out grenades.

WEAPON	RANGE	TYPE	S	AP	D	ABILITIES
Storm bolter	24"	Rapid Fire 2	4	0	1	-
Nemesis force sword	Melee	Melee	User	-3	D3	-
Frag grenade	6"	Grenade D6	3	0	1	-
Krak grenade	6"	Grenade 1	6	-1	D3	-
Psyk-out grenade	6"	Grenade D3	2	0	1	Each time you roll a hit roll of 6+ for this weapon when targeting a **Psyker** or **Daemon**, the target suffers a mortal wound instead of the normal damage.

WARGEAR OPTIONS	• Any model may replace his Nemesis force sword with an item from the *Grey Knights Melee Weapons* list. • For every five models in the unit, one Interceptor may replace his Nemesis force sword and storm bolter with an item from the *Grey Knights Special Weapons* list.

ABILITIES	**And They Shall Know No Fear, Daemon Hunters, Rites of Banishment, Teleport Strike** (pg 181) **Combat Squads:** Before any models are deployed at the start of the game, an Interceptor Squad containing 10 models may be split into two units, each containing 5 models.	**Personal Teleporters:** This unit can move across models and terrain as if they were not there. In addition, once per battle, instead of moving this unit normally in the Movement phase, you can choose for them to make a teleport shunt. At the end of the Movement phase, remove all of the models in the unit from the battlefield, then immediately set them up anywhere that is more than 9" from any enemy models.
PSYKER	This unit can attempt to manifest one psychic power in each friendly Psychic phase, and attempt to deny one psychic power in each enemy Psychic phase. It knows the *Smite* psychic power and one psychic power from the Sanctic discipline (pg 181).	When manifesting or denying a psychic power, first select a model in the unit – measure range, visibility, etc. from this model. If this unit suffers Perils of the Warp, it suffers D3 mortal wounds as described in the core rules, but units within 6" will only suffer damage if the Perils of the Warp cause the last model in the manifesting unit to be slain.

FACTION KEYWORDS	**Imperium, Adeptus Astartes, Grey Knights**
KEYWORDS	**Infantry, Psyker, Interceptor Squad**

Lunging from the seething tides of the warp, Interceptor Squads launch pinpoint strikes at the crucial moment.

PURGATION SQUAD

7 POWER

NAME	M	WS	BS	S	T	W	A	Ld	Sv
Purgator	6"	3+	3+	4	4	1	1	7	3+
Purgator Justicar	6"	3+	3+	4	4	1	2	8	3+

This unit contains 1 Purgator Justicar and 4 Purgators. It can include up to 5 additional Purgators (**Power Rating +7**). Each model is armed with a Nemesis force sword, storm bolter, frag grenades, krak grenades and psyk-out grenades.

WEAPON	RANGE	TYPE	S	AP	D	ABILITIES
Storm bolter	24"	Rapid Fire 2	4	0	1	-
Nemesis force sword	Melee	Melee	User	-3	D3	-
Frag grenade	6"	Grenade D6	3	0	1	-
Krak grenade	6"	Grenade 1	6	-1	D3	-
Psyk-out grenade	6"	Grenade D3	2	0	1	Each time you roll a hit roll of 6+ for this weapon when targeting a **PSYKER** or **DAEMON**, the target suffers a mortal wound instead of the normal damage.

WARGEAR OPTIONS	• Any model may replace his Nemesis force sword with an item from the *Grey Knights Melee Weapons* list. • Up to four Purgators in the unit may replace their Nemesis force sword and storm bolter with an item from the *Grey Knights Special Weapons* list.

ABILITIES	And They Shall Know No Fear, Daemon Hunters, Rites of Banishment (pg 181)	**Combat Squads:** Before any models are deployed at the start of the game, a Purgation Squad containing 10 models may be split into two units, each containing 5 models.
PSYKER	This unit can attempt to manifest one psychic power in each friendly Psychic phase, and attempt to deny one psychic power in each enemy Psychic phase. It knows the *Smite* psychic power and one psychic power from the Sanctic discipline (pg 181).	When manifesting or denying a psychic power, first select a model in the unit – measure range, visibility, etc. from this model. If this unit suffers Perils of the Warp, it suffers D3 mortal wounds as described in the core rules, but units within 6" will only suffer damage if the Perils of the Warp cause the last model in the manifesting unit to be slain.
FACTION KEYWORDS	IMPERIUM, ADEPTUS ASTARTES, GREY KNIGHTS	
KEYWORDS	INFANTRY, PSYKER, PURGATION SQUAD	

Purgation Squads annihilate all before them in a storm of heavy fire, and leave nought but riddled corpses in their wake.

NEMESIS DREADKNIGHT

NAME	M	WS	BS	S	T	W	A	Ld	Sv
Nemesis Dreadknight	*	3+	*	6	6	12	*	8	2+

DAMAGE

Some of this model's characteristics change as it suffers damage, as shown below:

REMAINING W	M	BS	A
7-12+	8"	3+	4
4-6	7"	4+	3
1-3	6"	5+	2

A Nemesis Dreadknight is a single model equipped with two dreadfists.

WEAPON	RANGE	TYPE	S	AP	D	ABILITIES
Gatling psilencer	24"	Heavy 12	4	0	D3	-
Heavy incinerator	12"	Heavy D6	6	-1	2	This weapon automatically hits its target.
Heavy psycannon	24"	Heavy 6	7	-1	2	-
Dreadfist	Melee	Melee	x2	-3	D3	If a model is equipped with two dreadfists, each time it fights it can make 1 additional attack with them.
Nemesis Daemon greathammer	Melee	Melee	x2	-4	D6	When a model attacks with this weapon, you must subtract 1 from the hit roll. Damage rolls of less than 3 count as 3 for this weapon.
Nemesis greatsword	Melee	Melee	+4	-3	D6	-

WARGEAR OPTIONS	• This model may take up to two different weapons from the following: - Heavy incinerator - Gatling psilencer - Heavy psycannon • This model may replace one of its dreadfists with a Nemesis Daemon greathammer or a Nemesis greatsword. • This model may take a Dreadknight teleporter.

ABILITIES	**And They Shall Know No Fear, Daemon Hunters, Rites of Banishment** (pg 181) **Force Shielding:** This model has a 5+ invulnerable save.	**Dreadknight Teleporter:** If this model has a Dreadknight teleporter, then during deployment, you can set it up in a teleportarium chamber instead of placing it on the battlefield. At the end of any of your Movement phases this model can teleport into battle – set them up anywhere on the battlefield that is more than 9" away from any enemy models.

PSYKER	This model can attempt to manifest one psychic power in each friendly Psychic phase, and attempt to deny one psychic power in each enemy Psychic phase. It knows the *Smite* psychic power and one psychic power from the Sanctic discipline (pg 181).

FACTION KEYWORDS	**IMPERIUM, ADEPTUS ASTARTES, GREY KNIGHTS**

KEYWORDS	**VEHICLE, PSYKER, NEMESIS DREADKNIGHT**

Nemesis Dreadknights tower over their hapless enemies as they stride into battle, guns blazing and blades flashing.

BATTLE-FORGED ARMIES

When picking a Battle-forged army for matched play, you will need to record the details of your army on a piece of paper (your Army Roster). Here we show one example of how you can do this; using several Detachment Rosters, at least one for each Detachment in your army, and the summarising main Army Roster itself. Over the page are blank rosters you can photocopy.

DETACHMENT ROSTERS

Each Detachment Roster details all the units it includes. Each unit has a small entry of its own where you can write down the name and type of unit, its Battlefield Role, the number of models it contains, and the weapons each model in the unit is equipped with. Details of how many models make up each unit and what weapons, options and upgrades each can take can be found on that unit's datasheet.

The points value of each unit's models and each individual weapon is then noted down by referencing the points lists in the appendix, and added together to give a points cost for the unit. The points cost of the entire Detachment is simply then the sum of the points costs of its units. This can be noted down alongside other useful information, such as the number of Command Points (if any) the Detachment gives you (see the *Warhammer 40,000* rulebook for more on Command Points).

Unit Champions

Many units are led by a champion of some kind such as a Sergeant. Unit champions often have better characteristics and weapon options than the models they command. With the exception of Wolf Guard Pack Leaders in Terminator Armour, unit champions have the same points cost as the others models in their unit.

Under-strength Units

Sometimes you may find that you do not have enough models to field a minimum-sized unit; if this is the case, you can still include one unit of that type in your army with as many models as you have available. In matched play games, you only pay the points

for the models you actually have in an under-strength unit (and any weapons they are equipped with). An under-strength unit still takes up the appropriate slot in a Detachment.

ARMY ROSTER

Once you have filled in all of your Detachment Rosters, you can then fill out the main Army Roster. The name and points value of each Detachment is noted down here for reference. The total points cost of your army is the sum of all the Detachment points costs in your army plus any reinforcement points you have chosen to put aside (see below). The points cost of your army should not exceed the points limit you are using for the battle.

There are lots of other useful things to write down on your main Army Roster, such as who the army's Warlord is (this should be done at the start of the battle) and the number of Command Points available to your army. Remember that all Battle-forged armies start with 3 Command Points, but certain Detachments, and occasionally certain models, can change this total.

Reinforcement Points

Sometimes an ability will allow you to add units to your army, or replace units that have been destroyed. You must set aside some of your points in order to use these units. The points you set aside are called your reinforcement points, and need to be recorded on your army roster. Each time a unit is added to an army during battle, subtract the number of points the unit would cost from your pool of reinforcement points.

ARMY ROSTER

PLAYER NAME:	Alex Smith	ARMY FACTION:	Adeptus Astartes
ARMY NAME:	Strike Force Calgar	WARLORD:	Marneus Calgar

DETACHMENT NAME	TYPE	CPS	POINTS
Lords of Macragge	Patrol	0+2	706
4th Battle Demi-company	Battalion	3	932
Ultima Task Force	Vanguard	1	362

WARLORD TRAIT		
FILL IN AT SET-UP:		

Total Command Points:	9
Reinforcement Points:	0
TOTAL POINTS:	2000

DETACHMENT ROSTER

NAME:	Lords of Macragge	TYPE:	Patrol

UNIT

UNIT TITLE: Marneus Calgar	BATTLEFIELD ROLE: HQ	NO. OF MODELS: 1	POINTS (MODELS): 250

WARGEAR:
Gauntlets of Ultramar and relic blade (all wargear points included in the model's points)

POINTS (WARGEAR): N/A

TOTAL POINTS (UNIT): 250

UNIT

UNIT TITLE: Tactical Squad	BATTLEFIELD ROLE: Troops	NO. OF MODELS: 10	POINTS (MODELS): 130

WARGEAR:
Chainsword (0), missile launcher (25), plasma gun (13), 7 x boltguns (0), 10 x bolt pistols (0), 10 x frag and krak grenades (0)

POINTS (WARGEAR): 38

TOTAL POINTS (UNIT): 168

UNIT

UNIT TITLE: Devastator Squad	BATTLEFIELD ROLE: Heavy Support	NO. OF MODELS: 5	POINTS (MODELS): 65

WARGEAR:
Combi-plasma (15), 2 x heavy bolters (20), 2 x lascannon (50), 5 x bolt pistols (0), 5 x frag and krak grenades (0), Armorium Cherub (5)

POINTS (WARGEAR): 90

TOTAL POINTS (UNIT): 155

UNIT

UNIT TITLE: Dreadnought	BATTLEFIELD ROLE: Elites	NO. OF MODELS: 1	POINTS (MODELS): 70

WARGEAR:
Assault cannon (21), Dreadnought combat weapon (40), storm bolter (2)

POINTS (WARGEAR): 63

TOTAL POINTS (UNIT): 133

Total Points (Detachment):	706	Command Points:	0+2

NOTES: All units in the Lords of Macragge Detachment are Ultramarines.
Gain 2 Command Points if Marneus Calgar is the army's Warlord.

ARMY ROSTER

PLAYER NAME: **ARMY FACTION:**

ARMY NAME: **WARLORD:**

DETACHMENT NAME	TYPE	CPS	POINTS

WARLORD TRAIT

FILL IN AT SET-UP:

Total Command Points:

Reinforcement Points:

TOTAL POINTS:

DETACHMENT ROSTER

NAME:

TYPE:

UNIT

UNIT TITLE:	BATTLEFIELD ROLE:	NO. OF MODELS:	POINTS (MODELS):
WARGEAR:			POINTS (WARGEAR):
		TOTAL POINTS (UNIT):	

UNIT

UNIT TITLE:	BATTLEFIELD ROLE:	NO. OF MODELS:	POINTS (MODELS):
WARGEAR:			POINTS (WARGEAR):
		TOTAL POINTS (UNIT):	

UNIT

UNIT TITLE:	BATTLEFIELD ROLE:	NO. OF MODELS:	POINTS (MODELS):
WARGEAR:			POINTS (WARGEAR):
		TOTAL POINTS (UNIT):	

UNIT

UNIT TITLE:	BATTLEFIELD ROLE:	NO. OF MODELS:	POINTS (MODELS):
WARGEAR:			POINTS (WARGEAR):
		TOTAL POINTS (UNIT):	

Total Points (Detachment):	Command Points:
NOTES:	

SPACE MARINES POINTS VALUES

If you are playing a matched play game, or a game that uses a points limit, you can use the following lists to determine the total points cost of your army. Simply add together the points values of all your models, as well as the wargear they are equipped with, to determine your army's total points value.

HQ

UNIT	MODELS PER UNIT	POINTS PER MODEL (Does not include wargear)
Captain	1	74
Captain in Cataphractii Armour	1	126
Captain in Gravis Armour	1	102
Captain in Terminator Armour	1	122
Captain on Bike	1	98
Captain with Jump Pack	1	93
Chaplain	1	72
Chaplain in Terminator Armour	1	115
Chaplain on Bike	1	95
Chaplain with Jump Pack	1	90
Land Raider Excelsior	1	300
Librarian	1	93
Librarian in Terminator Armour	1	145
Librarian on Bike	1	119
Librarian with Jump Pack	1	116
Primaris Lieutenants	1-2	70
Rhino Primaris	1	100
Techmarine	1	58
Techmarine on Bike	1	70

TROOPS

UNIT	MODELS PER UNIT	POINTS PER MODEL (Does not include wargear)
Crusader Squad	5-10	13
- Neophyte	0-10	11
Intercessor Squad	5	20
Scout Squad	5-10	11
Tactical Squad	5-10	13

DEDICATED TRANSPORTS

UNIT	MODELS PER UNIT	POINTS PER MODEL (Does not include wargear)
Drop Pod	1	103
Land Speeder Storm	1	80
Razorback	1	65
Rhino	1	70

ELITES

UNIT	MODELS PER UNIT	POINTS PER MODEL (Does not include wargear)
Apothecary	1	55
Apothecary on Bike	1	80
Cataphractii Terminator Squad	5-10	30
Centurion Assault Squad	3-6	73
Chapter Ancient	1	72
Chapter Champion	1	65
Company Ancient	1	63
Company Ancient on Bike	1	88
Company Champion	1	56
Company Champion on Bike	1	80
Company Veterans	2-5	16
Company Veterans on Bikes	2-5	34
Contemptor Dreadnought	1	98
Damned Legionnaires	5-10	25
Dreadnought	1	70
Honour Guard	2	21
Imperial Space Marine	1	60
Ironclad Dreadnought	1	120
Primaris Ancient	1	69
Servitors	4	2
Sternguard Veteran Squad	5-10	16
Tartaros Terminator Squad	5-10	31
Terminator Assault Squad	5-10	31
Terminator Squad	5-10	26
Tyrannic War Veterans	4-10	16
Vanguard Veteran Squad	5-10	16
Vanguard Veteran Squad with Jump Packs	5-10	18
Venerable Dreadnought	1	90

FAST ATTACK

UNIT	MODELS PER UNIT	POINTS PER MODEL (Does not include wargear)
Assault Squad	5-10	13
Assault Squad with Jump Packs	5-10	16
Attack Bike Squad	1-3	45
Bike Squad	3-8	31
- Attack Bike	0-1	45
Inceptor Squad	3	45
Land Speeders	1-3	80
Scout Bike Squad	3-9	25

FLYERS

UNIT	MODELS PER UNIT	POINTS PER MODEL (Does not include wargear)
Stormhawk Interceptor	1	85
Stormraven Gunship	1	172
Stormtalon Gunship	1	110

HEAVY SUPPORT

UNIT	MODELS PER UNIT	POINTS PER MODEL (Does not include wargear)
Centurion Devastator Squad	3-6	65
Devastator Squad	5-10	13
- Armorium Cherub	-	5
Hellblaster Squad	5	20
Hunter	1	90
Land Raider	1	239
Land Raider Crusader	1	244
Land Raider Redeemer	1	244
Predator	1	102
Stalker	1	90
Thunderfire Cannon	1	28
- Techmarine Gunner	1	36
Vindicator	1	160
Whirlwind	1	90

NAMED CHARACTERS

UNIT	MODELS PER UNIT	POINTS PER MODEL (Including wargear)
Captain Lysander	1	150
Captain Sicarius	1	132
Cenobyte Servitors	3	2
Chaplain Cassius	1	138
Chaplain Grimaldus	1	120
Chief Librarian Tigurius	1	130
The Emperor's Champion	1	108
High Marshal Helbrecht	1	170
Kayvaan Shrike	1	150
Kor'sarro Khan	1	107
Kor'sarro Khan on Moondrakkan	1	132
Marneus Calgar	1	250
Marneus Calgar in Artificer Armour	1	235
Pedro Kantor	1	170
Roboute Guilliman	1	360
Sergeant Chronus	1	58
Sergeant Telion	1	89
Vulkan He'stan	1	154

LORDS OF WAR

UNIT	MODELS PER UNIT	POINTS PER MODEL
Terminus Ultra	1	400

RANGED WEAPONS

WEAPON	POINTS PER WEAPON
Assault bolter	15
Assault cannon	21
Astartes grenade launcher	11
Astartes shotgun	0
Bolt pistol	0
Bolt rifle	0
Boltgun	0
Boltstorm gauntlet	25
Centurion missile launcher	25
Cerberus launcher	5
Combi-bolter	2
Combi-flamer	11
Combi-grav	17
Combi-melta	19
Combi-plasma	15
Conversion beamer	20
Cyclone missile launcher	50
Deathwind launcher	5
Demolisher cannon	0
Disintegration combi-gun	0
Disintegration pistol	0
Flamer	9
Flamestorm cannon	30
Frag grenade	0
Grav-pistol	8
Grav-cannon and grav-amp	28
Grav-gun	15
Grenade harness	8
Heavy bolter	10
Heavy flamer	17
Heavy plasma cannon	30
Hunter-killer missile	6
Hurricane bolter	4
Icarus stormcannon	17
Kheres pattern assault cannon	25
Krak grenade	0
Las-talon	40
Lascannon	25
Master-crafted auto bolt rifle	4
Master-crafted boltgun	3
Melta bombs	5
Meltagun	17
Missile launcher	25
Multi-melta	27
Orbital array	50
Plasma blaster	17
Plasma cannon	21
Plasma cutter	7
Plasma gun	13
Plasma incinerator	18
Plasma pistol	7
Predator autocannon	49
Reaper autocannon	18
Skyhammer missile launcher	24
Skyspear missile launcher	30

RANGED WEAPONS

WEAPON	POINTS PER WEAPON
Sniper rifle	4
Special issue boltgun	3
Storm bolter	2
Stormstrike missile launcher	21
Thunderfire cannon	30
Twin assault cannon	35
Twin autocannon	33
Twin boltgun	2
Twin heavy bolter	17
Twin heavy flamer	34
Twin heavy plasma cannon	34
Twin lascannon	50
Twin multi-melta	54
Twin plasma gun	20
Typhoon missile launcher	50
Volkite charger	6
Whirlwind castellan launcher	25
Whirlwind vengeance launcher	34
Wrist-mounted grenade launcher	4

MELEE WEAPONS

WEAPON	POINTS PER WEAPON
Chainfist	22
Chainsword	0
Champion's blade	0
Combat knife	0
Crozius arcanum	0
Dreadnought chainfist	46
Dreadnought combat weapon (Ironclad Dreadnought)	0
Dreadnought combat weapon (other models)	40
Eviscerator	22
Force axe	16
Force stave	14
Force sword	12
Lightning claws (single/pair)	9/13
Master-crafted power sword	10
Power axe	5
Power fist	20
Power lance	4
Power maul	4
Power sword	4
Relic blade	21
Seismic hammer	48
Servo-arm	12
Siege drills	0
Thunder hammer (**Characters**)	25
Thunder hammer (other models)	20

OTHER WARGEAR

WARGEAR	POINTS PER ITEM
Camo cloak	3
Combat shield	4
Storm shield (**Characters**)	15
Storm shield (other models)	5
Teleport homer	0

RANGED WEAPONS

WEAPON	RANGE	TYPE	S	AP	D	ABILITIES
Assault bolter	18"	Assault 3	5	-1	1	-
Assault cannon	24"	Heavy 6	6	-1	1	-
Astartes grenade launcher	When attacking with this weapon, choose one of the profiles below.					
- Frag grenade	24"	Assault D6	3	0	1	-
- Krak grenade	24"	Assault 1	6	-1	D3	-
Astartes shotgun	12"	Assault 2	4	0	1	If the target is within half range, add 1 to this weapon's Strength.
Bolt pistol	12"	Pistol 1	4	0	1	-
Bolt rifle	30"	Rapid Fire 1	4	-1	1	-
Boltgun	24"	Rapid Fire 1	4	0	1	-
Boltstorm gauntlet (shooting)	12"	Pistol 3	4	0	1	-
Centurion missile launcher	36"	Assault D3	8	-2	D3	-
Cerberus launcher	18"	Heavy D6	4	0	1	-
Combi-bolter	24"	Rapid Fire 2	4	0	1	-
Combi-flamer	When attacking with this weapon, choose one or both of the profiles below. If you choose both, subtract 1 from all hit rolls for this weapon.					
- Boltgun	24"	Rapid Fire 1	4	0	1	-
- Flamer	8"	Assault D6	4	0	1	This weapon automatically hits its target.
Combi-grav	When attacking with this weapon, choose one or both of the profiles below. If you choose both, subtract 1 from all hit rolls for this weapon.					
- Boltgun	24"	Rapid Fire 1	4	0	1	-
- Grav-gun	18"	Rapid Fire 1	5	-3	1	If the target has a Save characteristic of 3+ or better, this weapon has a Damage characteristic of D3.
Combi-melta	When attacking with this weapon, choose one or both of the profiles below. If you choose both, subtract 1 from all hit rolls for this weapon.					
- Boltgun	24"	Rapid Fire 1	4	0	1	-
- Meltagun	12"	Assault 1	8	-4	D6	If the target is within half range of this weapon, roll two dice when inflicting damage with it and discard the lowest result.
Combi-plasma	When attacking with this weapon, choose one or both of the profiles below. If you choose both, subtract 1 from all hit rolls for this weapon.					
- Boltgun	24"	Rapid Fire 1	4	0	1	-
- Plasma gun	24"	Rapid Fire 1	7	-3	1	See plasma gun
Conversion beamer	42"	Heavy D3	6	0	1	Attacks from a conversion beamer that target enemies at over half its range are resolved at Strength 8, AP -1 and Damage 2.
Cyclone missile launcher	When attacking with this weapon, choose one of the profiles below.					
- Frag missile	36"	Heavy 2D3	4	0	1	-
- Krak missile	36"	Heavy 2	8	-2	D6	-
Deathwind launcher	12"	Assault D6	5	0	1	-
Demolisher cannon	24"	Heavy D3	10	-3	D6	When attacking units with 5 or more models, change this weapon's Type to Heavy D6.
Disintegration combi-gun	When attacking with this weapon, choose one or both of the profiles below. If you choose both, subtract 1 from all hit rolls for this weapon.					
- Boltgun	24"	Rapid Fire 1	4	0	1	-
- Disintegration gun	18"	Rapid Fire 1	5	-3	D6	-
Disintegration pistol	9"	Pistol 1	5	-3	D6	-
Flamer	8"	Assault D6	4	0	1	This weapon automatically hits its target.
Flamestorm cannon	8"	Heavy D6	6	-2	2	This weapon automatically hits its target.
Frag grenade	6"	Grenade D6	3	0	1	-
Grav-pistol	12"	Pistol 1	5	-3	1	If the target has a Save characteristic of 3+ or better, this weapon has a Damage characteristic of D3.
Grav-cannon and grav-amp	24"	Heavy 4	5	-3	1	If the target has a Save characteristic of 3+ or better, this weapon has a Damage characteristic of D3.

WEAPON	RANGE	TYPE	S	AP	D	ABILITIES
Grav-gun	18"	Rapid Fire 1	5	-3	1	If the target has a Save characteristic of 3+ or better, this weapon has a Damage characteristic of D3.
Grenade harness	12"	Assault D6	4	1	1	-
Heavy bolter	36"	Heavy 3	5	-1	1	-
Heavy flamer	8"	Heavy D6	5	-1	1	This weapon automatically hits its target.
Heavy plasma cannon	When attacking with this weapon, choose one of the profiles below.					
- Standard	36"	Heavy D3	7	-3	1	-
- Supercharge	36"	Heavy D3	8	-3	2	For each hit roll of 1, the bearer suffers 1 mortal wound after all of this weapon's shots have been resolved.
Hunter-killer missile	48"	Heavy 1	8	-2	D6	A model can only fire each of its hunter-killer missiles once per battle.
Hurricane bolter	24"	Rapid Fire 6	4	0	1	-
Icarus stormcannon	48"	Heavy 3	7	-1	2	Add 1 to all hit rolls made for this weapon against targets that can FLY. Subtract 1 from the hit rolls made for this weapon against all other targets.
Kheres pattern assault cannon	24"	Heavy 6	7	-1	1	-
Krak grenade	6"	Grenade 1	6	-1	D3	-
Las-talon	24"	Heavy 2	9	-3	D6	-
Lascannon	48"	Heavy 1	9	-3	D6	-
Master-crafted auto bolt rifle	24"	Assault 2	4	0	2	-
Master-crafted boltgun	24"	Rapid Fire 1	4	-1	2	-
Melta bomb	4"	Grenade 1	8	-4	D6	-
Meltagun	12"	Assault 1	8	-4	D6	If the target is within half range of this weapon, roll two dice when inflicting damage with it and discard the lowest result.
Missile launcher	When attacking with this weapon, choose one of the profiles below.					
- Frag missile	48"	Heavy D6	4	0	1	-
- Krak missile	48"	Heavy 1	8	-2	D6	-
Multi-melta	24"	Heavy 1	8	-4	D6	If the target is within half range of this weapon, roll two dice when inflicting damage with it and discard the lowest result.
Orbital array	72"	Heavy D3	10	-4	D6	This weapon can only be fired once per battle. This weapon can target units that are not visible to the bearer. When targeting units with 10 or more models, change this weapon's Type to Heavy D6.
Plasma blaster	When attacking with this weapon, choose one of the profiles below.					
- Standard	18"	Assault 2	7	-3	1	-
- Supercharge	18"	Assault 2	8	-3	2	On a hit roll of 1, the bearer is slain after all of this weapon's shots have been resolved.
Plasma cannon	When attacking with this weapon, choose one of the profiles below.					
- Standard	36"	Heavy D3	7	-3	1	-
- Supercharge	36"	Heavy D3	8	-3	2	On a hit roll of 1, the bearer is slain after all of this weapon's shots have been resolved.
Plasma cutter	When attacking with this weapon, choose one of the profiles below.					
- Standard	12"	Assault 1	7	-3	1	-
- Supercharge	12"	Assault 1	8	-3	2	On a hit roll of 1, the bearer is slain.
Plasma gun	When attacking with this weapon, choose one of the profiles below.					
- Standard	24"	Rapid Fire 1	7	-3	1	-
- Supercharge	24"	Rapid Fire 1	8	-3	2	On a hit roll of 1, the bearer is slain after all of this weapon's shots have been resolved.
Plasma incinerator	When attacking with this weapon, choose one of the profiles below.					
- Standard	30"	Rapid Fire 1	7	-4	1	-
- Supercharge	30"	Rapid Fire 1	8	-4	2	On a hit roll of 1, the bearer is slain after all of this weapon's shots have been resolved.
Plasma pistol	When attacking with this weapon, choose one of the profiles below.					
- Standard	12"	Pistol 1	7	-3	1	-
- Supercharge	12"	Pistol 1	8	-3	2	On a hit roll of 1, the bearer is slain.
Predator autocannon	48"	Heavy 2D3	7	-1	3	-
Reaper autocannon	36"	Heavy 4	7	-1	1	-

RANGED WEAPONS CONT.

WEAPON	RANGE	TYPE	S	AP	D	ABILITIES
Skyhammer missile launcher	60"	Heavy 3	7	-1	D3	Add 1 to all hit rolls made for this weapon against targets that can FLY. Subtract 1 from the hit rolls made for this weapon against all other targets.
Skyspear missile launcher	60"	Heavy 1	9	-3	D6	Add 1 to all hit rolls made for this weapon against targets that can FLY. You can re-roll failed hit rolls for this weapon.
Sniper rifle	36"	Heavy 1	4	0	1	This weapon may target a CHARACTER even if it is not the closest enemy unit. If you roll a wound roll of 6+ for this weapon, it inflicts a mortal wound in addition to its normal damage.
Special issue boltgun	30"	Rapid Fire 1	4	-2	1	-
Storm bolter	24"	Rapid Fire 2	4	0	1	-
Stormstrike missile launcher	72"	Heavy 1	8	-3	3	-
Thunderfire cannon	60"	Heavy 4D3	5	0	1	This weapon can target units that are not visible to the firing model
Twin assault cannon	24"	Heavy 12	6	-1	1	-
Twin autocannon	48"	Heavy 4	7	-1	2	-
Twin boltgun	24"	Rapid Fire 2	4	0	1	-
Twin heavy bolter	36"	Heavy 6	5	-1	1	-
Twin heavy flamer	8"	Assault 2D6	5	-1	1	This weapon automatically hits its target.
Twin heavy plasma cannon	When attacking with this weapon, choose one of the profiles below.					
- Standard	36"	Heavy 2D3	7	-3	1	-
- Supercharge	36"	Heavy 2D3	8	-3	2	For each hit roll of 1, the bearer suffers 1 mortal wound after all of this weapon's shots have been resolved.
Twin lascannon	48"	Heavy 2	9	-3	D6	-
Twin multi-melta	24"	Heavy 2	8	-4	D6	If the target is within half range of this weapon, roll two dice when inflicting damage with it and discard the lowest result.
Twin plasma gun	When attacking with this weapon, choose one of the profiles below.					
- Standard	24"	Rapid Fire 2	7	-3	1	-
- Supercharge	24"	Rapid Fire 2	8	-3	2	On a hit roll of 1, the bearer is slain after all of this weapon's shots have been resolved.
Typhoon missile launcher	When attacking with this weapon, choose one of the profiles below.					
- Frag missile	48"	Heavy 2D6	4	0	1	-
- Krak missile	48"	Heavy 2	8	-2	D6	-
Volkite charger	15"	Heavy 2	5	0	2	-
Whirlwind castellan launcher	72"	Heavy 2D6	6	0	1	This weapon can target units that are not visible to the firing model.
Whirlwind vengeance launcher	72"	Heavy 2D3	7	-1	2	This weapon can target units that are not visible to the firing model.
Wrist-mounted grenade launcher	12"	Assault D3	4	1	1	-

MELEE WEAPONS

WEAPON	RANGE	TYPE	S	AP	D	ABILITIES
Boltstorm gauntlet (melee)	Melee	Melee	x2	-3	D3	When attacking with this weapon, you must subtract 1 from the hit roll.
Chainfist	Melee	Melee	x2	-4	2	When attacking with this weapon, you must subtract 1 from the hit roll.
Chainsword	Melee	Melee	User	0	1	Each time the bearer fights, it can make 1 additional attack with this weapon.
Champion's blade	Melee	Melee	User	-2	1	Each time the bearer fights, it can make 1 additional attack with this weapon.
Combat knife	Melee	Melee	User	0	1	Each time the bearer fights, it can make 1 additional attack with this weapon.
Crozius arcanum	Melee	Melee	+1	-1	2	-
Dreadnought chainfist	Melee	Melee	x2	-4	4	-
Dreadnought combat weapon	Melee	Melee	x2	-3	3	-
Eviscerator	Melee	Melee	x2	-4	D3	When attacking with this weapon, you must subtract 1 from the hit roll.
Force axe	Melee	Melee	+1	-2	D3	-
Force stave	Melee	Melee	+2	-1	D3	-
Force sword	Melee	Melee	User	-3	D3	-
Lightning claw	Melee	Melee	User	-2	1	You can re-roll failed wound rolls for this weapon. If a model is armed with two lightning claws, each time it fights it can make 1 additional attack with them.
Master-crafted power sword	Melee	Melee	User	-3	2	-
Power axe	Melee	Melee	+1	-2	1	-
Power fist	Melee	Melee	x2	-3	D3	When attacking with this weapon, you must subtract 1 from the hit roll.
Power lance	Melee	Melee	+2	-1	1	-
Power maul	Melee	Melee	+2	-1	1	-
Power sword	Melee	Melee	User	-3	1	-
Relic blade	Melee	Melee	+2	-3	D3	-
Seismic hammer	Melee	Melee	x2	-4	5	When attacking with this weapon, you must subtract 1 from the hit roll.
Servo-arm	Melee	Melee	x2	-2	3	Each servo-arm can only be used to make one attack each time this model fights. When a model attacks with this weapon, you must subtract 1 from the hit roll.
Siege drills	Melee	Melee	x2	-4	3	-
Thunder hammer	Melee	Melee	x2	-3	3	When attacking with this weapon, you must subtract 1 from the hit roll.

OTHER WARGEAR

Camo cloak	If every model in a unit has a camo cloak you can add 2 to saving throws made for models in the unit when they receive the benefits of cover, instead of 1.
Combat shield	A model with a combat shield has a 5+ invulnerable save.
Storm shield	A model with a storm shield has a 3+ invulnerable save.

ULTRAMARINES WARGEAR

RANGED AND MELEE WEAPONS						
WEAPON	RANGE	TYPE	S	AP	D	ABILITIES
Gauntlets of Ultramar (shooting)	24"	Rapid Fire 2	4	-1	2	-
Hand of Dominion (shooting)	24"	Rapid Fire 3	6	-1	2	-
Infernus	When attacking with this weapon, choose one or both of the profiles below. If you choose both, subtract 1 from all hit rolls for this weapon.					
- Flamer	8"	Assault D6	4	0	1	This weapon automatically hits its target.
- Master-crafted boltgun	24"	Rapid Fire 1	4	-1	2	-
Quietus	36"	Heavy 2	4	-1	D3	This weapon may target a CHARACTER even if it is not the closest enemy unit.
The Emperor's Sword	Melee	Melee	+2	-4	3	If you roll a wound roll of 6+ for this weapon, it inflicts D3 mortal wounds in addition to its normal damage.
Gauntlets of Ultramar (melee)	Melee	Melee	x2	-3	D3	-
Hand of Dominion (melee)	Melee	Melee	x2	-3	3	-
Rod of Tigurius	Melee	Melee	+3	-1	D3	-
Talassarian Tempest Blade	Melee	Melee	User	-3	D3	Any wound rolls of 6+ made for this weapon cause D3 mortal wounds instead of the normal damage.

IMPERIAL FISTS WARGEAR

MELEE WEAPON						
WEAPON	RANGE	TYPE	S	AP	D	ABILITIES
Fist of Dorn	Melee	Melee	+6	-3	3	-

CRIMSON FISTS WARGEAR

RANGED WEAPON						
WEAPON	RANGE	TYPE	S	AP	D	ABILITIES
Dorn's Arrow	24"	Assault 4	4	-1	1	-

BLACK TEMPLARS WARGEAR

MELEE WEAPONS						
WEAPON	RANGE	TYPE	S	AP	D	ABILITIES
Black Sword	Melee	Melee	+2	-3	D3	You can re-roll failed wound rolls when attacking with this weapon if the target is a CHARACTER or a MONSTER.
Sword of the High Marshals	Melee	Melee	+1	-3	D3	Helbrecht can make D3 additional attacks with this weapon if he charged in his turn.

RAVEN GUARD WARGEAR

MELEE WEAPON						
WEAPON	RANGE	TYPE	S	AP	D	ABILITIES
Raven's Talons	Melee	Melee	User	-3	D3	You can re-roll failed wound rolls for this weapon.

SALAMANDERS WARGEAR

RANGED WEAPON						
WEAPON	RANGE	TYPE	S	AP	D	ABILITIES
Gauntlet of the Forge	8"	Assault D6	5	-1	1	This weapon automatically hits its target.

WHITE SCARS WARGEAR

MELEE WEAPON						
WEAPON	RANGE	TYPE	S	AP	D	ABILITIES
Moonfang	Melee	Melee	User	-3	D3	This weapon has Strength x2 if the target is a CHARACTER.

BLOOD ANGELS POINTS VALUES

If you are playing a matched play game, or a game that uses a points limit, you can use the following lists to determine the total points cost of your army. Simply add together the points values of all your models, as well as the wargear they are equipped with, to determine your army's total points value. For units based on Space Marines datasheets, use the appropriate points values from pages 202-203.

UNITS

UNIT	MODELS PER UNIT	POINTS PER MODEL (Does not include wargear)
Baal Predator	1	107
Company Ancient with Jump Pack	1	72
Company Champion with Jump Pack	1	70
Company Veterans with Jump Packs	2-5	19
Death Company	5-15	17
Death Company Dreadnought	1	128
Death Company with Jump Packs	5-15	20
Furioso Dreadnought	1	122
Librarian Dreadnought	1	150
Sanguinary Guard	4-10	22
Sanguinary Guard Ancient	1	84
Sanguinary Novitiate with Jump Pack	1	60
Sanguinary Priest	1	69
Sanguinary Priest on Bike	1	94
Sanguinary Priest with Jump Pack	1	86
Techmarine with Jump Pack	1	91
Terminator Ancient	1	108

UNITS

UNIT	MODELS PER UNIT	POINTS PER MODEL (Including wargear)
Astorath	1	143
Brother Corbulo	1	94
Captain Tycho	1	95
Chief Librarian Mephiston	1	145
Commander Dante	1	215
Gabriel Seth	1	135
Lemartes	1	129
The Sanguinor	1	170
Tycho the Lost	1	70

RANGED WEAPONS

WEAPON	POINTS PER WEAPON
Angelus boltgun	9
Frag cannon	19
Hand flamer	8
Inferno pistol	20

MELEE WEAPONS

WEAPON	POINTS PER WEAPON
Blood talons	65
Encarmine axe	16
Encarmine sword	13
Furioso fist (single/pair)	40/50
Furioso force halberd	0

OTHER WARGEAR

WARGEAR	POINTS PER ITEM
Death mask	2
Magna-grapple	5

BLOOD ANGELS WARGEAR

RANGED WEAPONS

WEAPON	RANGE	TYPE	S	AP	D	ABILITIES
Angelus boltgun	12"	Assault 2	4	-1	1	-
Blood Song	When attacking with this weapon, choose one or both of the profiles below. If you choose both, subtract 1 from all hit rolls for this weapon.					
- Master-crafted boltgun	24"	Rapid Fire 1	4	-1	2	-
- Meltagun	12"	Assault 1	8	-4	D6	If the target is within half range of this weapon, roll two dice when inflicting damage with it and discard the lowest result.
Frag cannon	8"	Assault 2D6	6	-1	1	This weapon automatically hits its target.
Hand flamer	6"	Pistol D3	3	0	1	This weapon automatically hits its target.
Inferno pistol	6"	Pistol 1	8	-4	D6	If the target is within half range of this weapon, roll two dice when inflicting damage with it and discard the lowest result.

MELEE WEAPONS

WEAPON	RANGE	TYPE	S	AP	D	ABILITIES
The Axe Mortalis	Melee	Melee	+2	-3	D3	You can re-roll failed wound rolls for this weapon if the target is a **CHARACTER**.
The Blood Crozius	Melee	Melee	+2	-2	D3	
Blood Reaver	Melee	Melee	x2	-1	3	Each time you roll a hit roll of 6+ for this weapon, inflict 1 additional hit on the target.
Blood talons	Melee	Melee	x2	-3	D6	-
Encarmine axe	Melee	Melee	+1	-2	D3	-
Encarmine broadsword	Melee	Melee	+2	-4	D3	-
Encarmine sword	Melee	Melee	User	-3	D3	-
The Executioner's Axe	Melee	Melee	+1	-3	D3	Each time you roll a wound roll of 6+ for this weapon it causes 3 damage instead of D3.
Furioso fist	Melee	Melee	x2	-3	3	If a model is equipped with two Furioso fists, you can re-roll failed hit rolls when attacking with them.
Furioso force halberd	Melee	Melee	+4	-4	3	-
Heaven's Teeth	Melee	Melee	+1	-1	1	-
The Sanguine Sword	Melee	Melee	x2	-3	D3	-

DARK ANGELS POINTS VALUES

If you are playing a matched play game, or a game that uses a points limit, you can use the following lists to determine the total points cost of your army. Simply add together the points values of all your models, as well as the wargear they are equipped with, to determine your army's total points value. For units based on Space Marines datasheets, use the appropriate points values from pages 202-203.

UNITS

UNIT	MODELS PER UNIT	POINTS PER MODEL (Does not include wargear)
Deathwing Ancient	1	103
Deathwing Apothecary	1	75
Deathwing Champion	1	118
Deathwing Knights	5-10	45
Deathwing Terminator Squad	5-10	26
Fortress of Redemption	1	400
Interrogator-Chaplain	1	90
Interrogator-Chaplain in Terminator Armour	1	128
Interrogator-Chaplain on Bike	1	117
Interrogator-Chaplain with Jump Pack	1	101
Nephilim Jetfighter	1	123
Ravenwing Ancient	1	117
Ravenwing Apothecary	1	97
Ravenwing Attack Bike Squad	1-3	45
Ravenwing Bike Squad	3-8	32
- Ravenwing Attack Bike	0-1	45
Ravenwing Black Knights	3-10	50
Ravenwing Champion	1	106
Ravenwing Dark Talon	1	180
Ravenwing Darkshroud	1	128
Ravenwing Land Speeder Vengeance	1	122
Ravenwing Land Speeders	1-5	85

UNITS

UNIT	MODELS PER UNIT	POINTS PER MODEL (Including wargear)
Asmodai	1	145
Azrael	1	180
Belial	1	150
Ezekiel	1	145
Sammael in Sableclaw	1	216
Sammael on Corvex	1	183

RANGED WEAPONS

WEAPON	POINTS PER WEAPON
Avenger mega bolter	35
Blacksword missile launcher	0
Plasma storm battery	0
Plasma talon	0
Ravenwing grenade launcher	0
Redemption missile silo	0
Rift cannon	0
Stasis bomb	0
Twin Icarus lascannon	0

MELEE WEAPONS

WEAPON	POINTS PER WEAPON
Blade of Caliban	0
Corvus hammer	0
Flail of the Unforgiven	0
Halberd of Caliban	0
Mace of absolution	0

OTHER WARGEAR

WARGEAR	POINTS PER ITEM
Watcher in the Dark	5

DARK ANGELS WARGEAR

RANGED WEAPONS

WEAPON	RANGE	TYPE	S	AP	D	ABILITIES
Avenger mega bolter	36"	Heavy 10	6	-1	1	-
Blacksword missile launcher	36"	Heavy 10	7	-3	2	-
The Deliverer	12"	Pistol 1	4	-1	2	-
Lion's Wrath	When attacking with this weapon, choose one or both of the profiles below. If you choose both, subtract 1 from all hit rolls for this weapon.					
- Master-crafted boltgun	24"	Rapid Fire 1	4	-1	2	-
- Plasma gun	24"	Rapid Fire 1	7	-3	1	*See plasma gun*
Plasma storm battery	When attacking with this weapon, choose one of the profiles below.					
- Standard	36"	Heavy D6	7	-3	2	-
- Supercharge	36"	Heavy D6	8	-3	3	If you make one or more hit rolls of 1, the bearer suffers 3 mortal wounds after all of this weapon's shots have been resolved, and the plasma storm battery cannot be used for the rest of the battle.
Plasma talon	When attacking with this weapon, choose one of the profiles below.					
- Standard	18"	Assault 2	7	-3	1	-
- Supercharge	18"	Assault 2	8	-3	2	On a hit roll of 1, the bearer is slain after all of this weapon's shots have been resolved.
Ravenwing grenade launcher	When attacking with this weapon, choose one of the profiles below.					
- Frag shell	24"	Assault D6	3	0	1	-
- Krak shell	24"	Assault 2	6	-1	D3	-
Redemption missile silo	When attacking with this weapon, choose one of the profiles below.					
- Fragstorm missile	18-96"	Heavy 2D6	4	0	1	-
- Krakstorm missile	18-96"	Heavy D6	8	-3	D3	-
Rift cannon	18"	Heavy D3	10	-3	3	*See Ravenwing Dark Talon datasheet (pg 123)*
Twin Icarus lascannon	96"	Heavy 2D6	9	-3	D6	Add 1 to all hit rolls made for this weapon against targets that can FLY. Subtract 1 from the hit rolls made for this weapon against all other targets.
Twin storm bolter	24"	Rapid Fire 4	4	0	1	-

MELEE WEAPONS

WEAPON	RANGE	TYPE	S	AP	D	ABILITIES
Blade of Caliban	Melee	Melee	+3	-3	D3	-
Blades of Reason	Melee	Melee	User	0	D6	-
Corvus hammer	Melee	Melee	+1	-1	1	Each wound roll of 6+ made for this weapon causes D3 damage instead of 1.
Flail of the Unforgiven	Melee	Melee	+2	-3	2	Excess damage from this weapon is not lost; instead, keep allocating damage to another model in the target unit until either all the damage has been allocated or the target unit is destroyed.
Halberd of Caliban	Melee	Melee	+3	-4	D3	Each time the bearer fights, it can make D3 additional attacks with this weapon if the target unit contains 5 or more models.
Mace of absolution	Melee	Melee	x2	-2	3	-
Raven Sword	Melee	Melee	+1	-3	2	This weapon has Strength x2 if Sammael charged in the preceding Charge phase.
Sword of Secrets	Melee	Melee	+2	-3	D3	Each time you make a wound roll of 6+ for this weapon, the target suffers a mortal wound in addition to any other damage.
Sword of Silence	Melee	Melee	+1	-3	2	This weapon always wounds on a 2+, unless the target is a VEHICLE.
Traitor's Bane	Melee	Melee	+1	-3	D3	Add 1 to this weapon's damage if the target is a PSYKER.

SPACE WOLVES POINTS VALUES

If you are playing a matched play game, or a game that uses a points limit, you can use the following lists to determine the total points cost of your army. Simply add together the points values of all your models, as well as the wargear they are equipped with, to determine your army's total points value. For units based on Space Marines datasheets, use the appropriate points values from pages 202-203.

UNITS

UNIT	MODELS PER UNIT	POINTS PER MODEL (Does not include wargear)
Bjorn the Fell-handed	1	210
Blood Claws	5-16	13
- Wolf Guard Pack Leader in Terminator Armour	-	31
Cyberwolves	1-5	15
Fenrisian Wolves	5-15	9
Grey Hunters	5-11	14
- Wolf Guard Pack Leader in Terminator Armour	-	31
Iron Priest	1	58
Iron Priest on Bike	1	65
Iron Priest on Thunderwolf	1	80
Lone Wolf	1	75
Lone Wolf in Terminator Armour	1	115
Long Fangs	5-7	15
- Wolf Guard Pack Leader in Terminator Armour	-	31
Rune Priest	1	68
Rune Priest in Terminator Armour	1	120
Rune Priest on Bike	1	109
Rune Priest with Jump Pack	1	91
Skyclaws	5-10	16
Stormfang Gunship	1	155
Stormwolf	1	165
Swiftclaw Attack Bikes	1-3	45
Swiftclaws	3-11	31
- Swiftclaw Attack Bike	0-1	45
Thunderwolf Cavalry	3-6	45
Wolf Guard	5-10	16
Wolf Guard Battle Leader	1	60
Wolf Guard Battle Leader in Terminator Armour	1	92
Wolf Guard Battle Leader on Bike	1	85
Wolf Guard Battle Leader on Thunderwolf	1	97
Wolf Guard Battle Leader with Jump Pack	1	63
Wolf Guard in Terminator Armour	5-10	31
Wolf Guard on Bikes	5-10	34
Wolf Guard with Jump Packs	5-10	21
Wolf Lord on Thunderwolf	1	128

UNITS

UNIT	MODELS PER UNIT	POINTS PER MODEL (Does not include wargear)
Wolf Priest	1	90
Wolf Priest in Terminator Armour	1	144
Wolf Priest on Bike	1	135
Wolf Priest with Jump Pack	1	112
Wolf Scouts	5-11	11
Wulfen	5-10	37

UNITS

UNIT	MODELS PER UNIT	POINTS PER MODEL (Including wargear)
Arjac Rockfist	1	140
Canis Wolfborn	1	150
Harald Deathwolf	1	188
Krom Dragongaze	1	119
Logan Grimnar	1	190
Logan Grimnar on Stormrider	1	230
Lukas the Trickster	1	118
Murderfang	1	200
Njal Stormcaller	1	138
Njal Stormcaller in Runic Terminator Armour	1	167
Ragnar Blackmane	1	141
Ulrik the Slayer	1	133

OTHER WARGEAR

WARGEAR	POINTS PER ITEM
Blizzard shield	15
Camo cloak	3
Psychic hood	26
Runic armour	7
Runic Terminator armour	5
Storm shield (Thunderwolf Cavalry)	15
Wolf standard	10

RANGED WEAPONS

WEAPON	POINTS PER WEAPON
Helfrost cannon	25
Helfrost destructor	50
Helfrost pistol	15
Stormfrag auto-launcher	4
Twin helfrost cannon	30

MELEE WEAPONS

WEAPON	POINTS PER WEAPON
Crushing teeth and claws	0
Fenrisian great axe	40
Frost axe	10
Frost claws	15
Frost sword	7
Great frost axe	17
Great wolf claw	25
Runic axe	16
Runic stave	14
Runic sword	12
Teeth and claws	0
Tempest hammer	30
Trueclaw	0
Wolf claw (single/pair)	9/13
Wulfen claws	0

SPACE WOLVES WARGEAR

RANGED WEAPONS

WEAPON	RANGE	TYPE	S	AP	D	ABILITIES
Foehammer (shooting)	12"	Assault 1	x2	-3	D3	When attacking **CHARACTERS** or **MONSTERS**, this weapon has a Damage of 3.
Helfrost cannon		When attacking with this weapon, choose one of the profiles below. If a model suffers any unsaved wounds from this weapon but is not slain, roll a D6; on a 6, the target suffers a mortal wound.				
- Dispersed beam	24"	Heavy D3	6	-2	1	-
- Focused beam	24"	Heavy 1	8	-4	D6	-
Helfrost destructor		When attacking with this weapon, choose one of the profiles below. If a model suffers any unsaved wounds from this weapon but is not slain, roll a D6; on a 6, the target suffers a mortal wound.				
- Dispersed beam	24"	Heavy 3D3	6	-2	2	-
- Focused beam	24"	Heavy 3	8	-4	D6	-
Helfrost pistol	12"	Pistol 1	8	-4	D3	If a model suffers any unsaved wounds from this weapon but is not slain, roll a D6; on a 6, the target suffers a mortal wound.
Nightwing	12"	Assault D6	3	0	1	-
Stormfrag auto-launcher	12"	Assault D3	4	0	1	-
Twin helfrost cannon		When attacking with this weapon, choose one of the profiles below. If a model suffers any unsaved wounds from this weapon but is not slain, roll a D6; on a 6, the target suffers a mortal wound.				
- Dispersed beam	24"	Heavy 2D3	6	-2	1	-
- Focused beam	24"	Heavy 2	8	-4	D6	-

MELEE WEAPONS

WEAPON	RANGE	TYPE	S	AP	D	ABILITIES
The Axe Morkai	When attacking with this weapon, choose one of the profiles below.					
- One-handed	Melee	Melee	+2	-3	D3	-
- Two-handed	Melee	Melee	x2	-3	3	When attacking with this weapon, you must subtract 1 from the hit roll.
Claw of the Jackalwolf	Melee	Melee	+1	-2	2	You can re-roll failed wound rolls for this weapon.
Crushing teeth and claws	Melee	Melee	5	-1	1	After a model on this mount makes its close combat attacks, you can attack with its mount. Make 3 additional attacks, using this weapon profile.
Fenrisian great axe	Melee	Melee	+4	-3	D6	Each time the bearer fights, it can make 1 additional attack with this weapon.
Flurry of teeth and claws	Melee	Melee	5	-1	1	*See Logan Grimnar on Stormrider datasheet (pg 132)*
Foehammer (melee)	Melee	Melee	x2	-3	D3	When attacking CHARACTERS or MONSTERS, this weapon has a Damage of 3.
Frost axe	Melee	Melee	+2	-2	1	-
Frost claws	Melee	Melee	+1	-2	1	Each time the bearer fights, it can make 1 additional attack with this weapon. You can re-roll failed wound rolls for this weapon.
Frost sword	Melee	Melee	+1	-3	1	-
Frostfang	Melee	Melee	+1	-4	2	-
Glacius	Melee	Melee	+2	-2	2	If a model suffers any unsaved wounds from this weapon but is not slain, roll a D6; on a 6, the target suffers D3 mortal wounds.
Great frost axe	Melee	Melee	+3	-3	D3	The bearer can make 1 additional attack with this weapon on a turn in which it has charged.
Great wolf claw	Melee	Melee	+4	-2	D6	You can re-roll failed wound rolls for this weapon.
The Murderclaws	Melee	Melee	x2	-3	3	You can re-roll failed wound rolls for this weapon.
Runic axe	Melee	Melee	+1	-2	D3	-
Runic stave	Melee	Melee	+2	-1	D3	-
Runic sword	Melee	Melee	User	-3	D3	-
Staff of the Stormcaller	Melee	Melee	+2	-1	D3	-
Teeth and claws	Melee	Melee	User	-1	1	-
Tempest hammer	Melee	Melee	x2	-3	3	If a model suffers any unsaved wounds from this weapon but is not slain, roll a D6; on a 6, the target suffers a mortal wound.
Trueclaw	Melee	Melee	+5	-4	D6	You can re-roll failed wound rolls for this weapon.
Wolf claw	Melee	Melee	+1	-2	1	You can re-roll failed wound rolls for this weapon. A model armed with two wolf claws can make 1 additional attack with this weapon.
Wulfen claws	Melee	Melee	User	-1	1	-
Wyrmclaw	Melee	Melee	+2	-2	D3	-

DEATHWATCH POINTS VALUES

If you are playing a matched play game, or a game that uses a points limit, you can use the following lists to determine the total points cost of your army. Simply add together the points values of all your models, as well as the wargear they are equipped with, to determine your army's total points value.

UNITS

UNIT	MODELS PER UNIT	POINTS PER MODEL (Does not include wargear)
Corvus Blackstar	1	160
Deathwatch Bikers	1-5	34
Deathwatch Kill Team	5-10	
- Deathwatch Bikers		34
- Deathwatch Terminators		32
- Deathwatch Vanguard Veterans		21
- Deathwatch Veterans		19
Deathwatch Terminators	1-5	32
Deathwatch Vanguard Veterans	1-5	21
Watch Master	1	130

WATCH CAPTAIN ARTEMIS

UNIT	MODELS PER UNIT	POINTS PER MODEL (Including wargear)
Watch Captain Artemis	1	130

RANGED WEAPONS

WEAPON	POINTS PER WEAPON
Blackstar rocket launcher	15
Deathwatch frag cannon	30
Deathwatch shotgun	5
Guardian spear	0
Hand flamer	8
Inferno pistol	20
Infernus heavy bolter	25
Stalker pattern boltgun	4

MELEE WEAPONS

WEAPON	POINTS PER WEAPON
Heavy thunder hammer	30
Xenophase blade	7

OTHER WARGEAR

WARGEAR	POINTS PER ITEM
Auspex array	5
Blackstar cluster launcher	0
Combat shield	4
Deathwatch teleport homer	0
Infernum halo-launcher	5
Storm shield	15

DEATHWATCH WARGEAR

RANGED WEAPONS

WEAPON	RANGE	TYPE	S	AP	D	ABILITIES
Blackstar rocket launcher	When attacking with this weapon, choose one of the profiles below.					
- Corvid warhead	30"	Heavy D6	6	-1	1	Add 1 to hit rolls for this weapon when targeting a unit that can **FLY**.
- Dracos warhead	30"	Heavy D6	4	0	1	Add 1 to hit rolls for this weapon when targeting a unit that is in cover.
Deathwatch frag cannon	When attacking with this weapon, choose one of the profiles below.					
- Frag round	8"	Assault 2D6	6	-1	1	This weapon automatically hits its target.
- Shell	24"	Assault 2	7	-2	2	If the target is within half range of this weapon, its attacks are resolved with a Strength of 9 and an AP of -3.
Deathwatch shotgun	When attacking with this weapon, choose one of the profiles below.					
- Cryptclearer round	16"	Assault 2	4	0	1	You can re-roll failed wound rolls for this weapon.
- Xenopurge slug	16"	Assault 2	4	-1	1	If the target is within half range of this weapon, its attacks are resolved with a Damage of 2.
- Wyrmsbreath shell	7"	Assault D6	3	0	1	This weapon automatically hits its target.
Guardian spear (shooting)	24"	Rapid Fire 1	4	-1	2	-
Hand flamer	6"	Pistol D3	3	0	1	This weapon automatically hits its target.
Hellfire Extremis	When attacking with this weapon, choose one or both of the profiles below. If you choose both, subtract 1 from all hit rolls made for this weapon.					
- Hellfire flamer	8"	Assault D6	*	0	1	This weapon automatically hits its target. This weapon wounds on a 4+, unless it is targeting a **VEHICLE**, in which case it wounds on a 6+.
- Boltgun	24"	Rapid Fire 1	4	0	1	-
Inferno pistol	6"	Pistol 1	8	-4	D6	If the target is within half range of this weapon, roll two dice when inflicting damage with it and discard the lowest result.
Infernus heavy bolter	When attacking with this weapon, choose one or both of the profiles below. If you choose both, subtract 1 from all hit rolls made for this weapon.					
- Heavy bolter	36"	Heavy 3	5	-1	1	-
- Heavy flamer	8"	Assault D6	5	-1	1	This weapon automatically hits its target.
Stalker pattern boltgun	30"	Heavy 2	4	0	1	-
Stasis bomb	6"	Grenade 1	-	-	-	This weapon can only be used once per battle. If the attack hits, deal D6 mortal wounds to your target. If it misses, the bearer suffers D6 mortal wounds.

MELEE WEAPONS

WEAPON	RANGE	TYPE	S	AP	D	ABILITIES
Guardian spear (melee)	Melee	Melee	+1	-3	D3	-
Heavy thunder hammer	Melee	Melee	x2	-3	D6	When attacking with this weapon, you must subtract 1 from the hit roll. Each time you make a wound roll of 6+ with this weapon, that hit is resolved with a Damage of 6.
Xenophase blade	Melee	Melee	User	-3	1	Your opponent must re-roll successful invulnerable saves for wounds caused by this weapon.

GREY KNIGHTS POINTS VALUES

If you are playing a matched play game, or a game that uses a points limit, you can use the following lists to determine the total points cost of your army. Simply add together the points values of all your models, as well as the wargear they are equipped with, to determine your army's total points value.

UNITS

UNIT	MODELS PER UNIT	POINTS PER MODEL (Does not include wargear)
Apothecary	1	90
Brother-Captain	1	150
Brotherhood Ancient	1	128
Brotherhood Champion	1	113
Dreadnought	1	87
Grand Master	1	160
Interceptor Squad	5-10	23
Nemesis Dreadknight	1	130
Paladin Ancient	1	140
Paladin Squad	3-10	53
Purgation Squad	5-10	19
Purifier Squad	5-10	26
Strike Squad	5-10	19
Techmarine	1	91
Terminator Squad	5-10	44
Venerable Dreadnought	1	110

UNITS

UNIT	MODELS PER UNIT	POINTS PER MODEL (Including wargear)
Brother-Captain Stern	1	157
Castellan Crowe	1	125
Grand Master Voldus	1	190
Lord Kaldor Draigo	1	240

RANGED WEAPONS

WEAPON	POINTS PER WEAPON
Gatling psilencer	20
Heavy incinerator	40
Heavy psycannon	30
Incinerator	14
Incinerator (Terminator)	20
Psilencer	4
Psilencer (Terminator)	10
Psycannon	14
Psycannon (Terminator)	20
Psyk-out grenades	0
Storm bolter	2

MELEE WEAPONS

WEAPON	POINTS PER WEAPON
Dreadfist (single/pair)	25/35
Nemesis Daemon greathammer	15
Nemesis Daemon hammer	13
Nemesis falchion	0
Nemesis force halberd	0
Nemesis force sword	0
Nemesis greatsword	10
Nemesis warding stave	0

OTHER WARGEAR

WARGEAR	POINTS PER ITEM
Dreadknight teleporter	10

GREY KNIGHTS WARGEAR

RANGED WEAPONS

WEAPON	RANGE	TYPE	S	AP	D	ABILITIES
Gatling psilencer	24"	Heavy 12	4	0	D3	-
Heavy incinerator	12"	Heavy D6	6	-1	2	This weapon automatically hits its target.
Heavy psycannon	24"	Heavy 6	7	-1	2	-
Incinerator	8"	Assault D6	6	-1	1	This weapon automatically hits its target.
Psilencer	24"	Heavy 6	4	0	D3	-
Psycannon	24"	Heavy 4	7	-1	1	-
Psyk-out grenade	6"	Grenade D3	2	0	1	Each time you roll a hit roll of 6+ for this weapon when targeting a **PSYKER** or **DAEMON**, the target suffers a mortal wound instead of the normal damage.
Storm bolter	24"	Rapid Fire 2	4	0	1	-

MELEE WEAPONS

WEAPON	RANGE	TYPE	S	AP	D	ABILITIES
The Black Blade of Antwyr	Melee	Melee	User	0	1	-
Dreadfist	Melee	Melee	x2	-3	D3	If a model is equipped with two dreadfists, each time it fights it can make 1 additional attack with them.
Malleus Argyrum	Melee	Melee	x2	-3	3	-
Nemesis Daemon greathammer	Melee	Melee	x2	-4	D6	When a model attacks with this weapon, you must subtract 1 from the hit roll. Damage rolls of less than 3 count as 3 for this weapon.
Nemesis Daemon hammer	Melee	Melee	x2	-3	3	When a model attacks with this weapon, you must subtract 1 from the hit roll.
Nemesis falchion	Melee	Melee	User	-2	D3	If a model is armed with two Nemesis falchions, each time it fights it can make 1 additional attack with them.
Nemesis force halberd	Melee	Melee	+1	-2	D3	-
Nemesis force sword	Melee	Melee	User	-3	D3	-
Nemesis greatsword	Melee	Melee	+4	-3	D6	-
Nemesis warding stave	Melee	Melee	+2	-1	D3	A model armed with this weapon has a 5+ invulnerable save against attacks made in the Fight phase. If it already has an invulnerable save, add 1 to invulnerable saving throws you make for it in the Fight phase instead.
The Titansword	Melee	Melee	+4	-4	3	-